INJUSTICE

— IN —

FOCUS

In 1955 Cecil Williams and friend I. N. Rendall Harper stop at a segregated gas station, where each drinks from a "White Only" water fountain. The photo of Williams, embraced as an iconic image of defiance during Jim Crow segregation, has been appropriated for lapel pins, posters, magnets, and even face masks.

INJUSTICE

— IN —

FOCUS

THE CIVIL RIGHTS
PHOTOGRAPHY
OF CECIL WILLIAMS

CECIL WILLIAMS AND
CLAUDIA SMITH BRINSON

THE UNIVERSITY OF
SOUTH CAROLINA PRESS

Published by the University of South Carolina Press

Columbia, South Carolina 29208

uscpress.com

Manufactured in China

33 32 31 30 29 28 27 26 25 24

10 9 8 7 6 5 4 3 2 1

Library of Congress Cataloging-in-Publication Data
can be found at http://catalog.loc.gov/.

ISBN: 978-1-64336-437-7 (hardcover)

ISBN: 978-1-64336-438-4 (ebook)

PUBLICATION IS MADE POSSIBLE IN PART BY THE GENEROUS
SUPPORT OF THE WILLIAM E. DUFFORD FUND
FOR CIVIL AND SOCIAL JUSTICE PUBLICATIONS.

CONTENTS

CECIL WILLIAMS'S MISSION

I believe the civil rights movement did not begin with sports figures such as world heavyweight champion Joe Louis or Major League baseball star Jackie Robinson. I believe the movement did not begin with Rosa Parks refusing to relinquish her bus seat to a White passenger.

I believe the nation's slow and continuing transformation, from a segregated to a desegregated society, began with Black parents' determination that their children should receive an education equal to that of White children. And this was a divine transformation.

I believe that throughout our lives God uses us to do the work of good against evil or good for change. Surely God can click his fingers and make change happen. But he uses us to carry out missions and, in doing so, reflect his image.

Injustice in Focus is my opportunity to share my personal experience of the American civil rights movement and its true origin. My account differs from that of most historians and consequently differs from most people's understanding. For more than forty years I have been obsessed with remedying what my experiences tell me is an erasure of Black South Carolinians' involvement in the civil rights movement.

I believe the genesis of the American civil rights movement occurred in the late 1940s in Summerton, located in Clarendon County, South Carolina, about 35 miles from where I was born and grew up in Orangeburg. The petitioners of *Briggs v. Elliott* filed the first lawsuit attacking segregation in public schools and thus the first in a consolidation of five separate lawsuits known as *Brown v. Board of Education of Topeka*, the 1954 and 1955 United States (US) Supreme Court decisions that ended legal segregation in the American public school system.

Following the 1955 US Supreme Court ruling in *Brown v. Board*, Black parents in my hometown of Orangeburg petitioned for the desegregation of the county's schools. I believe that their actions served as the second catalyst of the civil rights movement. They organized the Orangeburg Freedom Movement, which began several months before the Montgomery bus boycott. From 1955 on, White Citizens' Councils (WCC) formed throughout the South to combat desegregation. With the goal of forcing petitioners to remove their names and never sign another petition, or, better yet, leave town or the state, South Carolina's WCC members kicked sharecroppers and tenant farmers off land, demanded repayment of mortgages, refused seed and fuel sales, and fired employees. To counter the WCC's economic terrorism, Orangeburg's Black citizens organized a boycott of White merchants. They were emboldened by the strength of the Summerton petitioners and by Thurgood Marshall, an attorney for the National Association for the Advancement of Colored People (NAACP), who challenged Black parents to test the Supreme Court rulings. The Montgomery bus boycott, led by Rev. Dr. Martin Luther King Jr. duplicated the Orangeburg Freedom Movement's strategic opposition to Jim Crow. (Let me say that I in no way intend to discredit King and others. But I was a witness to or a party to events that preceded the efforts of King, our beloved civil rights icon.)

Along with the descendants of *Briggs* petitioners and supporters, particularly members of the Harry Briggs, Joseph Armstrong "J. A." DeLaine, and Levi and Hammett Pearson families, I have persisted in sharing our story. I wrote four books (*Freedom & Justice, Out-of-the-Box in Dixie, Orangeburg 1968*, and *Unforgettable*, all out of print) that offered my personal account and documented my experiences and those of others that I photographed. In any and all of my efforts, I highlight civil rights events that prove the actions of Black residents of Clarendon and Orangeburg counties influenced a change in the mindset of Black citizens in South Carolina and elsewhere from that of accommodation to confrontation through nonviolent direct action.

Over the years I have spent thousands of hours speaking throughout the region and arranging exhibits of my civil rights photographs.

In 2019 I founded the Cecil Williams South Carolina Civil Rights Museum to preserve and exhibit supporting photographs, documents, and artifacts from the civil rights activists of South Carolina.

In 2021 I became engaged in an effort to petition the US Supreme Court to recognize the *Briggs* petitioners' historic accomplishments. I believe that the *Brown v. Board of Education* decisions should be renamed to acknowledge the first lawsuit, *Briggs v. Elliott.* In May 2022 President Joe Biden acknowledged *Briggs's* importance when he signed into law an expansion and redesignation of the Brown v. Board of Education National Historic Site in Topeka, Kansas. Now named the Brown v. Board of Education National Historical Park, the park includes the previously segregated Summerton and Scott's Branch schools in Summerton, and, in affiliation with the park, the schools represented in the Delaware, Virginia, and the District of Columbia lawsuits.

More needs to be done to tell the true story of a civil rights movement populated by thousands of people, not just a few larger-than-life heroes. The Black people of Orangeburg County never quit. From their desegregation petitions of 1955 through the boycotts and campus rebellions of the 1950s and 1960s, through the sit-ins and demonstrations, and the Orangeburg Massacre, they did not quit. The civil rights movement is described as a series of crises and pauses, but people such as my friends Rev. Matthew D. McCollom and James E. Sulton Sr. and students such as Fred Henderson Moore and Thomas Walter Gaither and Lloyd Williams exerted steady pressure into the 1970s.

I believe that *Injustice in Focus* will assist in providing a more authentic interpretation of Black South Carolinians' long journey toward freedom, justice, and equality.

CECIL J. WILLIAMS

ORANGEBURG, SOUTH CAROLINA
SEPTEMBER 2022

PREFACE

Cecil James Williams and I have known each other for so many years that neither of us remembers our first meeting. I worked as a senior writer, associate editor, and columnist for *The State* newspaper in Columbia, South Carolina, and am author of *Stories of Struggle: The Clash Over Civil Rights in South Carolina.* Cecil worked as a photojournalist in Orangeburg, South Carolina, but, really, his energy and entrepreneurial bent seem to place him everywhere. He loves art and science and business. He has created so much: remarkable photographs, a magazine, a newspaper, three Modern houses, a civil rights museum, a publishing company, even a device that allows photographers to digitize film, which he calls the FilmToaster.

In recent years, Cecil has been possessed by a mission. He wants to set right the civil rights record, which he believes simplistically focuses on a few stars, such as Rev. Dr. Martin Luther King Jr. For him, the petitioners of the *Briggs v. Elliott* case in Summerton, South Carolina, represent the beginning of the civil rights movement. *Briggs* was the first lawsuit of five consolidated into *Brown v. Board of Education of Topeka,* the 1954 and 1955 US Supreme Court decisions that ended segregated public education. For him, the second step of the movement arose with the NAACP-designed boycott of merchants who belonged to or supported the White Citizens' Councils (WCC) in Orangeburg, South Carolina, a boycott which preceded the bus boycott in Montgomery, Alabama. And both *Briggs* and the boycott illustrate the brilliant, complicated, and high-risk grassroots activism of South Carolina's Black citizens. Cecil knows; he was there. And it truly maddens him that others who should know do not.

When Cecil told me his photography books were out of print, that just seemed wrong. So here we are, thanks to the University of South Carolina Press, whose editors agree. *Injustice in Focus: The Photography of Cecil Williams* brings together a photographer and a writer, both experienced journalists. We—an eyewitness to the civil rights movement and a former reporter who loves interviews and research— offer an illustrated historical and biographical narrative. *Injustice in Focus* shows and tells the story of race, photography, and activism in the 1940s, '50s, and '60s as depicted by and lived by Cecil Williams during the busiest decades in Orangeburg and the larger civil rights movement.

Cecil and I worked hard to put this book together. Some of his film is decaying, some of it undeveloped, some unlabeled, much of it awaiting rescue from the Getty Images Photo Archive Grant for Historically Black Colleges and Universities (HBCUs), which includes Claflin University, Cecil's alma mater. Many of his stored digitized images are hiding, scattered as years passed among various data storage formats—floppy disks, compact disks, hard disk drives, and solid state drives. Then there is the issue of human memory. Cecil was born in 1937. Why was that photograph taken? Who is that in the second row? Who published it? We had a few discussions: his expertise, daily experiences, and personal knowledge versus my research, intuition, and weather reports.

And then there is Orangeburg itself. This also is a book about Orangeburg, the town and county. At times Orangeburg dominates in the story of Cecil Williams. Its residents and its two colleges of those decades—South Carolina State College, the only state-supported college for Black students, and Claflin University, affiliated with the United Methodist Church and Cecil's alma mater—are thoroughly documented, thanks to Cecil's work. As Cecil points out, civil rights activism in Orangeburg seemed never-ending, the result of infinite instances of White segregationists' intransigence and destructiveness and Black activists' inventiveness and persistence.

Because Cecil also took many portraits of himself with his many cameras, he too is documented from his teenage to his young adult years. But, in another way, Cecil is hard to find. Except for the self-portraits he is, after all, behind the camera. He is not a participant. He is an observer, a highly invested observer since he wanted, as he says, "freedom and justice" in his lifetime. He is an observer who makes a record.

He is physically on the edge or before or behind or even above what is happening. His role is not to participate but to pay attention, to instantly manipulate bodies in space by moving his own body. He must raise his camera and concentrate within seconds on focus, angle of view, texture, framing, timing, and, above all, dark and light and in between to collect light to collect images. There is nothing automatic about the cameras these days. Aperture, film speed, shutter speed, all have to be calculated and set. As a photojournalist and an events photographer, Cecil records the meetings, public and private; the speeches; the picketing, marches and protests; the conflicts and the aftermaths of the civil rights movement. With his photographs he tells the stories, as I do as a writer with words, but even in his own book, he is not exactly *the* story.

Cecil is hard to find in another way. Black-owned media were elsewhere, in Philadelphia and Chicago, for example, so their relationship with Cecil and South Carolina was always long distance. And because Cecil sent to them entire film rolls by mail, he lost access to his own work—until he started wearing two cameras at a time and trying to capture evanescent moments almost simultaneously. The Associated Press occasionally bought his photographs of noteworthy events. Orangeburg's local paper, the *Times and Democrat*, occasionally bought his shots of fires and car wrecks. But White-owned media had little to no interest in visually depicting Black life beyond the events it would have been bizarre to ignore even in a segregated society. So Cecil operated under censorship, and that is hard to grasp retrospectively, what is there versus what is not there.

Cecil supported himself not through his civil rights photography but through his photo store and studio and his yearbook photography for Black public schools and colleges. His living was made in wedding portraits and family portraits and high school portraits and special event documentation. He was almost invisible there too, the unfailingly polite director of flattering poses present as a voice behind a camera.

But he is so very present in what he wants his civil rights photos to tell you. Photography mentors Edward C. "E. C." Jones Jr. of Sumter and John W. Goodwin Jr. of Columbia and Cecil himself knew what to do about the bias of film—its calibration to White skin tones—while photographing, developing, and printing.

Consequently, whether Cecil photographed a march, a demonstration, an individual, or what journalists call a grip-and-grin, his photos celebrate the beauty of Black skin while illustrating the unbearable tensions of Black life.

Much would be unknown, forgotten, or mistaken without Cecil's photographs. I followed behind to collect Cecil's stories and curate his photos. The two of us completed dozens of interviews, most lasting two or more hours, and held countless telephone conversations. When time, death, memory, erroneous reports, and duplicitous officials cloud the past, here are his pictures and the stories behind them to tell the truth.

THE 1940S

A hand-me-down from his older brother determined the rest of nine-year-old Cecil James Williams's life. Alfred Leroy Williams had decided he was more interested in music—specifically, the saxophone—and gave his Kodak Baby Brownie Special to his younger brother. The little black box of shiny Bakelite looked art deco in design with its rounded corners. A rectangular viewfinder perched atop the body, the ivory-tinted film winder to the left. Below the centered lens an ivory-tinted shutter button poked out. A roll of 127 film produced eight $1^5/_8$-inch by $2^1/_2$-inch negatives. A rare treasure for a Black child in 1946, the camera cost $2.50.

Cecil Williams had been teaching himself to draw. "I learned how to draw a box, perspective, the four sides that make up a box. How to do shadowing and shading, how to draw faces and hands. I was mostly self-taught. I loved to look in books likes Sears," the popular Sears, Roebuck and Company catalog offering for sale most any object. Drawing was Williams's first crush; his favorite subjects were futuristic houses, cars, and spaceships. His brother's camera enchanted him "since it was, you might say, as electronic as you could get during those days. It was certainly interesting, a little magic box." At first he popped around the corners of his home, surprising family members. "I often took pictures of them in uncomfortable moments, getting dressed, brushing their hair. Then I branched out."

Wanting to make money lived in Williams almost as strongly as wanting to make art. Although a child, he knew "very few successful artists make a good living." On Sundays he walked two miles to Edisto Memorial Gardens and its five acres of azaleas. There he snapped strollers in their Sunday finery; collected names and addresses, and a dollar per photo; paid less than one dollar to develop the film

In 1946, Cecil Williams discovers the power of "a magic box" when older brother Alfred Leroy Williams passes on his Kodak Baby Brownie Special. Williams quickly moves from taking snapshots of his family to taking portraits of Edisto Garden visitors. He charges one dollar per photo and mails his subjects the commercially developed print.

roll at the drugstore; and then mailed the portraits in envelopes with three-cent stamps. "If I photographed ten or twelve people, I made a good little profit. With those dollars I could buy all the treats I wanted to eat." And with those dollars he also could buy kits for another of his consuming interests (he did nothing halfway): stick-built model airplanes.[1]

Williams took himself seriously, and so did his parents. He persuaded his mother that he needed a camera with a flash, and, thanks to the ever-helpful Sears catalog, they obtained an Argus Seventy-Five for $14.89. The camera's front panel and viewfinder hood gleamed with a satin-finished metal. The flash unit plugged into the camera's side, and a red shutter blade reminded the photographer that the shutter was cocked.

When Alfred left home—bound for New York City, music, and relatives—his bedroom became Williams's darkroom, the door removed, a thick quilt nailed to its frame, and blankets nailed to the windows. The patient parents accepted the acidic and sulfurous stinks of developer, stop bath, and fixer chemicals; the immersion of photographic paper in trays inhabiting the former bedroom or the kitchen sink or the bathtub; the drying prints hanging on clothespins in the bathroom. "I will never forget the magic of mixing up the chemistry and seeing that first picture come up in the solution, almost as if I were a magician," said Williams. "I worked mostly in the bedroom. After I printed the pictures, I had to take them to the kitchen sink. If I did a lot of pictures, I had to take them to the bathtub." His friend George Rufus Greene Jr. marveled, "a setup in his bathroom like you saw on television with little trays and all of sudden a picture is coming out like magic. Not many kids were doing stuff like that."[2]

At twelve years old Williams booked his first wedding, referred by an educator cousin, Dr. Charles H. Thomas Jr., who told a couple, "Oh, my cousin takes pictures." Williams survived his first venture. "During the entire wedding I shot only fifteen pictures. I made a twelve-page wedding album. They paid me $35." Williams began occasionally advertising his services on the back of the Sunday program for New Mount Zion Baptist Church. He had a business: Photos by Cecil Williams Photography.

Williams also worked for his father, Cecil Leroy Williams, who had made and tailored uniforms 100-some miles away at the Marine Corps' Parris Island during World War II. "That gave him the ability to tailor, and tailoring was very profitable in those days. He started doing it at home, then he got a shop downtown," Williams' Tailor Shop. The shop sat on Broughton Street, just a block off Main Street in Orangeburg, population 10,521, located in Orangeburg County, South Carolina, population 63,707. More attractive for the younger Williams was the store next door, Gus Browning Radio Sales and Service, home to the town's first televisions.

The elder Williams was the only tailor in town, and much of his work came from the local clothing stores—Belk Hudson, Limehouse Men's Store, and the Barshay and Marcus Company—the clientele overwhelmingly White for the clothing store owners and the tailor shop. The tailor's motto worked as a two-way promise, "A good job today means a customer tomorrow." On Saturdays the elementary school student delivered from merchants to his father any clothes needing tailoring and returned to the merchants the hemmed or altered apparel. "I would also collect the money as well. My father would give me a bill, little brown-colored paper with red ink and a carbon copy. I would take it to the merchant, collect the money, and bring the money back." The merchants treated him kindly, with conversation and dollar tips.

Williams's developing understanding of status and race was subtle. He figured out that the White customers perceived the Jewish clothing merchants as "one-down" from other White men in the southern hierarchy. He sorted it out this way: "They were less than White," but also "one-up" from him and other Black people. Williams also noticed status could be attained by whom you served. "Three doors down the street but across from my father's place was a barbershop. Two brothers were the barbers, and they were Black. But they didn't accept Black clients; they would only take White trade." His own family demonstrated that "race was very confusing. I had some family members that for all practical purposes were White." Light-skinned or not, life could be improved by moving north. His mother's younger siblings joined the Great Migration, the period from 1910 to 1970 when millions of Black Southerners moved to large north and northwestern cities. "My aunts and uncles, all of them migrated north, to New York," said Williams. "It was the only place to get a fairly respectable job. My Aunt Daisey was a New York City telephone operator. Her husband was a policeman. My Uncle James was a barber and also a bellhop. My Aunt Jesse was a nurse."

The work of Williams's father, mother, and grandmother, a tailor and two teachers, provided a fairly middle-class life. He also had the advantage of attracting mentors because he was such a well-dressed, well-mannered, determined, matter-of-fact child. First was family friend Robert E. Howard, who also loved photography. Howard rose from teacher and assistant coach to principal at Wilkinson High School during Williams's school years. Howard and his friend Edward C. "E. C." Jones Jr. had attended Orangeburg's Colored Normal, Industrial, Agricultural and Mechanical College of South Carolina at the same time. The state's only public college for Black students, it was known then as State A&M. Howard connected Williams to Jones, a fortuitous introduction.

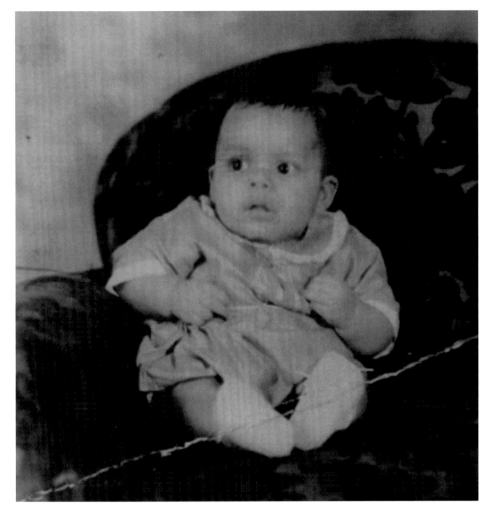

Cecil James Williams, the second son of Ethel Lillian Williams and Cecil Leroy Williams, is born on November 26, 1937. A midwife delivers him at the family's Quick Street home in Orangeburg, South Carolina.

Jones owned Majestic Studio in Sumter, an hour from Orangeburg. In the 1940s, not many people, young or old, owned a camera. But photo studios, including studios owned by Black photographers, could be found in most small towns. Orangeburg had two: White-owned Lackey's Studio and Black-owned Sharperson's Portrait Studio. People of small income could afford a studio portrait. Abolitionist Frederick Douglass himself posed for many a portrait and argued in lectures and essays, including his "Lecture on Pictures," that photography was accessible and a way to challenge the "social death" of slavery by offering self-representation, so important to a people objectified and caricatured. Douglass believed photography could further the social progress of Black people.[3]

Cecil Williams, left front, and cousin Maudelle Salley, right back, dress up for a family photo. Williams hates his striped blazer. Salley lives with the Williamses in Orangeburg during the school year while her mother works in New York City.

It occurred to Williams that there was room for him. He was not drawn to portrait photography, but he saw almost daily "this running thread with families in the community to have a photograph made of yourself. It meant you had reached a certain point and were proud and wanted to record it. It wasn't every person who could afford a five-dollar sitting fee and a picture that cost half that again. It was a symbol of the middle class to have a portrait. It was a status symbol."[4]

Event photography attracted Williams from the start. He enjoyed the interactions, the hustle and bustle, the recognition, even the pressure of being present, as in everywhere at once, and making something of it. It was art in action, and "It was the dominant force or drive in my life to create things," said Williams. Photography itself took a person places, its practice encompassing moments in need of documentation, cameras in need of tinkerers, darkrooms in need of chemists—truly a passport to adventure. Additionally, South Carolina's rigid racial segregation, enforced by laws, faced challenges that moved from the courts into the streets. That change and its drama needed a documentarian. With a camera, "I could do a lot of things most people couldn't do," said Williams—except that this was South Carolina in the 1940s.

After emancipation and Reconstruction, South Carolina and other Southern states passed laws—referred to initially as Black Codes and by the 1830s as Jim Crow laws—that maintained the political and social inequality of Black citizens. Jim Crow laws limited available jobs and voting rights. Jim Crow laws segregated schools, parks, beaches, state fairs, circuses, and hospitals. Jim Crow laws restricted where a Black person sat or stood on a bus, train, or streetcar. Jim Crow laws outlawed marriage to a person of another race and adoption of a child of another race. Jim Crow laws prohibited trying on clothes or shoes in White-owned stores or even being present downtown after sundown. Jim Crow customs required people of color to lower their eyes when passing a White person on the street and to go to the back doors of White-owned homes and to the side windows or back doors of White-owned restaurants.[5]

Williams rode his bicycle to and from his schools, Dunton Memorial School, and then Felton Training School on the campus of Claflin University, both built in the 1920s. Daily he cycled by a White-only playground on Russell Street, with its shinier swing sets and higher slides. "Living in Orangeburg was really strange because we had our own everything, but it was always not nearly as nice." So, "Several times, coming along there, absolutely nobody around, I went on those swings sets and that sliding board, and I played on their playground." He did so alone. Williams often made his points about race, with or without his camera, and if he had to do so alone, he did.

LIVING 'NOT WHITE'

Race determined every breath in South Carolina. Williams's family resided in an indeterminate and thus uneasy place, what Williams called "not white." The "not" mattered in South Carolina. "This was something quite often discussed because of the complexions of my family," said Williams. "We were caught between two worlds." At the dinner table, his parents—father Cecil Leroy Williams and mother Ethel Lillian Williams—talked freely about "others in similar situations who tried to pass, who did pass," meaning people they knew who lived as White despite birth in a family identified as Black. His own mother traveled to the White-owned hair salons of Columbia, the state capital. There, unknown in town, she could pass as White and get her straight hair cut and styled to her satisfaction.

The family also talked politics, and their son perfected—thanks to local radio station WTND, called by the family We Treat Negroes Dirty—an imitation of James Strom Thurmond, South Carolina's governor from 1947 to 1951. Thurmond ran in 1948 as the segregationist presidential candidate of the State Rights Democrats, also known as the Dixiecrats. "We were trying for freedom and justice," said Williams, "and he would come on and say, 'Colored people have got refrigerators, stoves, and cars. What else do they want now?'" At dinner, a conversation would stop for "Cecil, talk like Strom Thurmond!"

The Williams families' own ancestors illustrated the complications of the so-called "color line" and how often it was crossed. Sarah Donaldson (or Donalson or Danalson), Cecil Williams's maternal great-grandmother, born circa 1850 and perhaps a free person of color, bore nineteen children. She toiled as a farm laborer on rented land. Census enumerators labeled her variously "colored" or "mulatto" and the head of her household in Willow Township, Orangeburg County. Children born to her in the late 1800s carried the last name Evans. The census enumerator labeled them "mulatto." The White male enumerators did racial categorizing by sight or community perception and did not consult with the person being counted. Donaldson could neither read nor write, but the Evans children, who worked the land with her, could. Family research uncovered Cecil Williams's White great-grandfather, a landowner in Willow Township and a Confederate soldier who died in 1928 in Columbia's Confederate Soldiers Home.

In the census records of the early 1900s, the description "mulatto" was applied to generations of Cecil Williams's extended family, including James Howard Williams, Cecil Williams's maternal grandfather, born in 1888, a carpenter with a trade certificate from Voorhees Industrial School in Denmark, South Carolina. He taught industrial trades at State A&M and died at age thirty-four of typhoid fever followed by pneumonia. Lillian Estelle Evans Williams, Cecil Williams's maternal grandmother, was labeled "mulatto." Born in 1891, she attended college for a year, then

Several members of the 20th century Williams family move to New York City. The Orangeburg Williamses visit during summer and winter holidays, with the result that Cecil Williams, from his teen years on, drives to New York City to buy camera equipment and work short-term jobs in camera stores. The family gathers at Lackey's Studio in Orangeburg for this portrait.

Children, from left: Maudelle Salley, Cecil James Williams, Alfred Leroy Williams

Adults, from left, who are children of Lillian Estelle Evans Williams: James Williams, Lillian Estelle Evans Williams, Ethel Lillian Williams Williams, Jesse Williams Younger, and Andrew Williams.

worked as a schoolteacher. And Ethel Lillian Williams, his mother, was labeled "mulatto." Born in 1910, she was graduated from State A&M with bachelor's and master's degrees and worked as a schoolteacher.

On July 18, 1932, Ethel Williams and Cecil Leroy Williams married. They lived in the home that Ethel's mother, Lillian Williams, owned on Quick Street in Orangeburg. The children—Alfred Leroy, born in 1933; Cecil James, born in 1937; and their first cousin Maudelle Gloria Salley, born in 1934—were mostly raised by Lillian Williams while Ethel Williams Williams boarded and taught school in Calhoun County and Cecil Leroy Williams worked day and night as a tailor. Ethel Williams's schools lacked desks, blackboards, schoolbooks, heat, and water because White officials believed funding should go to White schools. She told her son that she boarded in homes where the outdoors could be seen through gaps in the floors and walls.

The photo Cecil Williams calls "Children of Segregation"—his blond, blue-eyed friends labeled "Negro" by the Orangeburg White community—illustrates for him "the hypocrisy of racism." Family friend and educator Robert E. Howard photographed the 1940s birthday party of I. N. Rendall Harper Jr., seen here holding his birthday cake.

Toddler crouching: Unidentified.

First row, left to right: Fraser Williams, Eugene Patterson, unidentified female, Thales Thomas "Skipp" Pearson, I. N. Rendall Harper Jr. (with birthday cake), Elaine Adams, John "Beanie" Sulton, Wayman Johnson, unidentified toddler.

Second row: Marion "Brother Burgess" Johnson, Raymond Lawrence, Melvin Adams, unidentified male, unidentified male, unidentified female, Reggie Dash, Wilma McCoy, Robert Jackson, Cecil Williams, William Hixson, Arnold Leroy "Bunt" Sulton Jr., Robert Funchess, unidentified male.

Third row: Barbara Jean Thompson, unidentified female, Carolyn Webber, Carolyn Harris, Miriam DeCosta, unidentified male, Betty "Burgess" Johnson, Robert "Bobby" Knight, unidentified female adult, Maudelle Salley, unidentified female.

And "After she would teach for a month, sometimes she had to go find the [White] superintendent to get paid. They [Black teachers] had to hunt him down."

For Cecil Leroy Williams, born in 1908, family life had been spare. When he broke his leg at a young age, a lack of medical care resulted in a lifelong limp. Cecil Leroy Williams's mother Lizzie Parler (or Parlor) Williams finished school with third grade. This was not unusual in a state where three-fourths of White and Black children attended five or fewer years of school. She worked as a washerwoman and died a widow in 1953. Cecil Leroy Williams's younger brother George Williams Jr. died young of a coronary blockage. However, younger sister Minerva "Minnie" Williams lived until age 90 and, at one time, worked for the Hungarian Consulate in New York City.

In 1940, the census enumerators labeled Cecil Leroy Williams as "Negro," although his branch of the family included White and Native American ancestors. The 1920 census was the last time the US Census Bureau used the categories of mulatto, quadroon, and octoroon, ending its recording of what was then called "mixed race" or "mixed blood." The 1930 census labeled people as either White, Negro, Indian, Mexican, or one of five Asian nationalities. Enumerators recorded people with both White and Black lineage as Negro and people with Black and Native American lineage as Negro, "no matter how small the percentage of Negro blood," and people with White and Native American lineage as Indian unless the community, by general consensus, regarded the person as White.[6]

Slaveholding colonies and states had held since the 1600s that any African antecedent made a person Black and that a child born of an enslaved mother was also enslaved. To preserve what was termed "white racial purity," the "one-drop rule" served as a legal principle of racial classification, codified into law in some states, and establishing, as one judge instructed, that "any Negro blood whatever" made a person and that person's descendants Black. Census counts enhanced a politics of race and control, as did Article 1, Section 2 of the US Constitution, which, in 1788, declared that any enslaved person be counted as three-fifths of a person when determining the population for congressional representation and taxation.[7]

Judge William Jay wrote, in 1853, "But who is a *colored* man? We answer, the *fairest* man in Carolina, if it can be proved that a drop of negro blood flowed in the veins of his mother." South Carolina's 1895 constitution declared, "The marriage of a white person with a Negro or mulatto, or person who shall have one-eighth or more negro blood, shall be unlawful and void." The constitution also stated, "Separate schools shall be provided for children of the white and colored races, and no child of either race shall ever be permitted to attend a school provided for children of the other race."[8]

In a neighborhood portrait of thirty-three children who attended I. N. Rendall Harper Jr.'s birthday party, Williams stood beside best friend Arnold Leroy "Bunt" Sulton Jr., a blond and blue-eyed child. The boys wore pressed, open-collar shirts and shorts, the youngest in rompers. The girls wore party dresses adorned with ruffled collars, smocking, and embroidery. Only people labeled Black, including the three blond celebrants, lived in Harper's segregated neighborhood.[9]

A few miles away in another Black neighborhood, Williams's backyard adjoined that of Bunt Sulton. "Where my backyard ended Bunt's backyard began. The field behind my house was overgrown, and I used to run through my backyard to Bunt's house, thinking that I would avoid any snakes if I ran. And Bunt had in his backyard a small shed, and that's where I smoked my first and last cigarette. That was our clubhouse where sometimes we would try unapproved chemical experiments. We would mix this and that." In a few years, friends Bunt Sulton and George Marion Crawford would delight in entering segregated territory as young White men, bringing Williams along as their "Spanish" visitor.

The Williams family's light skin and straight dark hair brought both privileges and attacks. When Williams was five, his mother took him downtown for a special purchase. They entered a dime store so that he could buy a toy car with the dollar his mother provided. "The car cost 89 cents, and when the lady slammed my change on the counter, I asked my mother about it." The woman had muttered, "Brass Ankles." Ethel Williams explained to her son that White people in Orangeburg did not like Negroes or Indians and perceived Brass Ankles as residing on an even lower rung. The saleswoman used a pejorative term. Brass Ankles referred, in general, to South Carolinians who may have had Native American, Black, and European ancestors. An isolated group lived at Crane Pond, the children attending the segregated Crane

Pond School in Orangeburg County. The families visited the town of Orangeburg occasionally, riding in wagons.[10]

FARM FIELDS, COURTHOUSES, AND COLLEGES

Williams worked at State A&M when he was ten years old. He dashed in and out of buildings, delivering messages and hovering around the edge of history in the making, thanks to an NAACP lawsuit. John H. Wrighten, who grew up on Edisto Island, had twice applied unsuccessfully to the College of Charleston in Charleston, South Carolina, for undergraduate education. Denied admission because of race, Wrighten attended State A&M and, upon graduation in 1946, applied to the University of South Carolina's law school. Once again denied admission because of race, he sued the university in January 1947 with the help of the NAACP. Wrighten's lawsuit asked for admission to the School of Law because the state provided no law school for Black students. Worried about higher education lawsuits that sought Black applicants' admission to White-only graduate schools in other states, the legislature preemptively appropriated $60,000 for graduate and legal education at State A&M.[11]

In July 1947, federal district judge J. Waties Waring ordered the state to make one of three choices: open a law school with "substantial parity" at State A&M by September, or accept Wrighten at the University of South Carolina, or close its law school. In September, without adequate professors, books, or space, State A&M offered a law degree as well as graduate degrees in English, education, and the social and natural sciences. As the decade ended, just eleven institutions in nine southern states offered Black students graduate degrees, mostly in teacher training programs. No Black college in the South offered a doctorate.[12]

"Equality" after the lawsuit worked this way: State A&M received $523,000 compared to the $8.2 million allocated for the five white institutions. At the same time the University of South Carolina (USC) received $3.5 million for its graduate schools while State A&M received less than $1 million. Modjeska Monteith

Simkins, corresponding secretary for the state NAACP, raged over "chump courses" that would "hoodwink" any "shortsighted Negroes" enrolled in unaccredited programs. Wrighten initially disdained the one-classroom, two-professor school that Thurgood Marshall, the NAACP's chief legal counsel, called "a Jim Crow dump." In 1949, still determined to be a lawyer, Wrighten joined fifteen other students at State A&M against Marshall's wishes. Wrighten's plight illustrated the NAACP's great fear associated with its strategy, that such lawsuits could entrench "separate but equal" rather than end it.[13]

Williams carried handwritten messages up and down the stairs and corridors of Wilkinson Hall and throughout the State A&M campus. His job provided a monetary thrill. He was paid for his work by check, "your name on a piece of paper. It was great!" He charmed the new law school dean, Benner Creswell Turner, a 1930 graduate of Harvard Law School who had practiced law for three years in Philadelphia, worked in real estate and taxes, and came to State A&M after serving five years on the faculty of North Carolina Central College of Law in Durham. Turner, viewed as aloof on and off campus, would stop Williams in the hall to chat or call Williams into his office to share his latest jokes. Working at State A&M put Williams in the know. He crossed paths with Essie Mae Washington, the not-so-secret daughter of Strom Thurmond and Carrie Butler, a 15-year-old Black servant in the Thurmond family home in Edgefield, South Carolina, when the 23-year-old Thurmond taught and coached at Edgefield High School. Washington enrolled at State A&M in Fall 1946, her parentage such common knowledge that even a young person such as Williams knew the story.[14]

Williams's work ethic paid off again when photographer Edward C. "E. C." Jones Jr. ushered him into a pivotal place and time, neighboring Clarendon County in 1949. Jones photographed for the NAACP. He did so while James Myles Hinton, state conference president, and Eugene A. R. "Skippy" Montgomery, the conference's executive secretary, nurtured the most radical of actions: a constitutional challenge to the "separate but equal" public schools by Black parents and children who knew firsthand that Black students' public education was barely funded. Jones and apprentice Williams became eyewitnesses and more; they worked as visual storytellers, record-makers, and historians.

When Jones drove pitted, narrow dirt roads bordered by Clarendon cotton fields and when he and Williams entered the rural churches, cameras in hand, they attended the blossoming of decades of plaintiffs' and attorneys' hard and dangerous work. In the 1930s the NAACP had designed and then implemented a way to end segregation through the use of lawsuits targeting graduate and professional schools. This strategy required challenging the 1896 *Plessy v. Ferguson* standard of "separate but equal" by demanding equal opportunities for Black students.[15]

At the NAACP's 1935 convention, the documentary film *A Study of Education Inequalities in South Carolina* made its shocking debut. The year before, Charles Hamilton Houston had trekked through rural South Carolina, including Chester, Orangeburg, Richland, and York counties. Houston, who was then the NAACP's chief counsel, had recorded, in flickering black and white, a decayed and condemned school building near the state capital, its Black students crammed into a nearby church; sixty-eight Black students lining up in front of a one-room school with benches but no desks or tables, no heat, and a privy located across a highway and railroad tracks; young Black children hiking ten miles across fields to school while White children cruised down the road in a school bus. The film ended with a rallying cry: "Negroes must ceaselessly protest discrimination in education by publicity . . . by test cases in court, by the ballot . . . until the State offers the identical quality and quantity of educational opportunity to all its citizens, regardless of race, color, or creed."[16]

In 1936 Lloyd Gaines applied to the University of Missouri School of Law. Denied admission because of race, he sued with the help of the NAACP. In 1938, in *Missouri ex. rel. Gaines v. Canada,* the US Supreme Court upheld "separate but equal" education but did not ignore the consequent lack of access. Black college graduates had to leave Missouri to study law, and that violated the Equal Protection Clause of the Fourteenth Amendment, the Supreme Court said. To preserve segregation the state created Lincoln University Law School, located in a former beauty salon. Gaines declined to attend and disappeared—permanently—before an appeal.[17]

Also in 1936, Donald Gaines Murray sought admission to the segregated University of Maryland School of Law. Maryland denied Murray access to the state's only accredited law school. Thus, Marshall argued, Murray was denied a "separate but equal" education. A court of appeals declared that Murray could attend while remaining separate, or segregated, within the university. Lawsuits continued in 1946 when Heman Marion Sweatt was denied admission to the University of Texas School of Law and Ada Lois Sipuel was denied admission to the University of Oklahoma College of Law because of race. Each sued.[18]

In 1947 Texas leased four rooms below street level for a Black-only law school that Sweatt declined to attend. In 1948 six Black students applied to a variety of Oklahoma's graduate schools, and all were denied admission because of race. George McLaurin, who had applied to the doctoral program in the College of Education, sued. The 61-year-old retired professor was admitted under the state's segregation laws as a student apart. He attended for two semesters—seated apart from classmates in an alcove, studying and eating apart at isolated tables in the library and student union, and using a restroom solely reserved for him in the education building.[19]

That same year Oklahoma slapped together a segregated law school for Sipuel—one room at the state Senate—and the NAACP successfully argued it was not equal. In June 1949 Sipuel entered the College of Law. The college consigned her to a chair marked "colored" in classrooms and to a guarded and chained-off area in the cafeteria. These "instant" law schools did not provide full-time professors, law libraries, course variety, historic prestige, or interaction with the majority of a state's law students and attorneys. Just so segregation within an institution also prevented educational equality, the ropes and chains and barricades of empty chairs blocking interaction with professors and classmates, thus preventing Black students from forming relationships that could enhance a future legal career. Sipuel graduated in 1951.[20]

Because Williams's mentors documented such great changes and because he was curious, ambitious, and invited to attend, he found himself in the midst of the transformation. Just down the road from him lived Clarendon County's sharecroppers, farmers, teachers, and ministers, a fair number of them World War II veterans who had decided that their children deserved more and it was long past time for change.

RECORDING HISTORY IN THE MAKING

The almost-successes in courts led the NAACP to gather leaders, including Hinton, in Atlanta in 1946 to discuss public education lawsuits in the South. Hinton, born in North Carolina in 1891, orphaned at four, and raised by an aunt in New York City, was among the few Black men serving as an officer, an infantry lieutenant, in World War I. Ending his service in Augusta, Georgia, in 1919, he joined Black-owned Pilgrim Health and Life Insurance Company, and opened territory on the East Coast before settling in Columbia in 1938. By 1939, he was running the Columbia NAACP branch and, in 1941, he followed the state conference's second president to leadership and quickly expanded membership to 15,000 and the number of branches from thirteen to eighty. Ferociously determined to end segregation, he had become expert in NAACP court challenges, earning the respect of NAACP legal counsel Marshall as he fostered a win in equal teacher pay, the end of the all-White primary, and the opening of the law school at State A&M.[21]

After an Atlanta NAACP strategy session, Hinton brought home a challenge, telling ministers at an Allen University-Benedict College summer session in Columbia to find a plaintiff who dared to ask for a school bus. In many Southern states, including South Carolina, White students rode school buses while Black students walked to public school. Requesting bus transportation seemed a logical starting place. In Clarendon County, farmers Hammett and Levi Pearson had already spent years on this, asking the county's school superintendent and school board, even the state Board of Education, for a school bus. Their Davis Station schoolchildren walked nine miles one way to reach Scott's Branch school in Summerton. The Pearsons rigged a truck for passengers, then, with the help of other parents, purchased one after another two worn and temperamental buses. They asked officials for funds for a driver, fuel, and repairs.[22]

The Pearson brothers—denied at every turn, but encouraged by Hinton and Rev. Joseph Armstrong "J. A." DeLaine, a Summerton minister, educator, and activist—dared take another unheard-of step. On March 16, 1948, Levi Pearson petitioned officials for school transportation and then filed a lawsuit with the aid of Hinton and Harold Boulware, local NAACP counsel in Columbia. Thwarted by

White officials' claims regarding school district boundaries, the lawsuit did not go forward, but something much further reaching did. Deciding that they had the courage and determination to petition for more than a bus, a Clarendon contingent persuaded Marshall that they should and could challenge the "separate but equal" legal doctrine in court.[23]

South Carolina's Black schoolchildren, denied a proportionate share of school funding, met in abandoned shacks and hunting lodges or donated cabins that lacked desks, blackboards, textbooks, heat, electricity, and running water. They toted to school their lunches and coal or wood for oil-drum fires, hauled well water, and used outdoor privies. White children attended brick schools with libraries, cafeterias, and playgrounds, with central heat, lighting, water fountains, and indoor toilets. In the 1939–40 school year, 265,845 White students and 215,905 Black students attended public school. The state superintendent's 1941 report valued school property for the White students at $45.8 million and that of Black students at $7 million. Per pupil expenditures amounted to $56.33 for a White child and $11.90 for a Black child. *Plessy v. Ferguson's* standard of "separate but equal" clearly meant only "separate" in South Carolina.[24]

Ethel Williams taught at such a rural school, Mount Carmel School, built in 1894. "It was a two- or three-room school in Cameron, a pot-bellied stove in the middle," said Cecil Williams. "The students before they received their education, they had to get firewood to burn in the stove. The schoolbooks were used and marked up, always secondhand. They had to draw water from a well. They had an outdoor privy, no separate bathroom for the teacher." But Ethel Williams did not complain. "This was what she had for herself too," as a child, said Cecil Williams.

At their 1948 annual conference, members of the South Carolina Conference of Branches of the NAACP approved a resolution opposing segregated education. The resolution said in part, "Equality of citizenship must begin in the school system, and our branches are instructed to carry on a campaign both in the Negro communities and in the cities and towns to end segregation in the elementary, high school, college and university levels." Eugene A. R. "Skippy" Montgomery, a former Marine who served in World War II and then earned a master's degree in social services from Atlanta University in Atlanta, Georgia, crisscrossed the county looking for people ready to sue or to support the court challenge. He met in churches with farm laborers, sharecroppers and tenant farmers, maids and cooks and janitors, blacksmiths and gas station attendants, teachers and principals, and small business owners. Hinton ensured a strong South Carolina Conference of Branches of the NAACP, well-supported local branches, statewide fundraising, and the commitment of attorney Marshall, who worried about the safety and staying power of such isolated and impoverished people.[25]

Throughout, Jones photographed with Williams at his side. They photographed gatherings, meetings, sermons, recognition ceremonies, and, later, celebrations. Jones would stop by the Williams home on a Sunday and drive the two of them the thirty-five miles to Clarendon County in his Ford Coupe. In the trunk, packed in fiberboard cases, rode a Graflex Crown Graphic and a Graflex Speed Graphic, the cameras' film sheets, film holders, flash units, and expensive flash bulbs that could be used only once. These were hefty cameras; the Crown Graphic's leather-covered wooden body weighed almost five pounds.

The two photographers preferred the Speed Graphic with its faster shutter speed designed to capture action. A viewfinder at the back of the camera required a black hood for focusing before film was inserted into a film holder. Designed to be a press camera, the Speed Graphic also provided an optical viewfinder and rangefinder atop its body. Jones and Williams preferred it for mobility's sake. Even so, taking photos was a cumbersome process. The photographers opened the front of the camera box, unfolded a bellows, and then turned knobs on the left and right of the camera body to move the lens back and forth, focusing by merging two images. They then set the shutter speed and f-stop with a knob on the right side; inserted into the camera's back a film holder with its two sheets of 4-inch by 5-inch film, the film sheets protected by opaque slides; cocked the shutter and pressed a lever on the right side to take a picture; pulled the film holder out and reversed it; then inserted it again for the second photo. Slow, despite *speed* in the camera's name? Yes. Complicated? Yes.[26]

There was Williams. He lugged the heavy camera cases. If Jones wanted to take several photographs, Williams pulled a loaded and unused film holder from one side of a camera case and handed to Jones the "double dark slide film holder." Each film

The Majestic Studio case sits below the first pew. To the right of the case are Gabriel Tindal, Gilbert Henry, and J. S. "Flutie" Boyd of Manning, a retired teacher and NAACP stalwart.

The Black residents of Clarendon County, determined to obtain an equal and desegregated education for their children, often meet at Liberty Hill AME Church, about three miles outside Summerton. Photographer Edward C. "E. C." Jones Jr., owner of Majestic Studio in Sumter, and apprentice Cecil Williams document speeches and meetings for what becomes Briggs v. Elliott, *the first of five lawsuits consolidated in* Brown v. Board of Education.

holder held only two sheets of film, each sheet of film shielded from the light by the intervening dark slide. Once used, "I would turn a little latch and 'lock' the film in, keeping the dark slide from sliding out and exposing the film," explained Williams, who would then carefully place the used film on the opposite side of the camera case from the unused. For longer exposures or for portraits, Williams set up a tripod that Jones used to support and steady the Crown Graphic. Indoors, for photos of an audience or congregation, the photographers held the hefty Speed Graphic high above their heads for a panoptic shot. They used Plus-X or Tri-X high-speed films. "I also had to keep Jones supplied with flashbulbs, which were almost as big as the bulbs that go in an incandescent light. We had a huge, shiny metal flash unit we attached to the camera for indoor pictures." The boy and the man possessed a rather dramatic presence, their bulky cameras held by a leather strap on the left side, the flash apparatus clamped to the camera and looming tall on the right, the flashbulbs ka-popping, melting, or exploding upon the shutter's release. Anyone in the foreground found themselves blinded by the flash's light.

Soon Williams began taking photos himself with Jones's spare camera and, later, with a Crown Graphic borrowed from school, and, still later, with his own Crown and Speed Graphic cameras. "Almost all journalists had a 4×5. If you didn't have a 4×5, you didn't count. The camera itself would immediately identify you as a professional photographer," a new dream of his.

Their photograph of more than a hundred men, women, and children looking at the camera from seats on long, polished church pews illustrated the challenges and the beauty of the team's work. The church, lit by tall double-hung windows, appeared both full and cavernous; the people appeared both waiting and ready, their faces glowing. Tucked under the front pew, squat and heavy, sat the Majestic Studio case, its three latches open.

The constant meetings, rallies, and celebrations to recruit petitioners and inspire them and their supporters occurred during and after services in several rural Clarendon County churches. The small, packed country churches could be heatstroke hot in spring and summer. At one church "they had a huge fan at the back of the church that made a lot of noise. It was an eight-foot fan for two hundred people in the church." Windows opened to the outdoors, roaring fans, restless children, shouted sermons, choirs singing: "It was very loud." A potluck or picnic might follow, but every time, "It would end up with appeals for funds," said Williams.

Williams's mother, who taught at a summer institute with Rev. DeLaine, described for her son the social and economic pressure inflicted on the Pearson and DeLaine families. White business owners and farmers denied the Pearsons seed, fertilizer, farm equipment, gas and oil, and loans. At night, cars roared down the rural roads, drivers and passengers shooting toward the Pearson homes, where the children slept on the floor for safety's sake. DeLaine, fired from his principal's post at Silver School in the summer of 1949, warned, "This will be rough. Some will fall on the wayside. Some will lose their jobs." And, as all knew, "Someone may die on the way." He did not exaggerate.[27]

On November 11, 1949, Black tenant farmers, sharecroppers, housekeepers, cooks, and gas station attendants of that small, impoverished county signed a petition—107 parents and their children at the home of Eliza and Harry Briggs—asking for more than a bus. They asked for buildings, books, furnishings, equipment, and buses equal to those of children in White-only schools. The petitioners of *Briggs v. Elliott* challenged "separate but equal" by petitioning for what DeLaine called "Equal Everything."[28]

Williams paid attention. Standing beside Jones, "the photographer of prominence in central South Carolina," he attended, a child helping document this revolution.

THE 1950S

In 1950, Cecil Williams was twelve years old, and he was a photographer. He entered the larger adult world of right versus wrong and good versus evil when he accompanied photographer and mentor Edward C. "E. C." Jones Jr. to Clarendon County. There they found themselves documenting not just events but a change: rural Black South Carolinians petitioning for their Constitutional rights. More than a youthful assistant, maybe more than a sidekick, "Very early on I became known as a photographer," said Williams. And very early on Williams suspected he had embarked on a "divine mission," that "Throughout history God uses us to do the work of good for change for humanity's sake."

After World War II, the speed of change accelerated, too much for some and not enough for others. Jackie Robinson had desegregated Major League Baseball. President Harry Truman had signed an executive order ending racial segregation in the armed forces. The Fellowship of Reconciliation (FOR) and the Congress of Racial Equality (CORE) had organized a Journey of Reconciliation, during which Black and White riders challenged segregation on buses in the South. CORE's Black and White members had attempted to desegregate public spaces such as restaurants. NAACP lawsuits, a state-by-state slog attacking "separate but equal" in graduate and professional schools, had chipped away at Jim Crow. And voting rights lawsuits had ended the all-White primary, which previously existed in eight Southern states, including South Carolina.[1]

The repeated protests challenged segregationists' long-held beliefs about their superiority and primacy and prompted a vengeful meanness. South Carolina's segregationists reinvigorated the KKK and founded White Citizens' Councils whose

Wilkinson High School students support their football team, the Wolverines, at the Fair Ground Stadium. Orangeburg's stadium accepts Black schools' sports events once a week on a weekday. Their 1938 campus on Goff Avenue has been replaced in 1953 on Belleville Road by what was called an "equalization school." The state built these schools for Black students to sustain segregation after Briggs v. Elliott's *challenge to segregated public schools.*

participants punished every petitioner while White politicians fought every lawsuit. But Black defiance, coming strong in Orangeburg, worked strategically on downtown streets, on campuses, and in court.

In Williams's 1950–51 school year, Black children made up 40 percent of enrolled students; 85 percent of them attended one-room schools. South Carolina valued public school property at $83.9 million for White students and at $19.7 million for Black students. Williams and his classmates, though, had it better than most at Felton Training School on the campus of State A&M, where Williams spent the remainder of his elementary and middle school years.[2]

Orangeburg offered what Williams called an "intellectual mecca." In 1938 the Works Progress Administration (WPA), a federal program that employed millions during the Depression to construct roads and public buildings, built Wilkinson High School, the city's first public high school for Black students. Attending a high school and, especially, earning a high school diploma remained rare in South Carolina, a rural state that denied transportation to all Black students and seldom provided them with upper-grade education. In 1950–51, South Carolina supplied 291 public high schools for White students but only sixty-eight for Black students. Yet Orangeburg was home to two of the state's eight post-secondary institutions serving Black students. And both Claflin and State A&M offered graduate education, although an NAACP lawsuit had forced South Carolina to provide graduate and professional education at State A&M.[3]

From their founding Southern Black colleges had functioned essentially as primary, secondary, and teacher-training schools. Laws had prevented literacy and the education of enslaved people, and the post-war peonage and poverty of formerly enslaved people meant that many freed people began a formal education self-taught. In 1869 Northern Methodists established Claflin University in Orangeburg. In 1872 Claflin president Alonzo Webster persuaded the state legislature to take advantage of the Morrill Land Grant College Act of 1862 and add an agricultural and mechanical college to Claflin. The two schools shared land, buildings, a president, faculty, and students. This forced relationship between a land-grant school and a private, Methodist-affiliated school sometimes felt too close for comfort. In 1896, legislation divided the two schools and established a separate Normal, Industrial, Agricultural & Mechanical College for the Colored Race, a public land-grant institution referred to as State A&M (and renamed, in 1954, South Carolina State College (SC State)). Claflin discontinued most of its elementary and all of its high school grades in the 1940s, retaining only the first to fourth grades for teacher training. State A&M eliminated its high school in 1933, retaining kindergarten through eighth grade at Felton for teacher training.[4]

Felton's four-room school building existed because the Rosenwald Fund of philanthropist Julius Rosenwald, co-founder of the Sears, Roebuck and Company, helped build 481 much-needed schools for Black children in South Carolina. Throughout the South between 1913 and 1941, the Rosenwald Rural Schools Initiative—with required community assistance in the form of funds, labor, and/or land donations—constructed more than 5,000 schools, the majority elementary schools. In 1924 in Orangeburg the Rosenwald Fund had provided $7,000 toward Felton, an on-campus brick school with heat, electricity, desks, and books. Students applied for admission. "It was an achievement to get into Felton," said Williams. One grade to a teacher, glass windows, flooring, and cots for naps: "Felton was upscale, like a private school," said Williams, "but mostly because State College buoyed it with instructional materials, audio visual equipment, art materials," and apprentice teachers to aid classroom teachers. "We had better school supplies, better books, art lessons with clay or drawing pads." Teacher Julia Etta Washington doted on Williams. "Every February she would give me a box of chocolates, a big box, not one of those dollar boxes, and say, 'When I get married, I want to have a little boy that looks like you.'"[5]

Williams's mother and maternal grandmother had attended college and taught school; his maternal aunts and uncle had attended college. In the town and county of Orangeburg college-educated Black citizens outnumbered White citizens with higher education. When challenging White authority this made possible independent, locally based strategies; a certain pride; and, for some, less economic risk. Inspired by the stoic persistence of *Briggs v. Elliott* petitioners, the Black people of Orangeburg began devising their own methods of confrontation. Years of terrorism and economic persecution in Clarendon and Orangeburg counties had heightened the sense of mission and urgency felt by many of Orangeburg's Black ministers and World War II veterans and by the Black colleges' faculty, staff, and students. "We knew we had important matters that we had to work on," said Williams.

The adults mentoring and employing Williams put him within the sphere of local activists. "In those days you naturally gravitated toward the people in the community doing what you wanted to do. They meant everything," said Williams of the adults he admired, those who opposed Jim Crow and those who took on apprentices or protégés. Observing local activists led Williams early to the belief that Black citizens of Clarendon and Orangeburg counties in the 1940s and '50s "created the civil rights movement." Black-owned *Jet* magazine, soon to employ Williams, concurred when describing the two counties as "Orangeburg (home of the Negro militant intelligentsia) and Clarendon (home of the original NAACP school bias fighters)."[6]

Williams did do what children do. He joined the Boy Scouts. He attended Bible School in the summer. "At Felton, I was in the school operettas. One time I played the leading role. I was Carlos. I had about three lines." But mostly he reached for the far future. He daydreamed about rocket ships and listened to *The Mysterious*

Traveler on the radio. He bought and pored over comic books featuring space exploration, such as *Space Adventures, Space War,* and *Mysteries in Space.* While other children drew the family house, car, and dog, "I usually put a futuristic twist on it." He drew fantastic rocket ships and spacescapes. He impressed his friend George Greene and at least one automobile manufacturer by designing a car of the future. Williams entered the annual model-building competition of the Fisher Body Craftsman's Guild, sponsored by the Fisher Body Division of General Motors. "I first made it of coat hangers for framing and stability and then kept building on it with clay" that his parents ordered after Williams discovered drugstore clay hardened too quickly. He placed with a four-door car design that anticipated the 1956 Studebaker Hawk, but he did not win. Greene remembers, "They sent him a lovely letter back saying he had a future, and when he got older, they would like to hear from him again."[7]

Williams also composed photo collages. "I would cut things out of magazines and paste them on my real pictures. When I got ready to send a Christmas card, it had my picture on it. It had the moon in the background and a miniature spaceship." Williams called that composition *Reaching for the Moon.* In more down-to-Earth compositions, "I would take pictures of myself, and I would then superimpose my picture on *Newsweek* and *Life* magazine covers and send those out."

That summer of 1950 it truly seemed Jim Crow's death approached. *Sweatt v. Painter* and *McLaurin v. Oklahoma* reached the US Supreme Court, and the plaintiffs won. NAACP attorney Thurgood Marshall exulted, "The complete destruction of all segregation is now in sight," even though the court's acceptance of the NAACP's Fourteenth Amendment argument did not include striking down *Plessy v. Ferguson's* "separate but equal" doctrine. On June 5, 1950, the Supreme Court ruled that Heman Marion Sweatt could claim "his full constitutional right: legal education equivalent to that offered by the State to students of other races." That same day the court ruled that the conditions imposed on George McLaurin "deprive him of his personal and present right to the equal protection of the laws." And that same day in *Henderson v. United States,* the court ended trains' segregated dining cars, which subjected persons to "undue or unreasonable prejudice or disadvantage" in interstate travel, as a violation of the Interstate Commerce Act.[8]

Black-owned newspapers celebrated. Pay your NAACP dues, wrote *Pittsburgh Courier* columnist Trezzvant W. Anderson. "Brethren, you owe it to the NAACP, so the NAACP can keep Thurgood and his giant-killers on the job, bringing us up into still brighter light." In July 1950, after a two-day conference of law professors with NAACP staff, attorneys, and state conference presidents, Marshall announced a focused drive to "strike down" segregation in public elementary and secondary schools, higher education, and interstate transportation. In November the *Afro-American* reported a total of 233 Black students studying in previously segregated universities in eleven states.[9]

A TRAIN BRINGS THE CHIEF LEGAL COUNSEL

That winter Williams's civil rights career began. The most famous civil rights attorney was coming to Charleston to argue *Briggs v. Elliott* in federal court. Shadrack Morgan, an Orangeburg attorney known as Squire, short for Esquire, called on Williams to record the moment. Morgan, a short and bespectacled man, had practiced law in Orangeburg since 1919, after graduation from Howard University School of Law. In 1938 he assisted Thurgood Marshall in a stymied effort by Charles Bailey, a Morehouse College graduate and Columbia resident, to gain acceptance to the University of South Carolina's law school. And, from 1943 to 1945, Morgan served as local counsel to the NAACP's Marshall in successful lawsuits to equalize the pay of Black and White teachers.[10]

An invitation from Morgan was an honor; Williams's parents gave permission for an overnight trip. *Briggs v. Elliott* would be heard on November 20, 1950, with Marshall arriving early for a pretrial conference. Morgan, Williams, and other greeters crowded under a shed roof and waited for hours for Marshall's train. Williams carried his own Argus 75 Twin Lens Reflex camera, smaller, lighter, and less expensive than the Crown or Speed Graphic cameras. He had armed himself with one flashbulb. At a dollar apiece frugality was necessary. In the dark before dawn, the six-foot, two-inch attorney stepped from the Champion, the train from New York City. "He just paused for a second," but Williams got his shot: Marshall

Thurgood Marshall comes to Charleston for the November 20, 1950, trial of Briggs v. Elliott, *but a voluntary dismissal of the initial challenge delays the trial for six months. Cecil Williams accompanies Shadrack "Squire" Morgan, an Orangeburg attorney, to photograph Marshall, also known as "Mr. Civil Rights." Williams uses his own medium format camera to capture Marshall disembarking from the train. Flashbulbs are expensive so he takes only one photo.*

in three-quarters profile during his descent of the train's steps, his fedora brim upturned, his trench coat buttoned and belted, his suitcase battered.[11]

During the drive from the train station to the house where the attorney would charm his hosts and then sleep, the teen was transfixed by Marshall's long arm stretching the length of the bench seat and startled by his earthy monologue, not trial worries but salty anecdotes peppered with profanity. He teased Williams, "Man, I'm going to have to give you some liquor before the night is over." The few minutes at the train station comprised Williams's only opportunity to photograph "Mr. Civil Rights," but he did well. His photo of Marshall made its way into Black-owned newspapers, and ten dollars per print made its way into his pocket.

Briggs v. Elliott did not go to trial then. A voluntary dismissal of the equality challenge, encouraged by federal Judge J. Waties Waring, made way for a new argument, a challenge to segregation. On December 22, 1950, the NAACP filed another petition, signed by twenty Summerton parents and their forty-six children, saying that South Carolina's segregated public schools denied children "equal educational advantages in violation of the Constitution of the United States," the first direct challenge to *Plessy v. Ferguson.* The petitioners had no chance for success in South Carolina, but a loss in district court could be directly appealed to the US Supreme Court.[12]

Ever the entrepreneur, Williams kept up with such news by selling *Jet,* which arrived by Trailways bus from Johnson Publishing Company in Chicago. Lee Alonzo "L. A." Blackman, a contractor in Elloree and president of its NAACP branch, had passed on Orangeburg circulation to Williams. Devoted readers received *Jet* by mail, but Williams could sell two dozen or so copies per week at the price of fifteen cents each, a nickel each to him. Pocket-size, printed in black and white, except for one bright color on the cover and in ads, *Jet* reported national and international news, human interest tales, and celebrity gossip through snappy summaries or brief stories collected into departments such as National Report, the Weekly Almanac, People Are Talking About (biracial "Adam and Eve" party in Columbia), Best Photos of the Week, Religion, Sports, Education ("S.C. NAACP Makes New Demand for Mixed Schools"), Business, Books, Science, Medicine, and, often, mayhem ("Near-Blind S.C. Wife Slashes Mate 85 Times"). First published on November 1, 1951, to meet a national hunger, by 1953 the Johnson Publishing Company had recalibrated. *Jet's* weekly entertainment, sports, and gossip mix was enhanced by breaking news, politics, and exclusives on civil rights. Fans called *Jet* the "Negro bible" and said, "If you didn't read it in *Jet,* it didn't happen." South Carolina's racist politics and violence guaranteed news for Black-owned publications, and Williams's big dream became photographing for *Jet.*[13]

In May 1951 Marshall returned to Charleston to prove—using testimony from experts who had surveyed the Black and White schools and educators who had studied the consequences of segregation—that South Carolina did not offer equal education to Black children and that this deprivation caused lasting harm. On May 28, 500 Black citizens squeezed into the courthouse halls. Hundreds more waited in the streets to hear what "the great special counsel" had to say during this "first head-on attack to end segregation," reported the *Afro-American* and *Pittsburgh Courier*. Williams did not attend, but one of his heroes did. Alexander M. "Alex" Rivera Jr. photographed petitioners, judges, attorneys, and onlookers for the *Courier* and reported that the "relentless" Marshall and the NAACP's education experts "blasted holes in the already crumbling walls of segregation." Williams thought of Rivera, whom he met while assisting Jones, as a "step above" his mentor because Rivera worked as a photojournalist, reporting with words and images. "I idolized him." Soon, Williams would work beside him.[14]

Black journalists traveled like foreign correspondents below the Mason-Dixon line, where they could not stay in White-owned hotels or motels or eat in White-owned restaurants, and might be run out of town. Black-owned media covered the Deep South from headquarters in the northeast and in a few larger Southern cities. Publications included the *Chicago Defender;* the *Pittsburgh Courier;* the New York *Amsterdam News,* in Harlem; the *Baltimore Afro-American (Afro-American)* and its regional editions in Washington, DC, Philadelphia, Newark, and Richmond; the *Atlanta Daily World;* the *Norfolk Journal and Guide,* in Norfolk, Virginia; and *Ebony* and *Jet* magazines in Chicago.

Rivera reported and photographed news in Virginia, North Carolina, and South Carolina for the *Pittsburgh Courier* from 1946 to 1957. He had graduated from Howard University and worked in naval intelligence in World War II. He had reported for the *Washington Tribune* in Washington, DC., and the *Norfolk Journal and Guide* in Virginia before becoming the *Courier's* regional reporter. John Henry McCray, reporter and editor of the *Lighthouse and Informer,* worked in Columbia, South Carolina, from 1941 until the newspaper closed in 1954. He worked the next eight years as a regional reporter and editor and wrote a weekly column "Need for Changing" for the *Baltimore Afro-American.* He took that column to the *Pittsburgh Courier* from 1960–62, along with a chatty people-oriented column, "Roving About Carolina." The field was open, but, because of race, the market was narrow.[15]

On Sunday, June 17, 1951, Williams accompanied Jones to Liberty Hill African Methodist Episcopal (AME) Church, three miles outside Summerton, to document a statewide testimonial honoring the *Briggs* plaintiffs. Speakers included James Myles Hinton, president of the South Carolina Conference of Branches of the NAACP; Eugene A. R. "Skippy" Montgomery, the state NAACP executive secretary; and Rev. Joseph Armstrong "J. A." DeLaine, a dedicated local activist. The NAACP presented Harry Briggs with a merit award honoring the plaintiffs, their children, and community leaders for their efforts "to stop segregation and discrimination as detrimental and alien to a Christian democracy." Jones and Williams fit nineteen children and almost fifty adult petitioners and supporters behind a church rail for one of several portraits.[16]

On another day in another portrait, this one outside St. Mark AME Church in Summerton, the women—wearing earrings, beads, and print dresses—smiled. The men—wearing white shirts, boldly printed ties, and lightweight suits—stared, mouths set. Every family had lost something. White landowners and merchants cancelled lines of credit, called in mortgages, kicked sharecroppers off land, refused the loan of farm equipment, and blocked sales of seed and fertilizer and gas and oil. The KKK encircled homes and fired shotguns; even children got death threats. But in this luminous photograph by Jones and Williams—taken at dusk, lit by the brilliance of a flashbulb's combustion—the Summerton petitioners and supporters seemed a united force, which they were. They sustained themselves and each other—secretly selling cotton and timber through friends, obtaining land and a home for an evicted sharecropper, collecting money to pay off a mule debt, sending a spouse north to work and mail home money—and kept their names on the petition.[17]

In October 1951 Williams stood on a Summerton dirt road beside Jones and the much-admired Rivera, all three photographing Rev. DeLaine, wife Mattie, and children Joseph Armstrong "Jay" DeLaine Jr., Brumit Belton "B. B.," and Ophelia. Williams photographed for himself now, even on excursions with Jones. "He allowed me on my own to do what I wanted to do," and what he wanted to do was take and sell photographs. The trio lined up the DeLaines on the foundation of their destroyed home, "We arranged for them to meet us there, and we took the same picture, almost from the same angle." The couple and their three children stood among charred bricks and askew chimneys, what remained of their home after an

First row: Unidentified children.

Second row, far left: Harry Briggs Sr., unidentified men, women, and children.

Standing at the back, from left: Robert Georgia, unidentified man, Edward Ragin, unidentified man, Gilbert Henry (slightly below), Rev. Edward Eugene "E. E." Richburg, Rev. James Washington "J. W." Seals, unidentified man, J. S. "Flutie" Boyd, Gabriel Tindal, Rev. Joseph Armstrong "J. A." DeLaine, S. J. McDonald, Modjeska Montieth Simkins, Bennie Parson (slightly below), James Myles Hinton, John H. McCray, Lee Richardson, Hammett Pearson, unidentified women.

A June 17, 1951, testimonial at Liberty Hill AME Church honors the twenty adults and forty-six children who signed a December 22, 1950, petition attacking "separate but equal" as unconstitutional. Petition signers, supporters, and NAACP leaders join in celebrating Briggs v. Elliott. Cecil Williams accompanies photographer Edward C. "E. C." Jones Jr. to Summerton to document the event.

October 10 fire that was surely arson. Firefighters had refused to put out the flames, and the FBI had refused to investigate.[18]

Over the next few years Williams would learn of violence against DeLaine: a murder attempt, a trumped-up libel lawsuit, and KKK efforts to run him out of Summerton and then Lake City. He learned of violence against Rev. James Washington "J. W." Seals of St. Mark AME Church: fired from his job, his mortgage called in, his home burned, and his pig farm destroyed. And he learned of violence against Rev. Edward Eugene "E. E." Richburg of Liberty Hill AME Church: kidnapping, and death threats, and his church and parsonage surrounded by armed KKK who were countered by armed parishioners.[19]

Edward C. "E. C." Jones Jr. documents Briggs v. Elliott, *the first of five lawsuits in* Brown v. Board of Education, *for the NAACP. Cecil Williams assists with the 4 × 5 Graflex Crown and Speed Graphics, which require film-holder changes and, sometimes, a tripod. Plaintiffs and supporters collect outside St. Mark AME Church in Summerton for this portrait.*

First row, left to right: Maxine Gibson, Mary Oliver, Sarah Ragin, Celestine Parson, Katherine Briggs (child), Eliza Briggs, Rebecca Richburg, Esther Fludd, Plummie Parson, Annie Gibson.

Second row, left to right: Robert Georgia, Edward Ragin, Roland Pearson (child), Gilbert Henry, Harry Briggs Jr., Harry Briggs Sr., James Bennett, Bennie Parson, Brumit Belton "B. B." DeLaine, Lee Richardson.

Third row, left to right: Gabriel Tindal, Hammett Pearson, Levi Pearson, Jessie Pearson, Jesse Pearson (child).

Fourth row: Charlotte Pearson, Rev. James Washington "J. W." Seals, Rev. Joseph Armstrong "J. A." DeLaine, Rev. Edward Eugene "E. E." Richburg.

From left: Rev. Joseph Armstrong "J. A." DeLaine, wife Mattie Belton DeLaine, elder son Joseph Armstrong "Jay" DeLaine Jr., Ophelia DeLaine, and Brumit Belton "B. B." DeLaine.

Williams wanted to add income and equipment by assisting Jones. "Sometimes the NAACP would not pay us cash or would not pay for the work" documenting events. "We'd end up selling pictures to various people who were participants; we'd sell prints for a dollar up to five dollars." DeLaine, who understood the importance of documentation and kept copies of his own and others' letters, essays, and sermons, often hired Jones and Williams and bought multiple copies of their 8 × 10 prints. So did the peripatetic Montgomery, who traveled the state seeking membership and support. Jones himself often did not pay Williams in dollars; he offered tutelage. Jones taught Williams photo composition, lighting, staging, and technical tricks to use in the field and darkroom. He also compensated Williams with photographic film and paper purchased at a discount from cold storage at Sumter's Shaw Air Force Base. The refrigerator storage meant their prints did not lie flat. Majestic Studio's and Williams's own prints all possessed a distinctive cold-storage curl.

Cecil Williams and mentor Edward C. "E. C." Jones Jr. take a time-delay self-portrait on the campus of SC State. Around Jones's neck hangs a Rolliflex. A Graflex 23 Speed Graphic mounted to a tripod is barely visible behind Cecil Williams. When Jones photographs for the NAACP or for Black colleges' yearbooks, he calls on Williams to assist him.

A CHEVY COUPE, A HASSELBLAD, A BELL AND HOWELL

Four wheels and a driver's license at fourteen made the apprentice a professional awaiting paychecks in the mail. With help from his mother and family friend Sarah Smith, Williams bought a two-door black Chevrolet Coupe for $350. His expanding network provided community gigs. He roamed the countryside, photographing Black life to hone his documentary skills. Through emulating Jones and with practice on his own, Williams learned how to override the racial skew of film, which was calibrated for White skin. Film emulsion contained grains of silver salt; larger grains required less light to break down into pure silver and so were "faster," the film speed represented by an ISO number. "We would never follow the film guide, a white sheet folded into the film box with the ISO recommendations," explained Williams. "White photographers seemingly did not know how to keep dark-skinned people of color the right tone." Black photographers knew to open their lens one f-stop wider than the recommended standard.

Jones and Williams took other steps. When photographing a group of Black people, "We would pose the lighter-skinned people on the ends, the darker-skinned

Cecil Williams buys a Chevrolet Coupe for $350, thanks to help from his mother and a family friend. His mother objects when he screws a "Press" plate onto his bumper's license plate. She believes this puts him in danger.

people in the middle because the light falls off on the end," said Williams. Outdoors, "A lot of the time, in order to enhance skin tones, we used a flash to brighten the shadows." But, if a White and a Black person stood side-by-side, "You would want to take your camera off flash so you could get more light on the dark-skinned person and let the White person be feathered" in light.

This Mount Carmel school bus offers Black children in 1952 a new experience: a "separate but equal" school bus ride. Before Briggs v. Elliott challenges segregation in public schools, White children ride school buses, and Black children walk. In an attempt to retain segregation, the state legislature approves funds to "equalize" school buildings, equipment, and services for Black children.

In the darkroom, Williams checked the chemicals' temperatures; hot summers or chilly winters affected the developer timing for film. Then came the stop bath, the fixer, and the wash. Sometimes Williams "pushed" film to compensate for low light. When printing he used a dodging tool to play with light or his loose fist to "burn" in a spot, trial and error determining the best exposure. Williams's arts-and-sciences talents fit well with photography's mix of magic and mad scientist. He loved "mixing up chemistry and seeing the pictures come up." He delighted in the unpredictability of light, focus, film, chemicals, and subject. "It was challenging yet fulfilling intellectually and artistically." He continued to make collages, using the camera's timer to photograph himself, then combining his and published images. "I would take a shot of the moon or the Earth, and I would place myself on the moon or the Earth out in space. I would take a picture of myself holding out my hand, and I would have a figure of me in my hand. People would be amazed at what I could do."

On June 23, 1951, the US District Court for the Eastern District of South Carolina ruled two to one in *Briggs v. Elliott* that removing inequities was all the relief

to be granted. "Separate but equal" remained the law. The 1951 state appropriations act, with Governor James F. Byrnes's insistence, shoveled money toward the
state's false claim of "equality of educational opportunity." The state came up with a
three-cent sales tax, South Carolina's first, to equalize and expand school programs;
statewide busing; increased and equalized teacher pay; a $75 million bond issue for
school building construction; consolidation of school districts—from 1,220 to 102—
and a requirement that every district offer a high school for each race. In March 1952
the district court accepted the state's prediction that still-segregated schools, White
and Black, would be equal by fall, and, on appeal, *Briggs v. Elliott* went to the US
Supreme Court. The state's new Education Finance Commission began authorizing
the building of Black schools, including a replacement for Wilkinson High School,
among the first of what were called "equalization" schools.[20]

These were good years for Williams. At Felton, "We became addicted to tennis,"
said his friend George Greene Jr. "We would get up at six and play before we'd go
to class." Between 1927 and 1968 the American Tennis Association (ATA) held its
national tournaments at historically Black colleges and universities. During the
1948 nationals at State A&M, Williams and Greene served as ball boys, "wearing
those little short pants and running out and grabbing balls," said Greene. Williams
aided Althea Gibson, a native of Silver, South Carolina. (In 1956 she became the first
Black player to win the Grand Slam title, following that with both Wimbledon and
US Nationals wins in 1957 and 1958.) An annual tennis clinic at State A&M drew
William C. Lufler, a tennis pro and University of Miami coach who praised Williams
and two competitors as "the most promising youngsters" encountered in years.[21]

At thirteen years old, Williams made the boys' semifinals in the ATA Nationals
at Wilberforce University in Ohio. During the Wilberforce years, from 1949–52,
the teens stayed in dormitory rooms and paid for their food. But "Those were very
lean times," said Williams. On one visit Williams and Frank DeCosta Jr., eating
cheap on French fries, ran out of money. They cadged lemons from classmates
drinking tea, added sugar to their water, and squeezed the lemons for lemonade.
On a bus ride home, they discovered a bag of fruit in the luggage rack. "During the
night Frank and I—there was a tiny hole developing in the bag—we made the hole
bigger. That was our meal—bananas, apples, tangerines—coming back because

we were hungry." At Bethune-Cookman College in Daytona Beach, Williams won three games in a set against a young Arthur Ashe, soon to be the first Black player on the US Davis Cup team. During high school Williams and Greene played on the college team.[22]

In 1952 sister Brenda Lillian Williams, instantly doted on by all, was born. In 1953 Williams and his classmates moved to the new Wilkinson High School on Belleville Road. Williams found himself in a privileged position. "I was one of the luckiest students," he said. "I had gained the complete trust of Mr. Robert Howard," the family friend who was now Wilkinson's principal. For the next two years, "I had a darkroom not only at my house but at Wilkinson. Not only that, I had a master key. I could be there in the evening and go into any room on the entire campus with that one key. He trusted me that much, and I never violated that trust." Williams served as editor and photographer for the school newspaper and yearbook, positions rich with peer and adult connections. The new Wilkinson offered a dedicated darkroom, set up in the first aid room, and new darkroom equipment, such as a better enlarger and all the chemistry and photo paper needed; and new cameras, a 4 × 5 Graflex Crown Graphic, a 4 × 5 Graflex Speed Graphic, a Rolleiflex, even a Hasselblad and a 16 mm Bell and Howell movie camera. "It was Christmas to me," said Williams.[23]

New equipment meant new skills and new opportunities. On November 7, 1953, WIS Radio launched a commercial television station, its VHF channel broadcasting from Columbia and reaching central South Carolina. Williams knocked on the WIS-TV door with footage of high-school basketball games. The impressed station manager handed him ten rolls of 16 mm motion-picture film and said, "Shoot everything you can and bring it to us." The high school furnished the camera; the station furnished the film. Williams shot sports, sometimes news, for twenty to thirty dollars a film clip.

This was what Williams did. He worked. Unlike many in the 1950s—almost half of adults—he did not smoke. "In Bunt's garage we experimented with our first cigarette. I almost choked to death, and from that moment on I never smoked again." He never drank beer, wine, or spirits. He decided young, after a chocolate habit, that he needed to control all things. At twelve years old, "Three times a week I would

In 1951 tennis pro William C. Lufler, far left, coaches and plays at the Ninth Annual Tennis Clinic, sponsored by SC State and the South Carolina Tennis Association. Wilkinson High School's clinic participants include, from left: Jimmy Green, Frank DeCosta Jr., and Cecil Williams. Lufler coaches at Presbyterian College in Clinton, South Carolina; the University of Miami; and the University of Southern Florida.

get a thirty-nine-cent of chocolate chip cookies, and I would eat almost half in one sitting along with Ovaltine," a chocolate malt powder and milk concoction that his favorite radio characters endorsed. Next, a chocolate-caramel-peanuts bar became a four-a-day obsession. "I would have a Snickers after breakfast, a Snickers at lunch, a Snickers about three or four o'clock, and a Snickers after dinner." And then there was the lure of Alfreda James's homemade pralines, a pecan candy. Recognizing a tilt toward extremes, "I had to break myself away."

So Williams stayed thin; he put his all into photography. His single-mindedness earned teasing from friends, who called him "CJ" and photography his "obsession." Friend James Whetstone Jr. claimed he would say, "Hey, CJ, let's go out and see some girls," and Williams would reply, "Okay, let me go get my camera." When Williams met a young woman whom he wanted to impress, he sent her a photographic greeting. "I took a picture of myself at my desk, like I was an executive. I had my feet up on the desk," reading a magazine with the invented nameplate *Fabulous Women.* "And I sent her a note saying, 'Thinking of you.'"

Williams had style. While his friend Rendall Harper Jr. liked the ever-popular t-shirts with khakis, Williams chose an open-collar, untucked, boldly printed beach shirt or the untucked, boxy, white or pastel guayabera with its vertical pleats. He combined his shirts with khaki pants and leather shoes from JC Penney or Sears. Preferring to wear his hair long, he cut it himself. He wanted a scissors cut rather than Black barbers' clippers cut. When that did not go well—"too long, too short, too crooked"—he sometimes got a crewcut. He and his friends wore a jacket and tie for church and proms, but that was also Williams's work attire.

Williams dated—after all, he had a car and an income—but did not become "super serious" with anyone. Segregation limited in-town dates to Railroad Corner, the convergence of Treadwell, Boulevard, and Russell streets into a Black business strip. Williams took dinner dates to Boyd's Dinette. The White-owned theaters required separate entrances and seating in the "crow's nest," so he preferred Railroad Corner's State Theater for movie dates. It offered cowboy and adventure films preceded by newsreels, cartoons, and short serials, "where kryptonite is about to get the best of Superman, and you'd come to the next week to see what happened."

Some weekends Williams, Greene, George Crawford, and Bunt Sulton attended a White-only drive-in. Crawford's family property adjoined a drive-in's field on US Highway 21. Once the movie began the teens ran through the Crawford back yard and crossed a ditch to the drive-in's last row, often empty. They commandeered unused speakers suspended from free-standing poles—speakers intended to hang on a car window—and stretched the speakers' coiled cables backward into the ditch. "And we would sit in the ditch and watch drive-in theater."

They enjoyed toying with racial boundaries. Greene and Crawford applied for driver's licenses together. Crawford's family was labeled Negro in Orangeburg, but he looked White. The counter worker evidently could not imagine a friendship between the young man who she assumed was White and Greene. So she handed the teens licenses that said "White" for Crawford and "Mexican" for Greene. "I left it like that for two or three months then thought I might get into some kind of trouble," said Greene, who showed the license and told the tale to every friend before seeking a correction. Forays to the drive-ins grew bolder. "A few times I played the part of a foreigner who could not speak English, and we drove in the front gate," said Williams. "George [Crawford] was the driver and portrayed a White person," and he would say of Williams, "'He doesn't speak English.'" When Greene accompanied them, he and Williams sat in the back seat. "We could have been their houseman or gardener," said Greene. "As long as you were with somebody White, you could go where you wanted to go."[24]

Segregation signs reminded people of color that they could not go certain places without challenge and fear of arrest. So Williams photographed a child leaving the segregated section of Columbia's train station, a door opened to let the light in, the sign above his head reading "Colored." Williams arranged to photograph a friend at the Clarendon County Courthouse, posing him beside a "colored rest room" sign, an arrow directing down the hall. Williams took several pictures until a sheriff's deputy said, "You can't do that in here," and ordered them to leave.

EQUAL PROTECTION OF THE LAWS

This interest in racial boundaries and crossing them paid off. South Carolina's White-owned newspapers mostly ignored Black communities and covered civil rights as outrageous challenges to "our way of life" by the federal government, federal courts, the NAACP, Communists, and what were termed "outside agitators." With just a scattering of Black weeklies throughout the state, accurate coverage depended on reporters such as Rivera, McCray, *Jet's* associate editor Francis Mitchell and managing editor Robert Edward Johnson, and *Ebony's* associate editor Lerone Bennett. Williams, still just a teen, stepped into the state's visual void, determined to emulate Rivera. He notified *Jet,* the *Afro-American,* the *Pittsburgh Courier,* and *The Crisis,* the NAACP's official publication, of what he called "tidbits" as well as potential news stories. He sold them his photos. When *Jet* sent a writer, he picked up the reporter at the airport and drove him around.

McCray bought the teen's photos for his columns and articles in the *Afro-American* and the *Courier*. "McCray only reluctantly took photos himself," said Williams. "He would weekly come around and get the most important pictures for his publications. He would come in for just about an hour, get your pictures, and pay you, and give you a credit line." During his visits, McCray coached Williams. Take "story-telling pictures," he would say and pay Williams five dollars per photo.

McCray spent his childhood in all-Black Lincolnville, South Carolina, graduated from Avery Institute in Charleston, and earned a bachelor's from Talladega College in Talladega, Alabama. NAACP state president Hinton loved him as a fearless investigator—angry White men ran McCray out of town more than once—an aggressive reporter, and an NAACP stalwart. He was an inventive politician, a founder in 1944 with Hinton and others of the Progressive Democratic Party to challenge the all-White state Democratic Party. He spent two months on a chain gang in 1949 for a libel conviction and parole violations, accompanied Hinton to identify and write about lynching victims, and called White politicians the names they deserved. He could be harsh, funny, sarcastic, a daring truth teller.[25]

Williams's role kept expanding. Jones, who photographed people and events for Claflin and State A&M yearbooks, ceded more and more of that work to Williams. "I took over for him, not intentionally but by way of convenience," said Williams. That furnished Williams a steadier income. He customized his cars, switching out grills for a modern, streamlined look. Fascinated by and adept with electronics, he asked Atomic TV in Columbia to install a police-band radio in his car. He monitored local law enforcement broadcasts and chased emergencies. "In one week I would have one or two pictures in the *Times and Democrat* for a fire or a wreck," earning $5 apiece. "I felt really like a correspondent."

Williams's parents wanted him to attend college, and he expected to do so. He dreamed of attending the modernist, professional-focused Art Center School in Pasadena, California. But "that was beyond my family's means." Despite no Black student ever attending Clemson Agricultural College, he decided that he wanted to study architecture there. His interests—in all things mechanical and electronic, in cars and rocket ships, in building darkrooms and radios—seeded this aspiration. In 1954 Williams and his guidance counselor sought an application form from segregated Clemson. They were ignored. Queries from Wilkinson High School could come only from Black students. Sometimes South Carolina paid to educate elsewhere Black students majoring in a subject unavailable in-state, not out of altruism but to avoid desegregation lawsuits. So Williams sent a handwritten letter to the governor's office requesting out-of-state grants. He was ignored. He figured special dispensation required "a little pull," the clout of the influential in bigger cities such as Columbia, Charleston, or Greenville. Months later, two Black soldiers in Cheraw also applied to Clemson, to study textile chemistry; they, too, were ignored.[26]

Williams already knew that "living in South Carolina there were great limitations to how far one could reach." He decided he did not need college. He bought himself a drafting table. At the library he searched for books on draftsmanship, home design, and construction. He studied architecture on his own.

By summer's end, he found himself in a battle zone, his hometown.

The US Supreme Court ruled, on May 17, 1954, in *Brown v. Board of Education of Topeka*—a consolidation of *Briggs v. Elliott* and lawsuits from Kansas, Delaware, Virginia, and the District of Columbia—that "Segregation deprived the plaintiffs of equal protection of the laws, guaranteed in the Fourteenth Amendment." The unanimous decision, short and clear, said, "We conclude that, in the field of public education, the doctrine of 'separate but equal' has no place. Separate educational facilities are inherently unequal." On May 31, 1955, in what was dubbed *Brown II*, the Supreme Court set no deadline for desegregation, just "all deliberate speed," responsibility resting with local school authorities and courts that originally heard the cases. On July 15, 1955, the district court continued to preserve White supremacy in South Carolina, ruling that the US Constitution did not require integration. The US Constitution merely forbade government the power to enforce segregation, according to the district court. NAACP legal counsel Marshall promised petitions to school boards not acting to desegregate. The state legislature decreed state aid would end to any schools accepting transfers of Black students. Orangeburg's Black activists reacted by veering from quietly determined to radical in their responses.[27]

On August 22, 1955, the White Citizens' Council organizes in Orangeburg. On August 30, 3,500, White county residents at Orangeburg's Mirmow Field listen as politicians vow that desegregation of schools "will never happen here." On September 1, the White Citizens' Council of Orangeburg opens a downtown office and publishes a front-page newspaper ad seeking members. Membership costs $2.

Williams owned the inside track, given his years-long friendships with local NAACP officers: Rev. Matthew D. McCollom, president; Hazel F. Pierce, vice president; James E. Sulton Sr., treasurer, and John E. Brunson, executive secretary; and in Elloree, Blackman. Williams had established himself as the go-to photographer.

"I'm an eye witness, a participant, a journalist," hanging a "Rollei" from his neck like a two-eyed pendant or clutching a Speed Graphic by its belt-sturdy strap. His on-the-spot advantage and ever-ready attitude also led to employment as a *Jet* stringer, meaning he regularly contributed film, although without contract or guarantee of acceptance of any photo on his film rolls. Williams's employment pleased local and state NAACP officers who appreciated the validation that publication provided. But Williams had to give up his negatives to achieve publication: For speed's sake, *Jet* required that photographers mail their undeveloped film, rather than prints, slipping entire film rolls into *Jet's* prepaid, air-mail envelopes. A month's earnings ran anywhere from $25 to $200.

Following his 1955 high school graduation, Williams continued to work for Jones. He photographed events for SC State and Claflin, for Allen and Benedict in Columbia, and for Morris College in Sumter. Marianna Davis, who taught English at Claflin, frequently called on Williams to take photos in Orangeburg and Columbia at what he called "high society kinds of things" that required black tie.

Williams added a job with John Williamson Goodwin Jr. who had opened Goodwin Photography in the state capital. He found room and board—one meal a day—at a Waverly neighborhood home just blocks from Goodwin's studio. "It was my first flight out of the family house. I thought I knew everything, and I didn't want to go to college anymore."

Goodwin, who had earned an associate degree in chemistry from Allen University, concentrated on event and portrait photography, and Williams assisted. "John Goodwin was a master lighting technician. He knew how to photograph people so that they looked more pleasing," said Williams. Goodwin coached Williams in the use of large-format studio cameras and, in the darkroom, taught Williams how to use the Adams Retouching Machine. The task of eliminating on negatives a subject's blemishes and wrinkles required a retouching pencil, patience, and finesse. But taking portraits was not Williams's career goal. "Goodwin was a portrait photographer, and I was an event photographer. I didn't want to just take pictures of people in studios." Besides, home was home to ferment and where Williams needed to be.

On July 31, 1955, fifty-seven Orangeburg parents submitted a petition reminding local officials, "You are duty bound to take immediate concrete steps leading to early elimination of segregation." The petition used wording from the national NAACP office and from local attorney Newton Pough. In early August in Elloree, twenty miles away, thirty-nine parents petitioned for desegregation. Ten WCCs quickly formed throughout Orangeburg County, segregationists elsewhere quickly following, yielding a state association on October 10, 1955. Founded in Mississippi after *Brown I,* the WCC sowed ruination, its members intent on firing petitioners and their relatives, calling in debts and mortgages, kicking sharecroppers and tenant farmers off land, refusing sales, denying credit, and anything else that buttressed White supremacy, or, as White-owned newspapers described it, "state sovereignty and racial integrity." South Carolina's governor George Bell Timmerman Jr. and lieutenant governor Ernest F. Hollings endorsed the councils. Timmerman called them "inevitable." Hollings praised founders "who had the guts to stand up when needed."[28]

Following an Elloree desegregation petition, a WCC organized there, the second meeting attended by a thousand White people. Mayor W. J. Deer promised to "fight the leaders of the NAACP from ditches to fence posts in order to keep Negroes out of white schools," saying that no one with an NAACP membership or connection would be hired or receive credit or loans and that many NAACP members had already been fired. Soon nine petitioners asked that their names be removed from the Elloree petition. In Santee, twenty-one miles from Orangeburg, fourteen of seventeen petitioners asked that their names be removed. On August 11, Orangeburg's *Times and Democrat* published the names and addresses of every Orangeburg and Elloree petitioner. When one petitioner signed a statement claiming a misunderstanding, the paper printed it in bold on the front page.[29]

On August 22, the WCC organized in Orangeburg, and on August 30, 3,500 White county residents crammed themselves into the Mirmow Field baseball stadium to hear state senator Marshall Burns Williams declare, "Integration of the races is out of the question." To "rousing cheers," he and attorneys Hugh Sims Jr. and T. B. Bryant Jr. urged the crowd to join the fight "against the NAACP and foreign agitators," who were "seeking to destroy our way of life." On September 1, the Citizens' Council of Orangeburg opened an office and published a front-page newspaper ad seeking members. Joining cost $2. Store credit ended for as many as 2,000

Rev. Matthew D. McCollom, on bicycle, serves from 1955 to 1962 as pastor of Trinity Methodist Church, headquarters for the Orangeburg Freedom Movement. Following 1955 petitions to desegregate local schools, WCC members fire Black employees and demand Black debtors pay back loans and mortgages. McCollom and others in the NAACP respond with their own boycott of WCC merchants. Cecil Williams sometimes set up a photo and then asked a bystander to take the picture, as he did here.

suspected NAACP members, *Jet* reported. Thirty-two of Orangeburg's petitioners asked that their names be removed.[30]

Williams photographed Pough and McCollom at the Orangeburg County Courthouse. He photographed the "Orangeburg Citizens Council Upstairs" sign on the Russell Street building that housed the newspaper downstairs and the WCC upstairs with WTND, "the radio voice of the *Times and Democrat*." He photographed those fired and evicted and felt sympathy for panicked petitioners withdrawing their names. "Some fell to the wayside." More than once prominent White customers delivered warnings to Williams's father, what Williams called "jerking your shirttail." His father would not repeat to him what was said. He would just note the incident. Despite the risks, neither parent discouraged Williams, saying only, "Be very careful."

INTIMIDATION, HARASSMENT, VIOLENCE

Many in the Black community fought back. In Orangeburg, Becker's Department Store cancelled the credit account of a petitioner, and "teachers and many prominent women closed out their accounts" in response, reported Rivera in the *Pittsburgh Courier*. A former Black customer called the clothing store's owner to explain why Black women closed their accounts and promised that more of them would follow suit. She told Rivera that the store owner said he was pressured to cancel the petitioner's account and regretted doing so.[31]

In Elloree, Burgess Butler asked a White man standing in his yard to stop cursing his family, who sat on their porch. The White man beat Butler to the ground with an axe handle. Butler ran inside his home, returned with his shotgun, and shot the man in the leg. Initially fined $100 for discharging a gun in town and let out on bail, he told *Afro-American* columnist McCray, "I could have but didn't want to kill him." A few weeks later, the Elloree WCC formed and organized punishment of school desegregation petitioners. Butler, an NAACP member, and his son were fired at the behest of the WCC from the Orangeburg plumbing company where they worked. Then Butler, but not the White man, was charged with assault, and, in 1956, Butler was sentenced to a year in prison. He wrote McCray, "God is my only judge, and in Him I find no charge against me."[32]

On a Saturday night, a Klan meeting and cross burning followed a parade in downtown Elloree. The night was dark; light from the cross dwindled. Twenty-five robed men shouted threats and abuse, saying that Blackman, the NAACP president, must be run out of town. Then Blackman showed up. A friend, who had promised backup, announced him. A robed Klansman demanded Blackman step into the light and state his plans. Blackman said nothing, just held his position, silent. Behind him stood his friends, more than a hundred, silent and armed. Uneasy, the Klansmen disbanded. Blackman, who signed a letter to the NAACP's national membership office as "L.A. Blackman, the immovable," did not leave town. Weeks later a Black resident told McCray, "It isn't Mr. Blackman alone who has made the fight down here. We made it."[33]

"Exposé! South Carolina's Plot to Starve Negroes" proclaims Jet magazine on its October 20, 1955, cover. Seven of Cecil Williams's photos illustrate the article, including photos of an NAACP relief team distributing clothes to a farm family devastated by the White Citizens' Council's economic "squeeze," and an Orangeburg merchant's sign, "NAACP members (white or colored) NOT WELCOME in this store." Among those backing the Black community's boycott is James E. Sulton Sr., shown here. He and brother Arnold Leroy "Roy" Sulton Sr. co-own Sulton's Servicenter and Esso gas station in Orangeburg.

Just so, economic warfare could work in both directions. As WCC members applied what they called "the squeeze" or "the freeze," Black customers stunned them by replying in kind. Activists largely independent of the White power structure—McCollom, pastor at Trinity United Methodist Church; James E. Sulton Sr., co-owner of Sulton's Servicenter and Esso gas station with brother Arnold Leroy "Roy" Sulton Sr.; Brunson, a barber at the Black-owned People's Barber Shop; and Father Francis Donlan, a White Redemptorist priest at Christ the King Catholic Church and its school—designed a boycott. The Orangeburg team crafted a selective buying list, copied by the thousands on the mimeograph machine of Modjeska Monteith Simkins, secretary for the NAACP state conference. The NAACP team distributed the first batch secretively at an SC State football game. "These firms are

When Orangeburg's Black parents petition for desegregated schools, White segregationists punish and terrorize those who sign the petitions as well as their relatives and members of the NAACP. Many Black citizens do not back off. Instead, they march downtown. They picket. They also boycott merchants who belong to or support the White Citizens' Council. Orangeburg's boycott precedes the Montgomery bus boycott by several months.

cooperating with the Citizens' Council. Let's fight back by not cooperating with the following firms ONLY!" said one of the pocket-size lists, which encouraged ending trade with the most fervent segregationists but continuing trade with the relatively benign White merchants. James E. Sulton Sr. placed one of the boycott lists in his wallet, the way other people might carry family photographs.[34]

This shrewd approach included not only focusing pressure on the most vehement WCC members but also occasionally winnowing the boycott list to distinguish those somewhat harmful from the truly harmful, thus creating dissension among White merchants distrusting one another's commitment. Mayor Robert H. Jennings Jr., an important target, held Sunbeam Bread and Paradise Ice Cream franchises and owned the Orangeburg Coca-Cola Bottling Co. He suspended deliveries to Black businesses. Jennings told the Black-owned *Amsterdam News,* "I have ordered all my businesses to stop serving these niggers who have signed that school petition. I have checked with the 30 or more nigger employees I have working for me, and if I catch any of them joining that NAACP or signing the petition, they might as well leave town." Hazel Pierce, then the local NAACP executive secretary, personally called Jennings to inform him of the impending boycott of his businesses. He claimed he told her, "Go ahead and crack your whip and then see our attorneys."[35]

The Black community quit drinking Coke and struck Sunbeam Bread and Paradise Ice Cream from grocery lists. "It was unanimous," said Williams. The NAACP's national office took action, getting rid of its vending machine, and informing branch offices, which started their own Coke boycotts. *Amsterdam News* columnist Earl Brown urged a national boycott. "Stop buying it at the soda fountain. Stop buying it at the grocery store. Stop drinking it." Brown called on Coca-Cola itself, saying the company should either order distributors to stop furthering "hateful discriminatory practices" or cancel franchises. Coca-Cola's Atlanta office denied having the power to do so.[36]

In Elloree, a town of 1,100, White merchants felt the boomerang. "Nobody has been buying uptown," a Black resident told McCray. A White merchant sold out and left town, announcing, "I'm damned tired of starving just to be white." In Summerton, an owner of the Grayson Elliott cotton gin no longer refused Black business. Yanking down a sign that said "No corn ground for NAACP members," he declared, "I'm here to make money." Worried about White merchants' lost business, a *Times and Democrat* editorial urged posting WCC window stickers to tag those "who fight for our way of life." Sure of their power, WCC members had not taken into account losing their customer base, even though Black residents made up two-thirds of the county population.[37]

In the midst of this, Williams attended a Klan meeting on Belleville Road, alerted by a newspaper notice. Obligated to first photograph a basketball game, he arrived late, as dampened embers cooled around a downed cross. The only two men remaining, a robed grand dragon and a uniformed patrol officer, chatted. Williams parked his car, and "I took my big 4 × 5 camera out, and I walked toward them, and they started looking at each other." He met the men's astonished stares and said, "Oh, it's all over." They agreed, "About thirty minutes ago," looked at each other again, and Williams turned to leave. Then one asked, "Do you want to take a picture?" The three—a Black teen, the Klansman, and the patrol officer—lifted the weighty, eight-foot-tall cross. The two men posed with arms crossed. Williams spent two flash bulbs on them but did not find a buyer. His parents were furious; Williams had driven the family car. The general tenor of the ensuing discussion was "You better watch out, boy!"

It was no secret who belonged to the WCC or the Klan and no secret that law enforcement officers belonged. In September the mayor and city council officially approved city employees joining the WCC. George L. Reed, Orangeburg County sheriff, declared his membership. On his car's scanner Williams daily heard law officers broadcasting racial slurs preceded by expletives, promising violence when referring to Black residents. A police car trailed McCollom wherever he went. Police showed up outside NAACP meetings to take license plate numbers. If several cars were parked in front of a Black family's home, firefighters burst in, shouting, "Where's the fire?" W. T. C. Bates, president of the local WCC, dismissed as "not serious" letters containing death threats that were sent to McCollom, Pierce, attorney Pough, and others. Pierce said she and others gave their letters to the FBI for handwriting comparisons and investigation. Forty White Catholics wrote to Father Donlan's superiors asking that he withdraw his membership from the NAACP or be transferred. Obscene phone calls occurred so frequently that those harassed telephoned one another and left the line open so no one else could call. McCollom would ask for a name and offer to pray for the caller. He destroyed the NAACP membership list sought by the WCC—he was offered a ten-thousand-dollar bribe for it by "unnamed whites," reported *Jet*—and told journalist McCray that he had "fortified his home against invasion."[38]

Tall and thin, with a fine-boned face bisected by a slender mustache, McCollom stood shoulders back, calm under attack. He rode a bicycle—dressed in bowtie and suit—around town and played a left-handed, fierce winning game of ping pong, stepping back from the table to deliver a hard, unreturnable spin. Tennis star Williams could not beat him. An educator in Williamsburg and Darlington counties in the '30s and '40s, he was fired as principal of Cades Elementary School for speaking out against peonage in Williamsburg County. Drafted in 1942, he served as an x-ray technician during World War II. Afterward, he finished a bachelor's degree at Claflin and a master's degree in divinity and in sacred theology at Atlanta's Gammon Theological Seminary.[39]

Williams photographed McCollom whenever and wherever possible, believing him as deserving of admiration and adulation as the Rev. Dr. Martin Luther King Jr. "He had a defiant kind of way. He was a very, very intelligent minister, very brave for the time he lived in." In Orangeburg "he's right out front. Trinity is the headquarters for all the demonstrations. We have meetings in the basement. We're taught to engage in nonviolence; he's establishing the morality of nonviolence." McCollom participated in the 1957 founding of the Southern Christian Leadership Conference (SCLC), King as its president, McCollom on the executive board. In notes entitled "Reaching Out for Spiritual Reality," McCollom wrote, "The Negro's very soul, his freedom and citizenship, his economic and (physical) security, his normal aspirations as an American and a Christian, all are at stake in his fight for integration." What he knew and the WCC did not—"Most of us, in the leadership at least, were ready to die."[40]

Williams sometimes thought of the NAACP as simply McCollom and James E. Sulton Sr., but other officers stood out, too. Like many female activists of the time, Hazel Fedrena Tatnall Pierce immersed herself in civic life. A graduate of A&M College in Normal, Alabama, she worked at Mayesville Institute in Mayesville, South Carolina, founded in 1882 for Black schoolchildren. There she met and married James A. Pierce Sr., the institute's superintendent for seven years. The family moved to Orangeburg in the early 1940s so that he could teach industrial arts at State A&M, his alma mater. She taught school, led Red Cross and tuberculosis drives, was a charter member of New Mount Zion Baptist Church and the Sunlight Club for young women, served on the board of women for the Baptist State Convention, belonged to the local League of Church Women United and the state Federation of Women's Clubs, and led scouting groups and the Wilkinson High School parent-teachers association. She rotated through NAACP offices, serving as membership chair, treasurer, executive secretary, and vice president over the years.[41]

"She was very outspoken," noted Williams. "She had many White as well as Black friends and associates, and having money, she was very influential." When Pierce complained to the *Times and Democrat* about its coverage of Black schools, the newspaper called her "the woman" but noted her objections. When questioned about the school petitions, she dared to tell the *Times and Democrat*, "We are no more anxious to socialize with whites than they are with us. We are only going by what the Supreme Court says is right, and if the Supreme Court says we should have complete integration, then that is what we want." She then observed, "I have just as many white relatives as I have colored."[42]

Brunson, father of two, worked as a barber at the People's Barber Shop on Boulevard Street, a downtown shop that catered to Black customers. "He was the only one I let cut my hair," said Williams. Alphabetically, Brunson's name sat first on the Orangeburg school petition. A 1938 graduate of Dunton Memorial High School's last class, Brunson led the Dunton Memorial School Club for ten years and belonged to McCollom's Trinity congregation, where he served as lay leader, president of its board of trustees, and member of many church committees. Possessor of a lifetime membership to the NAACP, he also rotated through the local NAACP offices of vice president, executive secretary, or treasurer. Unlike his colleagues, he was silent, seldom smiling, and less financially secure; like them, he was well informed. "A barbershop is a very important part of any community," noted Williams. "Barbers are always abreast of what's going on, the gossip, the news. People would come to the barbershop and sit down just to get the news."[43]

Heartbreaking news arrived on September 1 when an NAACP press release revealed the lynching of Emmett Till and discovery of his body in Mississippi's Tallahatchie River. *Jet* stunned a nation on September 15, 1955, when Simeon Booker and David Jackson reported on and photographed the opening of Emmett Till's coffin, Mamie Till Bradley's first sight of her dead son, and, in close-up, the child's face mutilated by gunfire, beating, and three days in the river. During a visit to his uncle in Money, Mississippi, 14-year-old Emmett Till had been abducted and murdered by half-brothers Roy Bryant and John William Milam, and perhaps others, supposedly because the teen spoke to and whistled at Carolyn Bryant, Roy Bryant's wife. Bradley insisted on an open coffin for her child's Chicago funeral. She said, "Let the people see what they have done to my boy." As many as 100,000 people walked by the pine casket. In Williams's circle, "Most of the conversations were that those who killed him were getting away scot free." And they did. An all-male, all-White jury did not convict Bryant and Milam, the only two charged after a national furor. On January 24, 1956, *Look* magazine published Roy Bryant's and John Milam's confession, obtained for a $3,150 payment to Carolyn and Roy Bryant and Milam and $1,260 to their attorneys for the story and signed releases.[44]

"You knew it was dangerous to do things like Emmett Till may have done, like whistle at a White lady or, for that matter, to personalize a conversation with White people at all," said Williams. "It shocked everyone, but knowing such violence took place was no surprise." Violence was expected. "L. A. Blackman used to tell me how many people in Elloree and the lower part of Orangeburg County just disappeared. If people raised a concern or had an issue, they would be killed. They would come get them in the night, and that was the end of it. People just disappeared. The family wouldn't know if they had gone away, or the family would find their bodies in the woods some place." A friend of Williams, who hailed from a prominent Black family and secretly dated a White woman, found himself "shipped to California," said Williams, who believed, "The family had to take drastic measures because they would get to you."

Intimidation and violence throughout South Carolina escalated. Timmerman announced support of a segregationist third party; signed into law six acts to preserve school segregation, including repealing compulsory school attendance and allowing local school officials to open, close, sell, or lease public schools; ordered the State Law Enforcement Division (SLED) to investigate desegregation petitions; and ordered the attorney general to investigate the NAACP as an out-of-state corporation. In South Carolina's first-ever statewide radio and television broadcast of a speech, the governor excoriated NAACP leaders as "professional agitators," produced from a nonexistent Orangeburg woman a quote disavowing the petitions and said court-ordered desegregation of any public school "would force the mixed school and the Negro school to close." A week later a cross burned at Manning Training School and shotgun blasts pockmarked the door of the Fleming-DeLaine Funeral Home, owned by William "Billie" S. Fleming, president of Manning's NAACP, and Robert DeLaine. White sales representatives—for meat, soft drinks and beer, candy, dairy, and breads—told Robert Smith, Mary Oliver, and Rebecca Brown that the WCC forbade deliveries to their grill, grocery store, café, and shop in Summerton.[45]

Orangeburg deliveries of national companies' goods—Lay's and its potato chips; Lance and its Nabs; Curtiss Candy Company and its Baby Ruth candy bars—ended to Black-owned businesses such as Carson's Grocery, Jones Grocery, and Murph Café. The two Black-owned gas stations, the Sultons' Esso and H. O. Harvey's Shell

Oil, were denied deliveries, and the national companies denied knowledge. In retaliation for Father Donlan's activism, Coble Dairy refused delivery to Christ the King Catholic School. The school switched to Coburg Dairy, which ended its delivery after an angry broadcast on WTND. Alex Lewis, a bricklayer and petitioner, found himself fired from six jobs in a row. The *Pittsburgh Courier* reported on the "satanic act" of denying home delivery of milk to his child, a son with hemophilia.[46]

The FBI reported the Klan as potentially more dangerous in South Carolina than at any time since the 1870s, a stunning statement. In 1871, President Ulysses S. Grant had suspended habeas corpus in nine Upstate counties in South Carolina after a federal investigation of KKK atrocities announced that no community "nominally civilized has been so fully under the domination of systematic and organized depravity." With evidence of more than eleven murders and 600 whippings in York County alone, mass arrests had followed. Such violence had never really ended. Of twelve Southern states, South Carolina ranked seventh per capita in lynchings between 1880 and 1940. Orangeburg County ranked fourth in the state in number of lynchings between 1877 and 1950.[47]

'GRASSROOTS' SLEDGEHAMMER

The Klan and the WCC in South Carolina starred in *Jet's* October 20, 1955, issue. So did Williams's photography. "S.C. Whites Burn Church to Chase Minister" described the burning of St. James AME Church in Lake City, a "bold bid to chase away militant Rev. J. A. DeLaine." DeLaine's bishop had moved him to the Florence County town, where Klansmen attacked his family, home, and church in what the KKK called Operation Shoot 'Em Up. The issue's lead story—"Exposé!" said the cover line—reported on "South Carolina's Plot to Starve Negroes," detailing the "vicious hate" of the WCC in Clarendon and Orangeburg counties. *Jet* published seven of Williams's photographs, including one of Roy Sulton Sr. by his empty Coke machine. For Williams this was the breakthrough, the assignment that placed him and Orangeburg within the movement's momentum and attracted *Jet's* attention. On November 3, in "Militant S.C. AME Minister Tells How He Outwitted Lynchers," *Jet* reported DeLaine's escape from Lake City, described as a 90-mile-per-hour chase following gunfire that resulted in the minister traveling all the way to New York, which refused his extradition.[48]

For Roy Sulton Sr., sharp-eyed and hand on hip in Williams's *Jet* photo, and for younger brother James, hard work and setbacks composed life as usual. Their father McDuffie Sulton and uncle John Jacob Sulton Jr. ran J. J. Sulton and Sons, the oldest continuous lumber operation in the South, founded in 1825 by their White great-grandfather John J. Sulton. The business employed fifty workers, produced seven million feet of lumber annually in the 1930s, and was the first to haul logs with a truck and trailer. The business survived the Depression and three fires and did not close until the brothers' retirement in 1958. James E. Sulton Sr., an Army veteran of World War II, attended Morehouse College in Atlanta, and then worked with Roy, an electrical contractor, instead of joining the family lumber business. In 1948, the two obtained a Standard Oil franchise, despite opposition by White business owners, and founded the Sulton Fuel Oil Company.[49]

"I think because James had gone into the service and come back to South Carolina, he was more interested in seeing South Carolina changed," said Williams. A German prisoner of war's taunt motivated James E. Sulton Sr. for life. The prisoner said Sulton was a fool to fight for a country that denied him his rights. Sulton returned home to see German immigrants, "with more liberties and opportunities than I had," he said, and Black people "treated as though they were the lowest form of life." Vowing to secure full rights, he decided "protests and marches for equal rights would someday make the difference." So that's what he did.[50]

James E. Sulton Sr. and McCollom functioned for Williams as exemplars—and taskmasters. Sulton was intrigued by Williams's career, "a frustrated wanna-be photographer," so Williams bought his very good friend a Rolleiflex and, later, a Nikon. Williams wanted to emulate Sulton's spine of steel. "James would not turn the other cheek." Sulton was pivotal in NAACP planning and summonses of Williams to make a record. McCollom put Williams's photographic skills to work enforcing the boycott. Alleys for deliveries ran behind downtown stores. Aided by a telephoto lens, Williams photographed back-door customers. McCollom posted the prints in Trinity's basement. The minister held a firm line. Shame was a tool; mercy was another. McCollom created a buying service for those in need. He, James E. Sulton

Thurgood Marshall, chief legal counsel of the NAACP, speaks at Claflin University on November 27, 1955. He tells his audience in Seabrook Gym that the "once Solid South" no longer exists and cannot be reestablished.

Seated back row, far left: Hazel Pierce, local NAACP secretary.

Front row: James Myles Hinton, president of the state NAACP; Clarence Mitchell, chief lobbyist for the NAACP; and Rev. Matthew D. McCollom, pastor of Trinity Methodist Church. To the far right sit Herbert Lee Wright, youth secretary for the national NAACP, and I. S. Leevy, founder of the Columbia NAACP branch and a four-time candidate for Congress.

Sr., and Modjeska Monteith Simkins worked with Manning's Billie Fleming on a national relief fund for Clarendon and Orangeburg counties. McCollom wrote of anyone desiring constitutional rights, "He must practice freedom as devotedly as he says his prayers."[51]

FOR sent Glenn E. Smiley, its national field secretary, to Orangeburg in November. An international peace organization founded in England in 1914 and established in the United States in 1915, FOR wanted to reestablish its work in the South. Smiley, a White Methodist minister, had studied Mohandas Gandhi's use of nonviolence, joined FOR's staff in 1942, and, in 1945, went to prison rather than serve

The Times and Democrat *sends reporters to cover Thurgood Marshall's 1955 speech at Claflin University. This is Cecil Williams's first experience photographing an event for Black people that White journalists cover. At the far right sits Dean B. Livingston, later publisher of the Orangeburg paper.*

in World War II or take a minister's exemption. He met petitioners in Orangeburg who had lost jobs and received "threats to life and property." He found "an almost total lack of communication between [Black and White] groups in the city." He arranged a secret meeting among Black and White ministers, distributed pamphlets on nonviolent direct action, and convinced McCollom, at least, that nonviolence worked. Smiley concluded the problems of Orangeburg were the problems of the entire South.[52]

On November 27 NAACP legal counsel Marshall spoke in Claflin's gym to an audience of 1,500 people, announcing that the "once Solid South" no longer existed and placing South Carolina in the "not-budging" category, trailing only Mississippi in violence. For visits by Marshall "the NAACP would hold a rally and pick up a collection," said Williams, who photographed stacks of dollars accruing on a worn folding table. The NAACP legal counsel, barnstorming after the 1955 *Brown v. Board* decision, "challenged citizens to test the Supreme Court ruling that segregation in public education is unconstitutional," said an impressed Williams. The stage, packed with dignitaries seated on oak office chairs, stood several feet high. So Williams climbed onto a chair, hefting his 4 × 5 Graflex, now with an attached film back for quick reloading. For the first time, he photographed alongside White journalists; the *Times and Democrat* sent three. "After *Brown v. Board of Education*, the press in Orangeburg began to take notice of what's happening," said Williams. "If they did cover anything at all they would say, 'This is outside influence coming to Orangeburg; our colored people are happy.'"[53]

Williams captured on stage a who's who, including local leaders McCollom and Pierce; Hinton, president of the South Carolina NAACP conference; Clarence Mitchell Jr., director of the NAACP's Washington Bureau; Herbert Lee Wright, youth secretary for the national NAACP; and I. S. Leevy, a founder of the Black-owned Victory Savings Bank, owner of Leevy's Funeral Home, and Black Republican candidate for Congress four times, including in 1954. And there sat Father Donlan, who offered the invocation as he had at the preceding NAACP state convention. White citizens took note of the presence of the round-faced and balding priest, and more complaints from White Catholics ensued. In July one of Claflin's White trustees had resigned to protest a Black trustee signing a desegregation petition. Now Thurgood Marshall's presence so offended two more White trustees that they resigned too.[54]

An unsigned invitation to the rally had included the current boycott list of twenty-three products and businesses, essentially a directory of WCC supporters. The invitation made twelve points, among them a clear warning:

> Let us prove to these merchants that they cannot fire our friends, foreclose mortgages, refuse to sell to our leaders, cut our credit and try to make fools of us, and then expect us to go ahead with big smiles and make them rich. Those days are gone forever.

In rebuttal to the WCC heat and propaganda, the invitation noted, "The leaders of the NAACP in Orangeburg are your ministers. They are not fanatical agitators." Determined but not foolhardy, the activists made a nominal adjustment for protection, deniability, and to deflect animus against the NAACP. The boycott became the product of what was initially called the Orangeburg Civil Rights Movement. In interviews with Black or White reporters, McCollom repeatedly denied NAACP knowledge of the boycott list.[55]

Others noted the innovative rebuttal of the Orangeburg movement. On December 1, 1955, seamstress Rosa Parks in Montgomery, Alabama, refused to give up her seat on a public bus, following years of the Black community pushing to end Jim Crow seating. On December 2 Black ministers and leaders, including Revs. Ralph Abernathy and Martin Luther King Jr., met at Dexter Avenue Baptist Church to finish designing a bus boycott. That weekend Roy Sulton Sr.; Julius I. "J. I." Washington III, owner of Washington Poultry Farm; and Earl M. Middleton, barbershop owner; drove to Montgomery. Frank Augustus DeCosta Sr.—former graduate school dean at SC State, new director of instruction at Alabama State College, and a lifelong NAACP activist—had summoned the trio to describe their months-old Orangeburg boycott. They drove into the night in Sulton's 1955 Buick Century.[56]

"They slept on Abernathy's floor and heard gunshots all during the night and the telephone ringing so they just had to take it off the hook," said Williams. At a Sunday morning meeting, December 4, the three provided their expertise, then returned home. On December 5, ninety percent of Montgomery's Black residents—40,000 people—refused to ride city buses. That afternoon local leaders agreed to extend the one-day boycott into a campaign. Middleton described the Orangeburg trio's ability to advise as a reassuring "lesson in independence." All owned businesses, so "there was no one to fire us." To Williams the consultation underlined Orangeburg's precedent-setting use of a boycott, Orangeburg as originator and Montgomery as emulator.[57]

Black-owned newspapers put Orangeburg's boycott on their front pages with Mississippi murders and the fledgling Montgomery bus boycott. McCray danced with glee in his *Afro-American* columns, writing of the Orangeburg WCC's faulty assumption that firing workers, cutting off credit, and "intimidating the 57 signers of an integration petition and NAACP supporters would nip the move in the bud." Instead, he wrote, "They got hit with the neatest 'grass-roots' sledgehammer as of record, and now regret they ever started it."[58]

William Douglas "W. D." Workman Jr., a correspondent for the Charleston *News and Courier* who mixed column writing and politicking, reluctantly agreed. Workman had joined in founding the Committee of 52, a group of White power brokers determined to retain segregation and to work with the WCCs to do so. On August 21,

1955, the Committee published a resolution, provided to newspapers and the legislature, that accused "outside forces and influences" and "the pressure and propaganda
of the NAACP" for Black South Carolinians' efforts to end Jim Crow. The Committee advocated "interposition," a states' rights argument to place state sovereignty
between segregated schools and the *Brown* decisions, an impotent theory because
it ignored the US Constitution's Supremacy Clause that federal law prevails when in
conflict with state law or state constitutions. At year's end the ubiquitous Workman
better understood just what Orangeburg's boycott represented. He acknowledged
"quality" Black leadership and "solidarity among Negroes." As if it were news, and to
many White readers it was, Workman announced that fellow segregationists could
"no longer delude themselves that these leaders do not seek integration."[59]

RAISING THE STAKES

A further step drove home that point. James E. Sulton Sr. and McCollom met with
Fred Henderson Moore, in his third term as president of the Student Government
Association at SC State. A 1952 graduate of Burke High School in Charleston, Moore
had won a competitive city scholarship to attend the one public college for Black
students. His family lived in Charleston and in Honey Hill on James Island, where
Black people owned land and possessed what Moore called "a spirit of independence." Mother Rosalee Milton Moore had been born in the former slave quarters
of the John Rutledge House; she sold vegetables on Charleston's Broad Street and
took in laundry. Father John H. Moore Sr. worked manual labor at the Charleston
Navy Yard. Moore's mother had three years of school, his father none. The last of
twelve children, Moore's use of his left arm and leg was limited by either a birth
defect or polio, but he toted tomatoes on the island farms and sold vegetables with
his mother, who won Charleston street-crier contests.[60]

When Fred Henderson Moore was seven his father died. Following what Moore
later called "a day of destiny," the Black child became companion to a wealthy White
child. He successfully navigated this alternate reality, conscious of his mother's dic-
tum "ain't nobody in this world better than you are." Good-humored, garrulous,
smart, and ambitious, Moore planned to be James Island's first Black attorney.

Cecil Williams photographs campus events for the SC State yearbook. In February 1956 he photographs college president Benner C. Turner, host in his on-campus home to members of the student government association. The month before state representative Jerry M. Hughes Jr. of Orangeburg had introduced a resolution to search for any NAACP activity at SC State.

Everyone who knew him could imagine him an attorney. As Williams noted, "He was a talker. He could go very deep in a conversation, maybe deeper than you wanted him to be."[61]

A visible role guaranteed misfortune since White business owners, officials, and politicians ran everything, including SC State. Many students did not want to risk their exceptional education opportunity and feared their parents' response if they did. In 1950 just 2.2 percent of Black adults nationwide had completed college. But Moore accepted the role of involving and guiding his classmates, despite a conversation with President Benner C. Turner during which Turner ordered no campus involvement in community affairs and promised Moore entry to his alma mater, Harvard Law School, if he complied. Moore and his Charleston friends involved themselves anyway. "He was very aware of the need to stand up for freedom and justice, and he realized that would cause some sacrifice," said Williams. Students started an underground newspaper, *The Free Press*. They supported the downtown boycott. Discovering that boycotted businesses supplied the dining hall's milk, bread, ice cream, and campus laundry service, they objected. State politics forced something more dramatic.[62]

Fred Henderson Moore, president of the student body at SC State, encourages participation in the 1955 boycott of downtown merchants belonging to the White Citizens' Council. A graduate of Charleston's Burke High School, Moore grew up on James Island and in the city, where his mother sold vegetables on Broad Street and took in laundry. His father, who died when Moore was seven, did manual labor at the Charleston Navy Yard. Moore's intelligence and articulate leadership earned him a college scholarship.

At the start of 1956, state representative Jerry M. Hughes Jr. of Orangeburg called for a special committee to investigate SC State, asking to what extent faculty and students belonged to or sympathized with the NAACP, which he said existed "to mislead the Negro citizens and foment and nurture ill feeling and misunderstanding."

But Turner, president of SC State since 1950, had never allowed the establishment of a campus NAACP chapter. Those wanting to join a college chapter joined Claflin's. To SC State and Claflin students an investigation became one of many last straws.[63]

In February the Klan burnt a cross in town, announcing their goal of frightening Father Donlan. With a different purpose, a few White leaders secretly approached James E. Sulton Sr.. "They were suffering," said Williams, always in the know. "They wanted to mediate a behind-the-scenes settlement. The merchants wanted this to stop. But the mayor didn't. And the White Citizens' Council, the racists, they didn't." The *Afro-American* reported, without naming anyone, that the Black community's "counterattack" remained effective through the participation of "high school and college students, religious and fraternal and social groups." Black leaders had shown goodwill by whittling down their boycott list from forty to twenty-three merchants when "the firms withdrew from support of the citizens' council program." However, White merchants' proffer required "repudiation of the alleged leaders," a nonstarter.[64]

In March the legislature not only okayed an investigation of the NAACP at SC State but also passed a proviso making unlawful NAACP membership by any school district, city, county, or state employee. In addition, the state appropriations act required closing any state-supported public college under court decree to desegregate—and closing SC State at the same time. Furious SC State students assembled at lunch on March 25. "They planned they would go in, get their food, and dump it into the trash as a demonstration of their commitment," said Williams. Always on the hunt for news and for yearbook photographs, he often got timely calls about "some activity." Some did dump their food; others poured water on their bread and refused the milk. All marched out of Floyd Hall to protest college purchases from Mayor Jennings's businesses. Preferring outdoor shots, Williams climbed atop a car and captured students' all-smiles exit from the dining hall and their pause to sing in celebration.[65]

The students also hanged Hughes and Turner in effigy, and 150 protested in front of Turner's campus home. In the morning light Williams photographed the scarecrow with its hot water bottle head and a stuffed body labeled "Turner" on one side and "This time it is Hughes" on the other. In news reports Turner denied the effigy existed. Faculty mailed Turner a resolution signed "Members of the South

On March 25, 1956, SC State students toss their lunches into trash cans to protest the school's purchases of food and services from businesses owned by White Citizens' Council (WCC) members. They throw away the dining hall's milk, bread, and ice cream, sold to the school by WCC members who distribute Sunbeam Bread, Coble Dairy, and Paradise Ice Cream. Cecil Williams climbs atop a car to photograph the students singing outside Floyd Hall.

Carolina State College Faculty and Staff" that objected to the NAACP investigation and pressure and intimidation from within and without. SC State and Claflin students held rallies, campus protests, and marches downtown. Chalk comments—"Be a Man" and "Uncle Tom" in front of Turner's residence—decorated sidewalks. Students attempted to sit at the local Kress and Fischer's Rexall lunch counters—four years ahead of the 1960 student sit-ins. The food boycott continued in Floyd Hall, where students tossed away milk and bread and picked up meals from nearby Lamar's Restaurant.[66]

Claflin students picketed downtown with signs encouraging "Join the NAACP" and naming WCC businesses to boycott. Daniel Moss, student body president,

linked their participation to unity, Christianity, and the US Constitution, adding, "We further believe that our actions are in keeping with the basic law of the land." Dean Leonard Haynes said that the university did not restrict student participation in orderly activities and that Claflin had ended its use of some WCC-affiliated products and services "as a matter of Christian practice." Its ministerial association and veterans' club made public their boycott support.[67]

On April 2 Turner received a second resolution, an intensely patriotic history lesson that was signed by 176 of 177 faculty and administrators. They also sent the resolution to the state governor and legislature and to the media. "We, as teachers and professors at South Carolina State College hold that education is conducted for the good of all and not to further the interests of any individual or group of individuals." The authors cited the Declaration of Independence, the Constitution, the Supreme Court, and the *Brown v Board* rulings. They all but shouted a challenge: if the state General Assembly found such beliefs hostile to "all the people of South Carolina," the legislature should discharge faculty and staff "and admit the entire student body of South Carolina State to its other institutions (white)." What about the NAACP? The resolution mentioned it "as simply one organization which gives vitality to these beliefs."[68]

SC State students hang in effigy state representative Jerry M. Hughes Jr. and college president Benner C. Turner, using a scarecrow with a hot water bottle head to represent "Turner" on one side and "This time it is Hughes" on the other. Cecil Williams receives an early morning call that brings him to campus; the resulting photos are published by Jet *magazine and the* Afro-American *newspaper.*

Anne Jamison, left, and friends carry food from Lamar's Restaurant into Manning Hall, a women's dormitory. SC State students start a food boycott in March and add a class boycott in April to protest excessive administrative control, their school's purchase of goods and service from White Citizens' Council members, and a legislative investigation of possible NAACP influence at the school.

'NOT A PRISON OR A CONCENTRATION CAMP'

Timmerman put the campus under surveillance by local and state law enforcement, who were ordered to look for "subversive elements."When SC State's 1,500 students returned from Easter break on April 9, they returned to campus but not classes. Their list of grievances, delivered to Turner, cited disciplinary hearings likened to inquisitions, personality-based decisions on leadership opportunities, and administrative control of the student newspaper. The students' membership in a larger world of friends, family, and work, all constricted by Jim Crow, meant such complaints constituted a slice among greater grievances: NAACP membership outlawed; a legislative investigation of any NAACP influence at the college; SLED investigations of desegregation petitioners statewide; surveillance of the campus; support bestowed on the WCC by a governor, legislators, their trustees, even their own college funds.[69]

Turner required professors count the students absent. The second day just 280 of the college's 1,500 students attended class. Moore told the press, "The general feeling is this is an institution of learning that needs peace of mind. It is not a prison or concentration camp." On April 11 the students hanged the governor in effigy. On April 12 Turner finally met with students and faculty. On April 13 he threatened the students with expulsion if they did not attend class but promised excused absences if they did. Students attended 7:30 a.m. classes, skipped the next session for an assembly, then returned to classes. "Fred Moore was running into trouble" as the highly visible leader, said Williams.[70]

Wallace C. Bethea, executive secretary of the SC State board and a member of the Committee of 52, insisted this was an "insurrection" fomented from without, namely by the NAACP, which he claimed was "trying to goad us into closing the school so they'll have an excuse to seek entrance at our white colleges." True, NAACP leaders and student and faculty leaders cooperated from the start. McCollom and James E. Sulton Sr. approached Moore. McCollom and Sulton assisted Rev. Alfred Isaac—assistant history professor, school chaplain, and pastor of New Mount Zion Baptist Church—with the faculty statement. Trustee Bethea and president Turner aspired to a moat-enclosed fiefdom, but journalist McCray wrote that the WCC had achieved in six months what Black activists had wanted for years, to "get our people together."[71]

On April 25 Moore got the blame, "along with a number of his Charleston friends," said Williams. The trustees, with Turner's recommendation, expelled the senior just before graduation. Moore said the trustees would not specify any charges; they only labeled him a bad influence. He left campus that evening but returned the next day to say farewell. Hundreds gathered, including Claflin students. Moore addressed them. He said he would do it all again: "Freedom has always cost something." Williams climbed atop a car to photograph endless farewell handshakes and a Moore-led convoy.[72]

The next day students held three prayer meetings, refused to eat at the dining hall, collected in front of Turner's residence to jeer him, and mailed newspapers a statement saying that Moore fulfilled his leadership role by expressing student opinion and Turner failed his leadership role by groveling to the WCC. Williams, who greatly admired Moore and wanted the full story for *Jet,* followed Moore to the coast, seeing poetic symbolism in photographing Moore crossing the James Island bridge to return home.[73]

Williams had photographed it all: the marches downtown, the Floyd Hall walkout, the effigy, the strike, and the farewell. He felt, "I was embedded as a journalist in that story. It helped me define my style as a journalist." He approached *Life, Look,* the *Saturday Evening Post, Time, U.S. News & World Report,* and the *New York Times* without success. However, the *Afro-American* and *Jet* used several photos. In May, Francis Mitchell hired Williams as a *Jet* correspondent, requiring him to send short news contributions three times a week, to call collect for urgent news, and to clip from local newspapers "all items relevant to Negroes," supplemented by personal up-to-date reports. In return *Jet* paid Williams about one hundred dollars each month, which included a flat fee of fifty to seventy-five dollars, more for special coverage, and two to five dollars for each short news item. He also earned a fee for escorting *Jet* reporters. He received a free newsletter and a free subscription. For assigned photos—"They wanted to keep a person on the ground at all times covering this unusual technique, the boycott"—Williams earned an additional ten to twenty-five dollars for any photo chosen from his film for publication in the magazine.[74]

On May 31 Turner notified fourteen students, eleven of them women, of one-year suspensions. Three faculty members resigned in protest. The college did not renew contracts of four faculty members, including those of Rev. Isaac and Florence Miller. An ally of the students and advisor of their newspaper, Miller won a thousand-dollar settlement with the assistance of an attorney and the American Association of University Professors. Isaac retained his Orangeburg ministerial post for a year. In September McCray reported that at least eleven faculty members had resigned. Moore, refused admission by Claflin's trustees, accepted an offer from Allen University, where he found himself a celebrity.[75]

The strike itself was over, but the state legislative hunt for any remaining whiff of the NAACP on campus launched with two on-site sessions, held on July 18 and August 30. The legislative committee possessed subpoena power to obtain testimony in secret and under oath. The *Times and Democrat* said the committee interviewed Turner, Bethea, the college's business manager, and had previously spoken to a few faculty members. But McCray uncovered the campus tour and nothing more, no interviews under oath of faculty or students, no revelations of NAACP hijinks.

SC State trustees expel Fred Henderson Moore, student body president and campus boycott leader, on April 25, 1956, just before graduation. Moore says the trustees labeled him "a bad influence." Students gather near Wilkinson Hall to cheer him, shake his hand, and participate in a parade of cars around campus. Moore graduates from Allen University in Columbia, South Carolina, and Howard University School of Law in Washington, DC. He returns to South Carolina to participate as an attorney in 1960s civil rights cases.

Despite a January 1957 deadline, the probe faded away, no more "agitators" located. A satisfied state senator, James Hugh McFadden of Clarendon County, praised the president, saying, "Dr. Turner is loyal to the South Carolina way of rendering an education to the two races."[76]

The undaunted Moore, elected president of Allen University's NAACP chapter, began a bus protest in Columbia, leading groups of students onto city buses' front seats. On these weekend ventures, students "in droves" shared seats with White riders who responded with nothing worse than unsuccessful elbowing. One White rider said, "Hell, they paid their 15-cent fare just like me." Rev. Isaac landed on his feet. He became pastor of Union Baptist Church in Harlem in September 1957; his wife, fired from Dunton Memorial School after refusing to sign an anti-NAACP teacher application, took a Harlem teaching job. Isaac visited Greenville in 1957 to evangelize. From pulpits he said, "Too many of you preachers are going around preaching about a Heaven 'Over Yonder' while there is nothing but hell on earth." An uninvited Isaac and McCollom attended a segregated public meeting of Orangeburg's all-White county delegation, where McCollom warned, "It is no longer safe to say that colored people like the way segregation pushes them around."[77]

Williams had not convinced White news editors to pay attention to Orangeburg, but he had reached a childhood goal, employment with *Jet*. He understood *Jet's* personality. "*Jet* had a *National Enquirer* side, not gossipy, but dealing with human curiosity," and "They liked exclusives, things that did not appear in any other publications." Anointed a member of what editor Mitchell called "a nationwide corps of top-flight newsgathering personnel," Williams could proclaim, "I'm from *Jet*," a national Black magazine, influential, timely, stylish, a photograph on almost every page.[78]

NO NAACP, NO TEACHERS

Williams did not neglect Elloree. His boycott photos included local NAACP president Blackman and petitioners who had been fired. The WCC had destroyed Blackman's contractor business, but he was undaunted in his support of Orangeburg and Clarendon petitioners. In the spring Elloree's White school superintendent and trustees launched their own NAACP investigation, empowered by the new state law forbidding the employment of NAACP members. Following the WCC squeeze in Elloree, membership in the local NAACP branch actually increased by ninety members to an all-time high of 250, in part due to an NAACP assistance fund, which reached $40,000, and dedicated loans from Victory Savings Bank in Columbia. Dr. Henry D. Monteith served as president of the state's only Black-owned bank, which had opened in 1921. Modjeska Monteith Simkins, his outspoken and politically powerful sister, was among the founders. She held positions at the bank, and, as corresponding secretary for the state NAACP conference, led efforts to assist those economically injured by the WCC. Blackman said the WCC "helped us a lot" by creating a general sentiment summed up as "I'm for the NAACP now 100 percent. To hell with the white folks."[79]

At Elloree Training School, which served 1,100 Black students, White super-intendent M. G. Austin distributed an NAACP-focused teacher application, to be signed and notarized. The new form asked for far more than a teacher's name, years of experience, and certification fields. Questions included, "Do you belong to the NAACP? Does any member of your immediate family belong to the NAACP? Do you favor integration of races in schools? Do you feel that you are qualified to teach an integrated class in a satisfactory manner?" Of thirty-one teachers, just seven turned in completed forms on the due date, May 14, 1956. The low response led Austin to add a day with the hope of more responses. At that time eighteen of the teachers resigned; three refused to sign the application or complete a resignation form. "We met with the superintendent," said first-grade teacher Elizabeth Lewis Cleveland. "We didn't make it easy. We did know we were in our rights to say no." She and Juanita Richburg Wells, a business teacher, felt as offended by the idea they were incapable of teaching White students as they were by the effort to extract a denunciation of the NAACP. "We felt we could teach anybody," said Wells.[80]

Principal Charles Davis called Williams to say, "I want you to come to the school tomorrow; we're getting ready to make an important announcement." Williams did not ask for details, nor were they provided. When he arrived, Davis surprised him by announcing, "We're all going to resign." The principal wanted a portrait of the soon-to-be-unemployed faculty. In the morning light of May 15, twenty-one teach-ers and Davis lined up outside the school, wrapped their arms around one another's waists, and smiled for Williams. Williams did his job; he took a group photo. But his and their feelings showed in the sunshine-lit smiles. "I found it amazing they would take such a step, give up such a hard-earned prize. I knew they were taking a dan-gerous stand." *Jet* took that into account and published the portrait in a two-page spread, tagging it "Martyred Teachers." An *Afro-American* series on the WCC and KKK also included the teachers' portrait and story.[81]

On May 16 the Elloree trustees announced that at least twenty-one teachers would not return in the fall. The *Times and Democrat* published every departing teacher's name. Elloree's Black parents issued a statement bemoaning the loss of respected teachers and academic freedom. Roy Wilkins, executive secretary of the NAACP, telegrammed Hinton to offer legal support and noted in a press release that

*On May 15, 1956, principal
Charles Davis of Elloree Training School calls Cecil Williams
and asks him to photograph
twenty-one teachers who will
be leaving the school. Eighteen
have resigned rather than sign
a re-application for their jobs;
three more have refused to sign
the new application or a resignation form. The re-application
form asks questions, not just
about qualifications but also
about personal and familial
affiliation with the NAACP
and beliefs about integration.
Jet magazine gives the photo a
two-page spread.*

*From left: Elizabeth Cleveland, Betty Smith, James Mays, Ola Bryan, Jestine DeLee, Betty C. Green, Rosa
Davis, Laura Prickett, Ernestine Dawkins, Clarence Tobin, Rosa Haigler, Mary Jackson, Hattie Fulton,
Robert Carmichael, Howard Shelton, Vivian Floyd, Lelia Mae Summers, Deloris Davis, Rutha Ingram,
Frazier Kiett, and principal Charles Davis.*

police states stamp out freedom of association and opinion. The Elloree trustees
announced the hiring of twenty-four replacement teachers, one trustee claiming,
"Anything can teach a damned nigger." In September attorneys Marshall and Lincoln C. Jenkins of Columbia filed *Bryan v. Austin* in federal court for seventeen of
the teachers, saying the school district's questionnaire forced compliance with the
state's anti-NAACP law and denied the teachers equal protection of the law and
freedom of speech and association.[82]

In court in October, Hattie Fulton Anderson confirmed her NAACP membership, making clear the First Amendment issues for any local or state employee. On
January 23, 1957, the district court referred the case to the state while keeping *Bryan v. Austin* on its docket. On April 23, the NAACP asked the US Supreme Court

to nullify the law prohibiting membership in the NAACP. The very next day Timmerman signed a law that repealed the NAACP prohibition and substituted another requirement, the disclosure of membership or affiliation with all associations and organizations, hoping to "cut the feet from under the NAACP appeal," said the state attorney general. In May, back at it, the state department of education reminded White school trustees that while the new law did not name the NAACP, it still barred members of the NAACP from public jobs, especially teaching. In June the Supreme Court returned *Bryan v. Austin* to the state court because the law no longer existed, and the state court dismissed the lawsuit. In the midst of this, the state also tried to shut down the NAACP by outlawing barratry, a term for instigating or encouraging a lawsuit without a direct interest in the relief sought.[83]

Williams did fit in his own adventures. He just sandwiched them in, putting business before pleasure. In March 1955 the Fourth Circuit Court of Appeals had ruled that segregation of public parks and beaches was unconstitutional. Within two months John Wrighten, now an attorney, threatened a lawsuit if Edisto Beach State Park were not desegregated, and, on July 23, attorneys Newton Pough and Thurgood Marshall filed the NAACP lawsuit. Of South Carolina's twenty-two state parks, Black people had access to four areas within segregated parks and exclusive use of the Pleasant Ridge State Park in Greenville County. White South Carolinians also deemed as their own the coast's fine sand and mild waves. Black coastal residents and visitors found themselves confined to about six seaside areas, such as Atlantic Beach, a Black-owned stretch of hotels, restaurants, clubs, and dancing pavilions near Myrtle Beach, and Mosquito Beach, a Black-owned creekside strip with a few restaurants and clubs on Sol Legare Island near Charleston.[84]

The pending lawsuit drew Williams and his friend Harper to the coast one sunny day. Rev. Isaiah DeQuincey Newman, first vice president of the state NAACP, planned to wade in the Atlantic Ocean from the "White Only" roped-off shore. *Jet* wanted Williams to document this, but Williams never located Newman. The trip did inspire the teens to quench their thirst at a gas station's "White Only" water fountain on the return trip. "On the way back, I stopped on Highway 21, coming from Hunting Island, to get a drink of water. So I pulled into a service station," said Williams. "The water fountain was over near the open bay where they fixed cars. I jumped out of my car and got me some water, and Rendall got him some water, and then I said, 'Hey, let's take a picture.'"

Williams decided that he did want to attend college after all. To him, SC State carried more prestige than smaller private colleges. But Turner said no. Offended by Williams's photos, he rescinded his previous offer of a full scholarship and monthly work stipend of $150. Rev. Hubert Vernon Manning, president of Claflin since June 1956, heard of Williams's plight through McCollom and James E. Sulton Sr. The 38-year-old former pastor of Wesley Methodist Church in Charleston knew Orangeburg; he had served as chair of Claflin's religion department from 1947 to 1951. He invited Williams to meet with him, to the great relief of Williams's parents. "They wanted me to go to college by any means." Manning replicated SC State's offer. "He told me, 'I will give you the same scholarship as Turner. We can't let Turner outdo us.'" Williams chose art as his major and revived Claflin's abandoned darkroom, which contained his best enlarger yet. For four years he took only Monday, Wednesday, Friday classes so "I could work and run around everywhere."

Turner, intent on controlling SC State, and Manning, intent on reinvigorating Claflin, understood quite well that Williams belonged to the movement's "we." At Claflin, that was just fine. Williams believed, "You could not avoid it, a student of my age." He attended rallies, two or three per week; he attended NAACP leadership meetings at homes or in Trinity's basement. "My role was to capture these events for the local NAACP," said Williams. "They knew that the media played an important role, and they knew local newspapers would not cover them. I was involved in planning, what they were going to do, so I could be there to capture it. They relied on me to get it into national publications."

DYNAMITE

Segregationists' violent responses to desegregation increased. At the University of Alabama, Autherine Lucy's third day in graduate school ended with a mob of 2,000 on campus protesting her admission, then her flight by patrol car, and her expulsion, which trustees said was for her own safety. In Clinton, Tennessee, twelve Black students entered Clinton High School safely, then the WCC and KKK fomented a Labor

Day weekend of riots quelled by state police and the National Guard. In Little Rock, Arkansas, nine Black students enrolled at Central High School; the governor blocked their entry with the state's National Guard. President Dwight Eisenhower put the National Guard under federal control and sent in a thousand soldiers to protect the students. Even so, the Black students continued to endure assaults throughout the school year, after which the governor closed all the city's high schools.[85]

South Carolina's Klan made its displeasure visible. One grand dragon estimated the state's Klan membership at 100,000, divided among competitive groups. The media documented at least one full-regalia rally or cross burning a month between January and July 1956. A *New York Post* series on the Klan featured South Carolina repeatedly, noting the reliable presence of the highway patrol directing traffic at rallies despite a 1951 South Carolina law, aimed at the KKK, that prohibited masks hiding identity and burning crosses in public spaces. In July a bomb threat and cross burnings at the private all-Black Mather Academy in Camden and threats by police about "mixing of races" chased away a youth group of White Christians. In November in Kershaw County, five fires that were deliberately set destroyed Black churches and a home, the house fire preceded by a cross burning. In December six hooded men abducted Guy Hutchins, director of the Camden High School band, pulled a sack over his head, tied him to a tree, held a gun to his neck, and beat him "80 to 90 times," according to Hutchins, who required hospital care. He said the assailants accused him of making a pro-integration speech. SLED arrested six men; a grand jury twice refused to indict them.[86]

In January 1957 at Rock Hill, a six-foot cross burned in front of integrated St. Anne's Catholic School. In July at Travelers Rest, eleven men beat Black farmer and Baptist deacon Claude Cruell with chains and clubs and abducted wife Fannie Cruell. The abductors forced her to walk miles home without shoes. The KKK attacked the Cruells because the couple temporarily cared for seven White children of neighbor Sherwood Turner while his wife was hospitalized. In November in Cherokee County, dynamite exploded at the home of Black farmer Lewis Ford. In December at Gaffney, a KKK time bomb of three dynamite sticks exploded (nine other sticks did not explode), shattering windows and cracking walls at the home of Claudia Thomas Sanders, one of twelve White contributors to *South Carolinians Speak: A Moderate*

Approach to Race Relations. Five men were arrested for three separate attempts to blow up the Sanders home. Charges against two were dismissed, a third died when a car fell on him, and a jury acquitted the final two of assault with intent to kill.[87]

In 1958 Williams photographed a tiny gas station that Black people called "the store of hate." On Highway 21 in Calhoun County sat a concrete-block, tin-roof store, barely more than a shed, where customers could pump gas and buy a snack but only if they were White. A tin sign on a post by the pumps announced, "No nigger or Negro allowed inside building." A wooden sign beside the screen door read, "No negro or ape allowed in building." A screed below one of the two windows and again above the door said, "Negroes not wanted in the north or south. Send them back to Africa where God Almighty put them to begin with. That is their home." The elderly owner, most often standing behind the counter, would run outside and scream obscenities if any Black person dared come on the property. So Williams photographed the store on a Sunday, when it was closed.[88]

In April 1958 in Fort Mill, George Tinker of the Association of Southern Red Shirts said "God, Himself, is the author of segregation." He attacked the current Klan as corrupt, claimed that the KKK as an organization had ended with Grant's 1871 intervention, after which Red Shirts, not the KKK, "ran the carpetbaggers and scalawags out in 1876." In May 1958 in Marion County, the Carolinas' Klan leader— former carnival barker and Free Will Baptist preacher James W. Cole—announced a run as a write-in candidate for South Carolina governor. He was free under bond while he appealed a North Carolina conviction for inciting a riot at a Klan rally. Several hundred armed members of the Lumbee Tribe shortcut the event by surrounding the speakers' platform, breaking the one platform light, and firing into the air.[89]

In January 1959 in Heath Springs, a cross burned before the home of a White couple who had taken to live with them two Black children, a niece and nephew of a grandfather's servant. The Klan disapproved; the sheriff consulted with the KKK; the couple returned the unwilling children to a home of seventeen starving relatives. In April 1959 in Washington, DC, Billie Fleming of Manning, and Newman, who would become the state NAACP president in 1960, testified before a constitutional rights subcommittee about beatings and whippings of Black citizens attempting to vote. In May 1959 Robert E. Hodges, representing the Association of South Carolina

Klans, arranged a one-day lease at Elloree's racetrack for a full-regalia rally, speech, and cross burning. Neither sheriff George L. Reed nor the county attorney objected. "Klavern 829 in Orangeburg is one of the largest klaverns in the state and is very active," said Hodges, who boasted of prominent local members.[90]

And the White Citizens' Councils? Fifty-nine councils with 40,000 members existed in South Carolina in December 1958, "carrying on their affairs openly and continuing, as in the past, under the leadership of leading citizens," according to FBI reports. But the Association of Citizens' Councils of South Carolina divided over arguments about inaction and Klan "infiltration" of the WCCs. State chairman Baxter A. Graham, a merchant and farmer in Olanta, had accepted Klan members while promising that the WCC would not become "dressed up Klans." A February 1959 walkout led to the election of John Adger Manning as chairman and Farley Smith as executive secretary. Farley Smith—son of Ellison "Cotton Ed" Smith, a virulent racist and six-term US senator; brother of Ellison Smith Jr., chairman of the Committee of 52—immediately announced the state organization's continuing "dedication to the separation of the races" and a push for public funds to support all-White private schools.[91]

Williams chose to believe the personal and communal tribulations transitory. "With the *Brown* decision behind us, the future looked brighter than the past." He wanted the world to know, "Not only do we boycott; we form buying services. In addition to marches and demonstrations, we go downtown to Kress and Fisher's Rexall to try and do sit-ins. And we start doing this in 1955. Orangeburg is the leader." Innovation and persistence in Clarendon and Orangeburg counties had contributed mightily to the civil rights movement: the first public-school desegregation lawsuit, *Briggs v. Elliott;* desegregation petitions after *Brown II;* a long and successful boycott preceding Montgomery's; the principled stand of Elloree teachers and SC State faculty; the risky yet committed protests of students, and, throughout, the use of nonviolent resistance.

"We did it first," became Williams's slogan. He and others ofttimes felt bewildered or annoyed by the attention paid elsewhere in the South, rather than Clarendon and Orangeburg counties. But credit or no, a slow seismic shift continued. "These were really exciting days where things all around were happening," said Williams. He had the proof: his photographs.

Public schools for Black children lack running water, heat, indoor toilets, desks, blackboards, and school supplies. Schoolbooks and library books are discards from White schools. This effort at a school library is in Williamsburg County.

In 1950 South Carolina spends $91.74 per white pupil and $58.82 per Black pupil. Because Black children's schools lack running water, the students often tote water from nearby residences' wells. In Colleton County, children pump their water on school grounds.

Ethel Lillian Williams, standing, teaches children and adults in Calhoun County. Her work at Mount Carmel in Cameron requires her to board with local families. Her husband, Cecil Leroy Williams, and her mother, Lillian Evans Williams, care for three children at home in Orangeburg.

Cecil Williams, who is sometimes labeled "Indian," and blond, blue-eyed Arnold Leroy "Bunt" Sulton Jr., who is labeled "Negro," are best friends. The two take advantage of confusion concerning appearance and racial classifications to enter together White-only spaces, such as Orangeburg's segregated drive-in theaters. Williams records their friendship by using a cable shutter release.

George Crawford, a close friend of Cecil Williams, attends Massachusetts private academies in junior high and high school. At 19 years old, he suffers spinal injuries from a car wreck and returns to Orangeburg. Williams later photographs his friend in front of the SC State Law School, where Crawford earns his juris doctor in 1965, as does classmate Laura Ponds, the school's only female graduate.

John Williamson Goodwin Jr., a chemistry major at Allen University, opens Goodwin Photography in Columbia in 1955. Goodwin poses here with wife Susan at Brooklyn's Coney Island. He hires Cecil Williams to assist in studio work after Williams's high school graduation.

Students at Claflin University encircle the Tree of Freedom on campus. Claflin and SC State campuses sit side-by-side. SC State students, facing penalties for civil rights activities on their campus, join Claflin students for speeches, meetings, and rallies, and become partners in the 1960s protests.

Cecil Williams photographs a shoeshine two blocks from the family home on Quick Street on a Sunday morning in 1956. The Jim Crow South limits the majority of Black people to manual labor, agricultural work, and menial labor such as shoeshiner, custodian, maintenance worker, laundress, housekeeper, or cook. For a better life in the 1940s, 1.4 million Black Southerners migrate North. In the 1950s, 1.1 million more do so.

On July 18, 1956, a state legislative committee with subpoena power comes to SC State to investigate NAACP activity on campus. Yearbook advisor Ira B. Davis asks Cecil Williams to document the visit. The legislature had approved in March of that year an investigative committee of nine. The state legislature also passed a provision to the appropriations bill that requires closing any segregated state college under court order to desegregate and requires, at the same time, closing SC State, the only state-supported college for Black students.

Sixty Southern Black ministers and civil rights leaders are invited to a 1957 conference that kicks off the founding of the Southern Christian Leadership Conference (SCLC). Rev. Matthew D. McCollom, pastor of Orangeburg's Trinity Methodist Church, is among the founding members. From September 28–30, 1959, the Rev. Dr. Martin Luther King Jr., SCLC president, visits Columbia for an SCLC conference that includes a testimonial dinner, mass meeting, and workshops to train leaders in nonviolence. Cecil Williams photographs King, center, at the Claflin University bandstand, where he makes a brief speech. He is framed by Claflin's president Hubert V. Manning, left, and McCollom, far right, facing camera.

Opposite Page: Cecil Williams majors in art at Claflin University, the only Black college in the state to offer a bachelor's degree in art. Each year professor Arthur Rose hangs the Fence Exhibit on the campus fence, inviting passersby to purchase student work.

The markers of segregation are everywhere. Southern bus and train stations segregate restrooms and waiting rooms, and, if a café is present, require Black customers to order from a back window or door and eat outside. Entrances and exits are segregated too, as illustrated by the sign above the Black-only waiting room at the Seaboard Air Line Passenger Depot on Gervais Street in Columbia.

Cecil Williams asks a friend to pose for this photograph at the Orangeburg County Courthouse; the sign directs Black citizens to segregated restrooms. The two leave when ordered out by a courthouse employee.

A painted Jesus stares from the window while a sign proclaims, "No Negro or ape allowed in building."
Black people call the tin-roofed, concrete-block store "the store of hate." Williams frequently passes the
store while driving on Highway 21 near Sandy Run in Calhoun County. After this photo is published in
Jet *and Williams's book* Out-of-the-Box in Dixie, *the owner's daughter writes to say she left home young*
to escape such hate.

THE 1960S

Throughout the 1960s Black citizens of Orangeburg marched, picketed, petitioned, and sued in a ceaseless demand for Constitutional rights. Parried by stalls and refusals, fines and jail, extrajudicial and state-sanctioned violence, they kept on. For Williams, perhaps the recording angel of the movement, "There was almost never a letup. From 1955 through 1968, no letup."

Williams did not allow a personal letup either. The Claflin student taught photography at both colleges. President Benner C. Turner's anger had cooled, and Williams added back yearbook photography for SC State. He never did just one or two things, so college studies and campus jobs were not enough. He further established himself as a professional photographer. He engaged in studio work by appointment at home or in rented rooms or apartments. "I would put up a sheet as my background. I had my lights, my stands; when somebody would come by, I would set up." Then he took a bigger step, opening a studio in the Black business strip on Boulevard Street, rent $150 a month. The display window announced Cecil J. Williams Commercial & Portrait Photographer. The street-side business sign—a modernist mélange of a circle, a slashing dart, parallelograms—announced Williams Photography Studio.

"I had cameras already; I had all my equipment. I got rent money together, and, when I opened, that generated other money so I was able to kick it off." Emulating his mentor Edward C. "E. C." Jones, he hired male students eager for apprenticeships. "They would get paid out of what they helped me to earn," he said. Williams and assistants traveled the state, taking photos for high school yearbooks and returning for prom portraits. At Georgetown's Howard High School, "I took so many pictures that when I got ready to leave, I had money in my pants pocket, my camera case, even my coat pockets."

When the College Soda Shop on Boulevard closed, Williams moved there, establishing Colorama Photography at 117 Boulevard. For his signature modern touch, he installed aluminum borders on the windows and a three-dimensional Colorama Photography sign above a glass-and-aluminum front door. A pavement-to-roof sign announced that Colorama—Complete Photo Services by Expert Camera Artists— offered the sale of Kodak film, 24-hour developing of black and white and color film, made-to-order rubber stamps, and plastic lamination service. Williams continued to shoot portraits and take yearbook and commercial assignments. He could be hired for birthday parties, family reunions, and weddings. He restored photos, difficult work eased by training at Goodwin Photography, sketching and painting in college art classes, and experimenting with an airbrush. He sold picture frames. He became a dealer for Japan's Nikon cameras, much admired by *Life* magazine photographers in the Korean War.[1]

During his senior year, Williams married schoolmate Constance Goode. *Jet* published a wedding reception photo in its "Society World" pages, but, within a few years, they divorced. He graduated from Claflin in May 1960. He rented a house to live in from his aunt Jesse Williams Younger, a nurse in New York City. Conveniently, each of his Boulevard studios sat across the railroad tracks from the colleges. When SC State, Claflin, and Wilkinson students took to the streets, their demonstrations garnered more media attention than their elders' picketing and boycotting. Williams could dash out of his studio to document the protesters on their way downtown.[2]

At Colorama, Williams put his electronics fascination to work, installing a rotating antenna behind his studio. Inside, on a long table, sat the antenna rotor controller; a business band radio; a scanner tuned to receive city police, county sheriff, and highway patrol broadcasts; and a reel-to-reel tape recorder to capture conversations. Above the table hung a large state map so that he could pinpoint where he might head and how he might get there. An alley separated Colorama from The People's Barber Shop, and Williams parked his car there, backing it in for quick getaways. A citizens band (CB) radio and scanner in his car tracked city, county, and highway patrol broadcasts, which was "very handy during civil rights marches and demonstrations," noted Williams. His CB license was KDD3598. "I was everywhere," he said.

He did seem everywhere. He attended concerts and plays at the colleges and, always on the job, he photographed numerous celebrities. He photographed performers: James Brown, Cab Calloway, Sam Cooke, Aretha Franklin, Ramsey Lewis, Gladys Knight, and Otis Redding. "Just about everybody in music," Williams said. He photographed actors: Ossie Davis, Lena Horne, and Sidney Poitier. He photographed athletes: Joe Louis and Jackie Robinson. He photographed civil rights leaders: Ruby Hurley, the Rev. Dr. Martin Luther King Jr., Constance Baker Motley, and Roy Wilkins. Such well-known activists represented "a long line of individuals who came to Orangeburg as a result of our activities. Often I would get the behind-the-scenes pictures, the meetings in the president's office, visits in the community." He photographed civic and sports events. Because these were moments in Black lives, disdained by White-owned media, his record often became the only record.

He photographed the movement's youth leaders, attorneys, and speakers, their meetings and fundraisers, the marches and arrests and bail bond releases, the signs that picketers carried, the lunch counter stools that they could not sit upon, and the fire hoses that doused them. He photographed as the Sixties—war, assassinations, massive demonstrations, armed soldiers and tanks on the streets—unsettled, overwhelmed, and rearranged a nation.

SIT DOWN; GO TO JAIL

For Williams, 1960 began with a personal thrill. In Professor Harold I. Robinson's political science class, Williams and classmates discussed US Senator John F. Kennedy's political future. In a straw poll only Williams chose Kennedy. Robinson said a Catholic could not win. Williams believed Kennedy would run and win. He was a fan. On January 2 in the Senate caucus room, Kennedy announced his candidacy. Visiting family in New York City during winter break, Williams read of a Kennedy press conference at the elegant Roosevelt Hotel and decided to attend.

Lacking press credentials, Williams chanced barging into the hotel ballroom. Security guards spotted the only Black guest and escorted Williams out—just as

When US Senator John F. Kennedy announces his run for the presidency, Cecil Williams is visiting family in New York City. He attends a press conference at the Roosevelt Hotel, where he is the only Black press representative, and is escorted out. Kennedy interrupts, introduces himself, and escorts Williams to a front-row seat.

the senator and wife Jacqueline Kennedy arrived. "As they are rushing me out, my cameras banging around my neck, Kennedy stops them. He makes them let go of me, and we have a discussion right in the middle of all these journalists from ABC, NBC, CBS, UPI, AP." Kennedy asked Williams's name and whom he represented—Williams said that he worked freelance for *Jet*—and if Williams thought he could win. Williams, who often sounded definitive when answering questions, replied, "There is no doubt in my mind."

Kennedy offered a card with contact information, invited Williams to send his best shots, and escorted him back into the ballroom—to the front row with NBC broadcasters Chet Huntley and David Brinkley. Williams felt grateful, thrilled, and a bit suspicious that Kennedy "probably was using me to show that he was an equal-opportunity candidate." Yards in front of other photojournalists, who were confined in the back with TV camera operators, Williams was guaranteed the best pictures. "This was a good thing because I didn't have my telephoto lens," said Williams, who hobnobbed with the White media stars before photographing the senator close-up, capturing Kennedy's trademark alert and engaged charm. This paid off. During South Carolina campaign stops, Kennedy's team invited Williams onto the Convair 240 *Caroline,* the first-ever private plane used for presidential campaigning.

On November 8, 1960, Kennedy beat Vice President Richard M. Nixon with 50.31 percent of the vote. Analysts credited some of that skin-of-the-teeth prize to Kennedy winning 51 percent of the popular vote in South Carolina and 68 percent of the Black vote nationally. But before that surprising win, the South found itself the center of a youth-driven civil rights movement. The hyper-energetic Williams had to run to keep up with his peers.[3]

On Monday, February 1, 1960, four college students in Greensboro, North Carolina, supercharged their contemporaries' engagement. Ezell Blair Jr., Franklin McCain, Joseph McNeil, and David Richmond, friends studying at North Carolina Agricultural and Technical (A&T) College, made purchases at the downtown F. W. Woolworth Co., then sat at its lunch counter from 4:30 to 5:30 p.m., a popular time for White customers. Jim Crow law and custom required that Black customers order food while standing and then leave to eat.[4]

On Tuesday more Black students came to Woolworth, where they sat on counter stools and read from their textbooks. On Wednesday around 150 protesters participated, some at Woolworth, some at S. H. Kress & Co. lunch counters. White antagonists, several armed with sheathed knives, blocked Kress's store aisles and occupied counter seats. On Thursday Black high-school students attempted sit-ins at both stores, joined by supportive White students. On Friday about 300 sit-in participants and opponents arrived. Police escorted White men and women from the stores for using abusive language and arrested a White man for setting on fire a Black student's coat. On Saturday hundreds arrived to join or oppose the sit-ins, which ended with bomb threats. A&T students voted late in the day to pause the protests for two weeks.[5]

Close to perfection in its ability to illustrate the racist strictures of Southern custom and law, sit-ins allowed participants to make a peaceful and powerful statement by sitting on a counter stool, a schoolbook or Bible at hand, doing their best to ignore irate White men prowling behind them, cursing and pushing them, pouring food and drinks on them. The protesters made a simple, understandable point: if they could purchase goods elsewhere in the stores, why could they not also sit down, order food, and eat? Sit-ins suited group leadership and barebones organizing: pick a store, set times, spread the word, use safety in numbers, sit silently and stoically, and then return to school. The dignity and courage that the students brought to their task compelled attention, drew media, and inspired emulation.

Sit-ins spread to Durham and Winston-Salem and then to Fayetteville, Charlotte, and Raleigh, North Carolina. Gordon Carey, a field secretary for the Congress of Racial Equality (CORE), advised students in Greensboro and Durham. CORE dispatched to Rock Hill, South Carolina, its other field secretary, James Thomas "Nooker" McCain Sr., a native of Sumter, South Carolina. CORE hired McCain in 1957 as the organization's first Southern and Black field secretary. McCain helped found Sumter's NAACP branch in the late 1930s and supported Black teachers' equal-pay lawsuits in the 1940s as president and treasurer of the all-Black Palmetto State Teachers Association. Fired twice from principalships for refusing to disavow the NAACP, he joined CORE. Calm, focused, and devoted, McCain took on the difficult task of teaching nonviolent direct action. The peaceful refusal to accept injustice was developed from Mohandas Gandhi's principals of *satyagraha*, sometimes translated as "truth force" or "holding onto truth." Up and down the East Coast CORE's McCain helped youths and adults anticipate, endure, and survive the violent responses of others.[6]

The NAACP offered expertise in court challenges, and the 1950s had been all theirs. CORE offered expertise in nonviolent protest. The biracial organization emerged in 1942 in Chicago from the Fellowship of Reconciliation, founded in England before World War I to help conscientious objectors. Several of CORE's American founders and members served prison time rather than fight in World War II or the Korean War. In the 1940s and '50s, small interracial groups in northern and southern cities ate together at segregated dime stores, drugstores, and department stores. CORE leaders negotiated immediate desegregation with management before attempting to dine together or, if necessary, negotiated during a meal and afterward too. The 1960 sit-ins forced the NAACP and CORE to fit together, albeit uncomfortably. CORE taught the students nonviolent direct action, soon referred to as "soul power" and sent them forth. The NAACP raised funds to bail out the protesters and defended them in court. The NAACP wanted a few petitioners asserting constitutional rights in court. However, CORE supported dozens or hundreds of students in nonviolent confrontation—with the NAACP often stuck paying attorneys and putting up bonds or paying bail.[7]

On February 10 McCain arrived in Rock Hill to train Friendship Junior College students in nonviolent protest. On February 12 about 150 Black students walked into Woolworth and McCrory's variety stores and Good and J. L. Phillips drugstores. They encountered heckling and tossed bottles filled with ammonia. A White man punched a male student; another kicked a female student. When bomb threats ended the two hours of sit-ins, police escorted the students back to campus through a large and hostile crowd. "The North Carolina-born passive resistance movement also spread into South Carolina—thus into the heartland of the Deep South's total segregation," reported the Associated Press (AP).[8]

Williams and Orangeburg NAACP leaders were puzzled by the national attention and the rocket-fast spread of sit-ins. After all, NAACP members and SC State and Claflin students had conducted sit-ins off and on, spontaneous or planned, for years. But the current set of students was not interested in the old guard. They felt inspired by young people like themselves. "When we started the sit-ins in Orangeburg, we were not absolutely certain we would be backed by the adults, so we flew out on our own," said Thomas Walter Gaither, vice president of Claflin's student body, president of the NAACP's youth council, and a much-admired classmate of Williams. "We were idealists enamored with the possibility of using nonviolence to work for social change. Our approach was fundamentally different. We weren't interested in getting one person arrested and having a court case and ruling to say, 'You guys can sit at a lunch counter.' This was our movement, our time to move."[9]

A native of Great Falls, South Carolina, Gaither's childhood included attending NAACP meetings with his parents and watching his father lose jobs because he belonged to the NAACP and asked pointed questions about unfair practices. Gandhi's success and McCain's tutoring led Gaither to distinguish between a passivity he rejected and what he called the "high moral plain" of nonviolent direct action that he embraced. His ability to articulate this made him a campus hero and a national spokesperson. Within weeks "Gaither was traveling all over the place. He was making national news," said Williams. Claflin classmates celebrated Gaither as the most-traveled student for his speeches coast-to-coast. Gaither often was joined by James Farmer. A CORE founder in 1942, Farmer served as the NAACP's activities director and sit-in coordinator from 1959 through 1960.[10]

'WE ARE ALL LEADERS'

During evenings in Claflin's Seabrook Gymnasium, students met with McCain. They participated in sociodramas, taking turns in the role of peaceful protester or violent opponent to familiarize themselves with what might happen and to test their own responses. They studied and discussed *CORE Rules for Action* and King's *Stride Toward Freedom*. "Could each one of us trust our God and our temper enough not to strike back even if kicked, slapped, or spit upon?" wrote Gaither for a CORE report. Claflin's gym became headquarters for SC State students too. They were constrained by the 1956 expulsion of Fred Henderson Moore and by Turner's dicta, which included administrative control of student activities and an ongoing ban of the NAACP. Participants chose Claflin's Gaither and SC State's Charles Frederick "Chuck" McDew as copresidents of the Orangeburg Student Movement Association. Then they planned their first sit-ins. Scouts timed walks downtown, chose three routes to Kress, even counted the number of counter stools. A few dozen students confident that they could remain nonviolent would march and sit-in.[11]

On Thursday, February 25, about forty-five students, most from Claflin, walked to Kress. Around 11 a.m., about fifteen students sat on lunch counter stools and attempted to place orders. Within minutes employees put up signs that the counter was closed "in the interest of public safety." The original group left. Twenty more students stepped up. The manager began removing the stools' padded seats; each seated student stood when approached. No one was arrested, but White customers

doused students with mustard and ketchup and strode behind them with large knives and baseball bats.[12]

On Friday approximately sixty students participated. In the morning a small group watched behind a rope as the manager replaced seats, stacked on the floor until White customers arrived. Students stood from 11 a.m. until 3:30 p.m., their number growing as classes let out, until about forty stood rows deep. White youths and adults attacked a Claflin student when he tried to take a seat, according to the NAACP. Police arrested a Black student and a White adult. At 4 p.m. the store closed.[13]

Williams photographed the Orangeburg students marching. He photographed Gaither and Lloyd Williams showing a Kress employee their small purchases to prove they were customers deserving of seats. He photographed bewildered White customers at Kress's dismantled counters. The AP provided accounts of this; the

Students at Claflin University and SC State carefully plan their first large sit-in of 1960, following the protest philosophy of the Congress of Racial Equality (CORE). The students study nonviolent direct action, and they use sociodramas to practice responses to attacks. On February 25, 1960, about forty-five students, mostly from Claflin, walk to S. H. Kress & Company. There they take turns sitting at the lunch counter.

Thomas Walter Gaither, left, and Lloyd Williams, right, follow Congress of Racial Equality (CORE) guidelines at Kress by initiating conversation and hoping for negotiation. Gaither is a Claflin University student and copresident of the Orangeburg Student Movement Association. Lloyd Williams, SC State coordinator of sit-ins, is chair of the state NAACP youth conference. When possible, students buy small items to emphasize that they are customers deserving of a seat at a lunch counter.

Times and Democrat did not. Instead, the local paper, published in a county that was 60 percent Black, said in an editorial, "In the case of Orangeburg County, the majority is not yet ready to change most of the basic customs of this community."[14]

On Monday, February 29, twenty-five students with police clearance to picket began pacing outside Kress but stopped when police said a new ordinance required that they furl their signs or face arrest. Kress employees had stacked trash cans on the lunch counter. Only two Black customers at a time could enter the store. This was not even a speed bump. On Tuesday, March 1, hundreds of students—the police chief said six hundred to seven hundred students while Gaither reported one thousand students—marched downtown. Demonstrators walked two abreast in small groups, stayed off the grass, waited for red lights, and used hand signals instead of

The manager of Kress thwarts sit-ins by removing the padded seats to lunch counter stools, willing to lose White customers to avoid serving Black people. A few years later the lunch counter remains segregated, but the manager no longer swears out arrest warrants during sit-ins..

shouts. They carried signs saying, "Segregation is obsolete" and "No Color Line in Heaven," which they rolled up upon the order of Joseph Preston "Pete" Strom, chief of the State Law Enforcement Division (SLED). He told McDew that any violence would result in students being charged with inciting a riot. A first-generation native of Massilon, Ohio, McDew came to SC State to play on its championship football team, as had his father. McDew possessed a broad and easy smile, a strong sense of irony, and the ability to hold his own with White adults after having grown up in a desegregated steel town. He advocated nonviolent direction action as a pragmatic choice, saying it was the only way to survive since White people had all the guns.[15]

"The students came to Claflin and State—and to Allen and Benedict and Morris and Voorhees—awakened. They came knowing they deserve to be citizens," said

Williams, at twenty-two years old a protest veteran. "Their parents have warned them, 'I'm sending you to school,' but still they get involved. The students thought the adults were too slow and didn't want to go as far. And it was true the adults would be approached by the local leadership, their efforts neutralized; they would give in a little bit. But the students wouldn't give in; they wanted the whole hog."[16]

Jet chose one of Williams's many photos of marchers in two-by-two formation to illustrate an article that offered contrasting viewpoints. A White city official described the well-dressed and business-like Black students as "the most frightening thing I have ever seen." But reporter John Brehl, a White journalist from Canada's *Toronto Daily Star*, called the students "awesome" for pledging themselves "to take blows without returning them and yield to an arrest without a fight." Brehl also interviewed Rev. Matthew D. McCollom, who was pastor of Trinity Methodist Church, a local NAACP leader in the 1950s, state NAACP vice president in 1959, and state NAACP church committee chair in 1960. McCollom told him, "Sometimes I think the white man really thinks we are a different kind of human being. He doesn't seem to understand us; he doesn't realize how many times the human spirit is murdered every day."[17]

South Carolina governor Ernest F. Hollings described the sit-ins as "purely to create violence and not to promote anyone's rights," and sent SLED officers to Rock Hill and Orangeburg. Mayor S. Clyde Fair announced an Orangeburg Catch-22, a permit required for marches and a concern for public safety that prohibited issuing permits. With no intention of stopping, students from the state's historically Black colleges met on March 5 in Columbia to form the South Carolina Student Movement Association.[18]

Orangeburg's student association applied for a march permit, the police refused, and Claflin, SC State, and Wilkinson High School students marched anyway on Tuesday, March 15, more than a thousand participants in a coordinated effort by the state association. In Rock Hill, Friendship Junior College students held sit-ins at the bus stations and a lunch counter and picketed city hall; police arrested sixty-five students for breach of peace and five for trespassing. In Columbia, Benedict College students attempted sit-ins at a downtown pharmacy, where five were charged with breach of peace, and at the Union Bus Depot, where students were arrested but not charged. In Sumter, Morris College students gathered at the courthouse to sing patriotic songs and left when police arrived.[19]

In Orangeburg, students intended to pray and sing at Confederate Square, where a 33-foot-tall monument with a Confederate soldier had guarded the city since 1893. Lloyd Williams's group did not make it far, just to the local Piggly Wiggly before police ordered all to turn around. When police asked him if he were the leader, students behind him shouted, "We are all leaders. If one is arrested, we will all be arrested." Police arrested Lloyd Williams, who was president of the state NAACP's youth conference. He told the *New York Post* that the police chief instructed, "'All right, get them niggers,' and firefighters turned their hoses onto the group." He added, "No one ran away." Instead, they tried to sing.[20]

FIRE HOSES, TEAR GAS, A STOCKADE

It was cold and gray, the day's temperature ranging from twenty degrees into the forties. Orangeburg did not have enough jail cells for the 500-plus students arrested. After filling city and county jails and calling in buses to transport students to the penitentiary in Columbia, law officers confined protesters outdoors, where they were penned in by a chain-link fence. "The weather was sub-freezing, and we were completely drenched with water from the hoses," reported Gaither, arrested after he and about 200 students circled the courthouse to protest the mass arrests.[21]

Williams rushed about. "I very rapidly just photographed whatever was in front of me, left, right, events happening in front of me, no pre-planned script, everything spontaneous." After the mass arrests he climbed onto a warehouse loading dock beside the jail; it overlooked a fenced-in area now converted to a stockade. He photographed stern-faced students, fenced in, huddled together, clutching blankets tossed over the fence. At one point the students sang "God Bless America." Williams's bleak photo inspired J. Saunders Redding, a Black professor, author, and Guggenheim fellow. Redding wrote in *Jet*, "In that fenced-in jail yard in Orangeburg, S.C., the youngsters sang in defiance of those who seek to hold back the dawn."[22]

Firefighters had turned their hoses on four different groups. The high-pressure water knocked down Gilbert "Gigi" Zimmerman, the SC State yearbook editor who

*Matthew J. Perry, left, legal
counsel for the state NAACP,
pulls together teams of attorneys
to deal with mass arrests in
Orangeburg. James E. Sulton
Sr., right, long-term treasurer
of the NAACP's Orangeburg
branch, raises money for fines
and bail bonds. Sulton's financial independence, as co-owner
of Sulton's Servicenter and Esso
gas station, allows him a public
activism others might not dare.*

was less than four feet tall. His classmates rescued him by surrounding him. The
water knocked down Willa Mae Dillard, a blind seventeen-year-old SC State student. The firefighters held streams of water on targets, breaking one young woman's kneecap, hitting another young woman in the face and knocking out three
teeth. Police also shot two tear gas cannisters at students, gassing themselves in
the process. "I tried to avoid any direct contact or getting too close to officers," said
Williams. "I didn't know what they would do, like swing a club or take my camera
away from me."[23]

Matthew J. Perry Jr., state NAACP legal counsel, called in a team of attorneys, including Lincoln Jenkins, W. Newton Pough, and Willie T. Smith Jr. They achieved a bond reduction from $200 cash apiece to $10.00 surety bonds. In all, the city of Orangeburg charged 388 students with breach of peace. The nation took note of an AP photo of students penned in "an outdoor cage," said the *San Francisco Chronicle*, "like animals," said *Jet*. When reporters quizzed President Dwight D. Eisenhower at a press conference, he said that he deplored the use of any violence to prevent Negroes from exercising their Constitutional rights. In an April count of student demonstrations, Orangeburg led the way. No fewer than 1,359 students had been arrested in the South. South Carolina accounted for 448 arrests, 388 of them in Orangeburg. In fines, Orangeburg led the region, with $17,500 levied. Orangeburg's protesters had no intentions of stopping.[24]

Tired of the ensuing claims that "outside agitators backed by Communists" instigated and directed students' protests, Black business people decided to hold their own sit-ins, said Williams. Everyone knew the White businessmen's ritual of 10 a.m. coffee at Kress or Fischer's Rexall drugstore. On one occasion Williams joined James E. Sulton Sr., co-owner of Sulton's Servicenter and Esso gas station; Earl M. Middleton, a barber shop owner; and John Samuel Robinson, a sales representative of morticians' supplies, all three war veterans. The four men sat without coffee at Kress. On another occasion Williams and other local business owners left Trinity Methodist Church for Kress, and "On the way down people blew their horns because they knew us. They raised their fists in a 'go on ahead.'" In each venture some protesters took a seat while others shopped until a seat became available. Some White customers left; some moved a seat or two away.[25]

One time Williams sat two empty seats from Dean Livingston of the *Times and Democrat*. The two knew each other because Williams sold photographs to the newspaper. Waitresses met coffee requests from the aspiring Black customers by shaking their heads "no" or scurrying by. "Some wouldn't even come near us," said Williams. So Williams decided to ask an acquaintance for help. "I said, 'Dean, would you order me a cup of coffee?' He shook his head and said, 'Sorry, I can't do that.'" Private kindnesses might occur, but public allies could not be found.[26]

Lloyd Williams, left, and Raymond Weston, right, both students at SC State, attempt to obtain applica-
tion forms at the University of South Carolina on April 26, 1961. Cecil Williams accompanies them into
the administration building, his camera hidden under a coat, to snap a photo of the inevitable refusal.
A secretary tells the students that registration blanks and admission booklets are out of print.

In the spring Raymond Weston and Lloyd Williams decided to apply to the University of South Carolina. Cecil Williams arranged to join the two SC State students on Tuesday, April 26. They knew they would be conspicuous on a campus where the only Black people present were housekeepers, groundskeepers, custodians, or cooks. But no one stopped the three young men in suits and ties as they entered the administration building. The predicted high for the day was ninety degrees, but Cecil Williams also wore an all-weather trench coat. Warmth was not its purpose. Cecil Williams hid his Nikon within "so I wouldn't arouse suspicion. I kind of covered it up when I went in."[27]

Weston and Lloyd Williams walked into an office and sat down without invitation. "They got only as far as the secretarial desk," said Cecil Williams, who snapped a photo through the door, capturing a seated Lloyd Williams. Told registration blanks and admissions booklets were out of print, they left. "They were serious about attempting to get applications, but they knew in advance it would not be fruitful," said Cecil Williams. The attempt made news statewide, but only a university spokesperson was interviewed. Referring to a 1958 registration attempt by Columbia's Allen University students, the AP article noted, "Procuring blanks would serve no purpose because the university would not admit Negroes."[28]

As the school year wound down, the national NAACP reported 1,400 students arrested and $100,000 paid in fines in the South. South Carolina accounted for 600 arrests, the highest in the region. The NAACP celebrated students "far less interested in the legal position than in the moral justice of their cause. . . . They seek demolition of the entire Jim Crow structure and recognition of the dignity of the Negro as a human being entitled to all the rights enjoyed by other persons."[29]

For Williams, the year resembled his adored movie serials, one thing after another. He photographed a packed basement during a mass meeting at Trinity Methodist Church, all but one spindle-back chair taken. He photographed Lloyd Williams carrying his worn Bible as he and others followed police officers to their March 18 arraignment. He photographed Gaither in his "Jim Crow Must Go" tie. He photographed McDew beaming from a line of marchers. He photographed the signs they carried: "We died in War I We Died in War II We Will Fight Segregation III" and "Freedom," and "What do I have to do Bleach myself."

Charles Frederick "Chuck" McDew, far right, partial view, leads a protest group on Russell Street. Behind him, holding aloft a poster, is James Reeder, a Claflin University student. McDew is an SC State student, copresident of the Orangeburg Student Movement Association, and among the founders of the Student Nonviolent Coordinating Committee (SNCC). He serves as SNCC chair from fall 1960 through summer 1963, dropping out of college to focus on civil rights.

A DETOUR, ALMOST A DISASTER

In the fall of 1961, a photograph cost Williams dearly. On October 8, a Sunday, Williams parked his car across from St. Paul's Methodist Church on Amelia Street. On the steps of the imposing entrance—two sets of double doors set into the corner of a tower, the tower set into a corner of the white-brick sanctuary—stood Claflin students Dorothy Vann and Emmanuel Hixson. Williams had received a heads-up from a mutual friend and caught up with Vann and Hixson as they approached the church. It was a few minutes after 11 a.m., and the doors were closed. Vann and Hixson knocked.

"When the door opened, I was there. The mayor came out, and he said, 'You can't worship here. Go worship with your own people,'" said Williams, who stood close enough to hear and to photograph the mayor filling the doorway, the students listening. Vann said the church was pretty; they had hoped to worship there; why couldn't they? The two did not argue with the mayor's refusal. They joined Williams on the sidewalk, and the three left.

Thomas Walter Gaither, left, and Julie Varner Wright, right, work for civil rights organizations upon their May 1960 graduations. Gaither becomes a field secretary for the Congress of Racial Equality (CORE); Wright becomes assistant youth secretary for the NAACP. Gaither helps design and scout CORE's 1961 Freedom Rides. Julie Wright works with Herbert L. Wright, the national NAACP's youth director, then with Medgar Evers, NAACP field secretary in Mississippi, until his 1963 assassination.

Williams processed the film and delivered a print to the AP in Columbia. On October 9, newspapers nationwide published the photo of the church and its tall white doors, one ajar; a white-haired man filling the open space, blocking two supplicants. The photo, with captions such as "Turned Away," got far more column inches than usually awarded a daily news illustration. The AP interviewed the mayor and the students, and the story traveled in all directions, even as far as Guam and Germany. The *Times and Democrat* spent paragraphs describing "nothing but an NAACP stunt" before repeating the AP text and the mayor's line, "This is a segregated church."[30]

Within weeks the local draft board summoned Williams. While a full-time college student Williams had felt somewhat safe from the draft. Young men enrolled in higher education escaped the draft through student deferments. Upon graduation from Claflin, Williams had enrolled at SC State to pursue a master's and retain his deferment. But local draft boards determined who would be drafted, and only White men sat on Southern draft boards. "African-Americans were targeted, especially in

Emmanuel Hixson and Dorothy Vann, Claflin University students, ask to worship at St. Paul's Methodist Church in Orangeburg on October 8, 1961. Cecil Williams, standing on the sidewalk, hears Mayor S. Clyde Fair say, "You can't worship here. Go worship with your own people." The Associated Press distributes the photograph worldwide; Jet *prints the photo and Fair's rejection. Although Williams has a graduate student deferral, he gets a call from his draft board, likely as a consequence.*

the South," said Williams. He did not imagine a cabal deciding to punish him, "But I'm sure the draft board saw my name in newspapers and said, 'Isn't he eligible for the draft?' found out, 'He's got a deferment,' and said, 'Yeah, let's get him anyway.'"[31]

When Williams entered the draft board's office, he saw a White woman retrieve his folder from a cabinet. "The newspaper clipping kind of floated in the air, spun around, and dropped on the floor. I had no doubt about why they had called me in. They told me I had thirty days to clean up my affairs because I was subject to be drafted. They had rejected my deferment." The man he dealt with joked, "You'll make a good infantry photographer." Williams thought, "This is going to be it."

Williams talked to NAACP attorney Perry, who said he did not see a civil rights case, explaining, "'We have to take cases where there's a pattern of this happening.'"

Next, Williams visited an Air Force recruiter. He could enlist, attend eight weeks of basic training, then go to Florida to teach photography. He signed up. He sold his studio. He said farewell to work with SC State and Claflin. By year's end he had sold all his equipment, except for one Hasselblad, and traveled to Lackland Air Force Base in San Antonio, Texas. There he tucked his Hasselblad and an 80 mm lens into his trainee's trunk, which held all allowed worldly goods.[32]

Williams settled into the first desegregated environment of his life. On the weekends, "sometimes we were allowed to go into San Antonio. We would go to the movies, explore the city, hop on the bus to go places, whistle at the girls, go to a soda fountain, by the way always integrated." In a classic Williams move, on Sundays "I had a little hustle." Williams photographed recruits and airmen, developed the film at a camera store, charged ten dollars a print, "and I would make money off the other recruits. We would usually go to where they had airplanes parked," for an impressive photographic background, even though during basic training "they wouldn't let us near airplanes."

In the sixth week, during a 2:30 a.m. fire drill, as recruits hustled downstairs, a hefty White friend from Arizona fell against Williams, knocking him over another Arizonan. "He slipped and knocked me down the stairs on my back, bump, bump, bump." Trundled to the base emergency room on a stretcher and x-rayed every which way, Williams was then hospitalized. He received antibiotics for lacerations from the wooden stairs and injections and medications for swelling in his head, neck, and lower and middle spine. After several days he graduated from a wheelchair to one crutch. While an ambulatory patient—"I could walk, but I couldn't march or train with the rest of the airmen. I walked like a mummy"—Williams spent two weeks assisting the bedridden. "I had to help serve airmen who were worse off than I was. I would take their plates to them, a cane in one one hand." He ate ice cream sandwiches for lunch and dinner, gained weight, and worried about what was next. He would have to repeat and complete all eight weeks of basic training, and he had missed his chance at the Florida opening. "I grew weary of waiting around. Finally, I said, 'Is there any way I can get out of this?'" The officer in charge was not pleased, but in March 1962 Williams received an honorable discharge and a few thousand dollars in compensation.

Once home Williams began again. He opened a studio, reclaimed clients, watched his competitors sink, and soon got back his Boulevard site. "I was right back taking pictures as if I never left." His friends crafted a much-repeated joke. "Cecil was in the Army for two weeks, and they threw him out." But for years afterward Williams feared the Army would still come after him.

A COCA-COLA CRATE
OR AN ARMCHAIR

Back in October 1961, Gloria Blackwell Rackley had taken on the town, starting with Orangeburg Regional Hospital. Over the next few years Rackley and daughters Lurma and Jamelle became legends through inventive opportunism—Orangeburg offered so many opportunities—and persistence. Gloria Blackwell grew up in the tiny community of Little Rock, North Carolina. Father Harrison Blackwell owned a barber shop, all his customers White. Mother Lurline Thomas Blackwell, known as "Mrs. B.," worked as a schoolteacher, a piano teacher, and, among her many community activities, tutored illiterate adults. Mrs. B's father was a Methodist minister, and she insured that her two sons and daughter understood the social justice aspect of Methodism. Active in the NAACP, the Blackwells took their children to meetings and had them knock on doors for voter registration. "It was just a part of life, like going to church," explained Gloria Blackwell.[33]

At 16, Gloria Blackwell entered Claflin, her mother's alma mater, married a senior at SC State, left, and returned to Orangeburg after World War II. In 1951, divorced and the mother of three, she and her children suffered injuries in a car accident and daughter Ramona died. Encouraged by her parents to finish college, she completed an education degree at Claflin in 1953, taught school, attended SC State to earn a master's, and married Larney G. "Jack" Rackley Jr., SC State's director of educational extension services.[34]

In Orangeburg, "There was a gap, and there was a need," said Rackley, who served as third vice president of the state NAACP and chair of its Women's Auxiliary. She and Rev. Isaiah DeQuincey Newman teamed up to shake things up. Newman knew Orangeburg well. He attended high school at Claflin and earned a bachelor's

in 1934 from Clark College and a bachelor of divinity in 1937 from Gammon Theological Seminary, both in Atlanta. In 1940 he returned to Orangeburg, helped found
the Orangeburg NAACP branch in 1943, and served as pastor of Trinity United
Methodist Church until 1952. From 1948 to 1958 he served as vice president of the
NAACP state conference, in 1959 as its president, and, in 1960, as the state conference's field director. Newman preferred negotiation to confrontation, could read and
write five foreign languages, took pride in building relationships with White leaders,
and cultivated a dapper distinction, often wearing a bowler from Harrods in Lon-
don, a bow tie, a moustache, and sometimes a goatee. Williams often photographed
for Newman or offered photos of NAACP events. "Rev. Newman, in particular, did
not like to write, so he'd often use my pictures, write a caption, and send it off to the
[national] NAACP, and that would be his report."[35]

Newman frequently held NAACP meetings at the Rackley home. There, local
NAACP officers agreed that the segregated Orangeburg Regional Hospital ranked
high on the list of concerns, 200 of its 280 beds reserved for White patients, the one
wing for Black patients understaffed, "awful, unsanitary, unclean," said Rackley.
Who, needing care, dared sue? Or, as Rackley put it, "Who will bell the cat?" On
October 12, 1961, Rackley's fourteen-year-old daughter Jamelle dislocated a finger
during gym. Pulled from teaching her third-grade class at Whittaker Elementary
School, Rackley rushed to the emergency room to calm her daughter, upset after an
x-ray. Jamelle was given a sedative and moved for treatment.[36]

A nurse directed Rackley to the waiting area for Black visitors, located next to a
vending machine and furnished only with upturned Coca-Cola crates for seats. The
segregated hospital did have waiting rooms for White visitors, rooms with uphol-
stered chairs and lamps on tables. Rackley seated herself in that room, where she
read its Bible and prayed. A White man appeared, pointed at her, rushed away; she
rushed to follow, concerned about her daughter. But no. "There's a waiting room
for you down there," he said, pointing to the vending machine. Rackley returned to
the furnished waiting room. The chief of police arrived to notify her she would be
arrested if she did not leave the room. She waited for her daughter in the corridor.[37]

On October 26, Rackley and Jamelle returned. The cast removed, Jamelle was
taken to x-ray. Rackley entered the White-only waiting room. A doctor appeared

and asked her to join her daughter. Rackley said she would wait where she sat. A hospital administrator appeared to ask if treatment of her daughter was done. She said no. When notified treatment was complete, Rackley again said she would wait; Jamelle could find her. Jamelle arrived; the two sat in the room. Two police officers appeared, arrested Rackley, and walked her to a back exit. Helen "Hallie" Thompson, an NAACP member, saw Rackley's police escort, asked, "What's wrong, honey?" and took charge of Jamelle. Rackley rode in an unmarked car that was escorted by police cars in front and behind. At the jail none of the arresting or escorting officers wanted to take responsibility for the arrest or charge; the police chief charged her with trespassing. Rackley was pleased. "It was just so fortuitous, no one with a serious injury. It was almost like a miracle" that the NAACP had a case and plaintiffs to pursue it.[38]

On her day in court, October 31, 1961, Judge Fred R. Fanning locked up Matthew Perry, her attorney. Perry had asked hospital administrator Richard Roach several times and in different ways whether the hospital allowed Black people in the waiting room where Rackley was arrested. Fanning disliked the aggressive questioning. When Perry said he knew how to protect the rights of his clients, Fanning ordered him jailed for contempt. That lasted fifteen minutes. Fanning released Perry, said he understood his zeal, and made an unprecedented apology. Perry replied that he meant no disrespect, but he did not withdraw his questions.[39]

As March 1962 ended, Rackley and her daughter sued, with the assistance of the NAACP Legal Defense Fund (LDF), for desegregation of the county's only hospital. Their lawsuit and other health-discrimination complaints fit into "an all-out legal attack on segregated health facilities," said Jack Greenberg, director-counsel of the LDF. Williams hit a *Jet* double with news briefs on April 5 and 25, although the latter's headline mistakenly said Rackley's husband sued. His SC State contract not renewed, Professor Rackley left Orangeburg to complete a doctorate at the University of Oklahoma and joined the faculty at Florida A&M. The Rackley lawsuit, dismissed in district court, traveled to appellate court, and then back to district court as the hospital ignored a 1964 judge's order to answer questions regarding its separate wards and facilities. In 1965 Judge Robert W. Hemphill noted the hospital's paltry defense, that patients were separated by race because they were "'comfortable' in a segregated society." He ruled that the hospital, the recipient of more than $1 million in federal funds, could not, under the Fourteenth Amendment, practice racial discrimination. Issuing a permanent injunction, Hemphill allowed 105 days for the hospital to file a desegregation plan and put it into effect.[40]

Rackley seized other opportunities. As she ferried elderly John Jacob "J. J." Sulton Jr. to an NAACP meeting, a White driver crashed into the back of her car. Summoned to court on April 24, 1962, she and J.J. Sulton Jr. sat and chatted with McCollom and a White professor. Prior to Judge Fanning's entrance a bailiff waved his hand to direct White people to one side of court, Black people to the other. Rackley found herself on the "Black side," so "I got up and went across the aisle to what I thought was the traffic problem side," where the White driver sat. As Fanning entered, the bailiff tapped Rackley on the shoulder. "There I was, an affront to justice and civility." Directed to move, she said, "No, I am where I'm supposed to be." When she did not stand, the bailiff lifted her by the back of her arms and marched her out of the courtroom, down a stairway, and into a basement cell, its walls and floor oozing, its latrine open. Dressed up for court and carrying a magazine to read, Rackley placed her magazine on the floor, removed her high heels, and stood on the magazine until the bailiff returned. Fanning ignored Rackley asking if she were arrested, talking over her to deal just with the traffic issue, then left.[41]

McCollom wrote Mayor Fair that Fanning had resorted to "oppressive, illegal measures to enforce segregation in his courtroom." The state's Advisory Committee on Civil Rights sent to Washington, D.C., Rackley's complaint of being held in an "indescribably dirty cell" because she did not comply with segregated seating.[42]

THE CHILDREN OF '63

Turmoil filled the summer of 1963. In Birmingham, Alabama, on May 2, police arrested and jailed hundreds of marching children organized by the Southern Christian Leadership Conference (SCLC) and other organizations. On May 3, newspaper photographs and television broadcasts documented the children and teens of the Children's Crusade injured by high-pressure fire hoses and attacked by police dogs. By May 6, 2,500 protesters filled the city jail. On June 12, NAACP field secretary

Medgar Evers was shot to death at his home in Jackson, Mississippi, by a local WCC member. On August 28, 1963, the March on Washington for Jobs and Freedom drew 250,000 to the Lincoln Memorial, where King told a nation, "I still have a dream." Cities north and south experienced 758 demonstrations and 14,733 arrests before summer ended.[43]

In South Carolina that summer fifty NAACP leaders—exasperated, angered, fed up—met in Manning and again in Columbia. They had not reached the "forever free" of President Abraham Lincoln's Emancipation Proclamation of January 1, 1863. On Wednesday, June 5, field secretary Newman announced an "all-out attack on discrimination." The NAACP chose eight cities: Charleston, Columbia, Florence, Greenville, Orangeburg, Rock Hill, Spartanburg, and Sumter. Demonstrations would begin within two weeks if the governor, mayors, and business leaders did not take good-faith actions. The goals, familiar by now, included desegregated public eating places, hotels and motels, public libraries, parks, and public schools.[44]

Also familiar was the response. On June 6, L. Marion Gressette, head of the state's Segregation Committee, received a standing ovation in the state senate when he railed against the NAACP. He called the NAACP announcement a "virtual ultimatum," which it was, and said the NAACP held "no purpose other than integration," which was somewhat accurate. To the senators these were fatal flaws. Gressette described US Supreme Court decisions ending segregation as illegal, immoral, and sociologically misguided and claimed civil rights demonstrations "only lead to violence, friction, bitterness, and the hardening of resistance on both sides."[45]

But demonstrating for constitutional rights had become a "badge of courage" among the young, said Williams. "In fact, sometimes those that didn't go would be stigmatized." Inevitably, "parents got worried about their children, so to protect the NAACP and branch leadership, you had to bring back a signed permission from your parents to participate." That did not stop a seemingly endless supply of intrepid youth. "It was fun yet it was serious civil rights work." On marches "there were jokes along the way. Guys would say 'those girls ahead of us, they're going to break their neck with those high heels shoes on.' And 'that's so-and-so's last suit; he's going to jail with his best suit on.' Sometimes they would compare notes, 'Oh, man, I've been to jail five times. You haven't been but one time? Oh, man.'" In jail, the determined strung overcoats into hammocks. "And guys would joke, 'I haven't changed my underwear in three days.'"

NAACP leaders began their campaign in Charleston's 90-degree steamy heat. The Charleston Movement started with church, a march, and prayers at city hall by more than 200 participants on Sunday, June 9. The following days and nights filled with picketing and marches; sit-ins, church kneel-ins, beach wade-ins, theater stand-ins; and mass meetings as large as 2,500. "It seems evident the Negro will no longer accept tokenism," wrote Claude Sitton, who had been covering civil rights for the *New York Times* since 1958. As summer waned, Newman counted 700 arrests, $300,000 raised in bail bond, and the desegregation of seven restaurants, seven soda fountains, and four motels in Charleston. Most remarkable, on August 23, district court ordered the admission of eleven Black children and teens to Charleston schools, asserting the right of "all pupils to freely choose to attend a racially nonsegregated school."[46]

Orangeburg's summer of dissent began July 29 with a downtown boycott. Rev. Chappelle M. Davis of Williams Chapel AME had visited Mayor Fair weeks before the summer campaign began in Charleston. Afterward, officials said that demonstrating against "traditional and accepted practices" would yield the same result as a 1961 march when 400 people were arrested. On August 1, children, students, and some adults began picketing downtown. On August 20, dentist Harlow E. Caldwell, chair of the Orangeburg Freedom Movement, and businessman Earl M. Middleton, the secretary, presented to city council the Movement's objectives: a biracial committee, removal of segregation ordinances and signs, employment in city and county departments, desegregation of playgrounds and recreational facilities, and use of council influence to desegregate businesses, the hospital, and school districts.[47]

Steering committee members included the ever-vigilant James Sulton Sr. and John E. Brunson, as well as professors Charles H. Thomas Jr. and Arthur Rose, and pastors Davis and James W. Curry, the minister leading Trinity Methodist Church since May 1962. And, of course. there was Rackley, who had earned the nicknames "Miss Movement" and "Glorious." She became the face of the Orangeburg Freedom Movement, a terror to the White power structure, a heroine to those walking with her. In the parlance of the time, she was "uppity," said Williams, meaning White

From left: Rev. Herbert J. Nelson, St. Luke Presbyterian Church; Rev. J. W. Curry, Trinity Methodist Church; Rev. Chappelle Davis, Williams Chapel AME Church; John E. Brunson, a barber at The People's Barber Shop; Elease Thomas; Charles H. Thomas Jr., director of the South Carolina Voter Education Project; and Gloria Blackwell Rackley.

On September 15, 1963, an 11-year-old and three 14-year-old girls die in the bombing of the 16th Street Baptist Church in Birmingham, Alabama. On Sunday, September 22, "mourning marches" are held throughout the United States. The Torch, *the Orangeburg Freedom Movement's underground newsletter, reports that one thousand Black citizens march to Confederate Square to pray.*

people believed she did not know what they called her "place," while she knew exactly where she belonged, which was where she chose. In other words, as Williams noted, "She was brave." It mattered that a woman had stepped into a visible, audible leadership role. "Leadership by women was very important," said Williams. "About half or more of people marching were women, young women."[48]

An underground newsletter called the *Torch* encouraged and informed the Black community, its weekly issues distributed at mass meetings and passed around. The *Torch* packed its mimeographed pages with to-do lists, honor rolls of those arrested, and accounts of police violence. A weekly "DON'T SHOP DOWNTOWN!!" accompanied the reminder of the Saturday shopping trip, 9 a.m. to 3 p.m., to Columbia and back for free. The *Torch* occasionally leavened its fare with cartoons—Fair meeting a Black St. Peter at the pearly gates—or a word game—"How can we remove the SUP from Orangeburg's PRESS?" Charles Cottingham, the round-faced and stocky secret editor, had served in World War II, earned a doctorate in botany and plant pathology at Michigan State University, and joined the SC State faculty in 1960. He possessed an essential within his office, a mimeograph machine.[49]

Not until the end of September did media take notice of Orangeburg, but 684 arrests in three days demanded attention. The *Torch* was diligently reporting arrest counts and telling details. On August 24, when police turned over six youths to juvenile authorities and charged eight others with breach of peace, Judge Fanning refused to set bond for Jimmy Irick, identified by the *Torch* as "one of the Freedom Fighters." Fanning sentenced Irick to thirty days on a chain gang. When Irick's seven friends also refused bond, Fanning sentenced them to a chain gang. On September 6, the *Torch* reported the arrest of sixteen more juveniles. "Some were locked in cells—the boys with a murderer and the girls with a drunk." The *Torch* kept track of assaults ignored by police: a picketer struck in the mouth, picketers pelted by rock-throwing boys, and three youths physically ejected from a restaurant, including Jamelle Rackley, who was lifted up then dumped onto the sidewalk.[50]

Rackley made the *Torch's* arrest list on August 31, again with 14-year-old daughter Lurma on September 7, and again with Lurma and 16-year-old Jamelle on September 12. The *Torch* praised "positive actions in the form of deeds . . . going to jail." Then, on September 15, one 11-year-old and three 14-year-old girls died in the bombing of the 16th Street Baptist Church in Birmingham. The next Sunday, September 22, one thousand Black citizens knelt and prayed at Orangeburg's Confederate Square, "race conscious, civic minded, freedom loving, Christian, American Negroes— organized and united!!" said the *Torch*. "Suddenly, my sad heart was joyful." Williams photographed the procession, which was led by ministers J. Herbert Nelson, of St. Luke Presbyterian Church, Curry, and Davis. The silent participants walked to Confederate Square, proceeding single file down a tree-shaded street on a softly sunny day. At the city square they knelt and bowed their heads in prayer. "There were so many adults," said Williams, "so they marched very slowly and intently. It was very peaceful. They weren't about to go to jail that day." Throughout the nation tens of thousands attended memorial services or walked in "mourning marches."[51]

On Saturday, September 28, approximately 300 women, teens, and children walked, sang, clapped, and yelled their way downtown in a heavy rain. Waiting were city police, county sheriffs, the highway patrol, SLED, and city firefighters with fire hoses connected to hydrants. Rackley left the marchers to object to the fire hoses; she was arrested. Teens attempted sit-ins at Kress and at a drive-in restaurant; they were arrested. Police picked out fifteen march leaders, most of them women, to arrest. Police Chief C. H. Hall said they had to be "forcibly removed." Newman reported to the FBI that local police were "slapping, boxing, and manhandling" the women. The *Afro-American* described the beating of Nettie Tilley, dragged by police from her car, pummeled, then arrested and charged with resisting arrest and assaulting an officer. Unable to cram 175 more people into already full jails, authorities packed two buses with girls and women and confined them at the state penitentiary in Columbia.[52]

The next day, Sunday, police arrested 200 morning marchers. In the afternoon those confined in the county jail cheered on 130 more who passed by fire trucks, their fire hoses uncoiled. Arrests continued. By habit, Williams jogged to the front of this Sunday march, turning to face the demonstrators and photograph the scene. He waited on the corner of Russell and Middleton streets for marchers to approach law enforcement officers. "I'm right where the road is bigger, about a half-block from Kress. I have a great picture framed from a low angle. I'm getting ready to dramatize this; I'm down on my knees." Two highway patrol officers walked up behind Williams, lifted him by his arms, and escorted him to their car's front seat. The officers had already crammed people into the back. One officer took Williams's Nikon, a 35 mm single-lens reflex camera. From inside the car Williams could hear him rip out the film and toss the camera into the trunk. "This is my property. So they've arrested my camera too. I hear not only a thud but a tumble." This was the worst of indignities to Williams.[53]

The officers left to arrest others. Williams reached for the many wires connecting their Motorola two-way radio to the car. He unplugged the wires. "It was the only

thing I could think of doing, immobilize the radio and make it difficult for them to communicate back and forth." Eventually, car packed, an officer drove all to the city jail, where "they took all my money and belongings. When a new group of students came in, I borrowed a dime and called AP. I said, 'Everybody down here is in jail. I'm in jail. Can you send somebody here to cover this? The local paper won't cover it.'" Attorney and law professor Earl W. Coblyn, working for the NAACP, bailed out Williams for $100.[54]

Williams retrieved his camera, returned to the streets, and then climbed—as he had before—onto the warehouse loading dock beside the jail. Law officers had packed protesters into the jail and the stockade, as they had in 1960. They also filled busloads more for the state penitentiary. One bus got a late start when the keys went missing. "I don't recall penitentiary buses used in any other city," said Williams. He wondered, "How could they lock up more than the number they could put in the

At Confederate Square, children and adults kneel to pray. Cecil Williams climbs stairs in a building across from the green to photograph from a window. No arrests take place on this day, but thousands of arrests take place throughout 1963. Beginning with the summer's start, NAACP branches in Orangeburg and seven other cities hold almost daily mass protests against segregation in restaurants, hotels, employment, public spaces, and public schools.

jails?" Busing protesters to the penitentiary, as well as three nearby prison farms, was the answer. That day's total of 305 people arrested, most of them students who did not post bond, contributed to empty classrooms on Monday at SC State and Claflin. More than a third of the colleges' students sat in jail.[55]

By Wednesday, October 2, the governor had sent at least fifty highway patrol officers to Orangeburg and at least 900 protesters had been arrested. The day ended close to disaster when demonstrators sat on downtown curbs. SLED's Strom threatened them with the charge of inciting to riot; firefighters pulled out hoses; police held back at least 300 White onlookers. The October 3 *Torch* listed those arrested, four pages' worth, including Williams, Rackley and daughter Lurma.[56]

The *Afro-American* sent staff correspondent George Collins, a native of Bennettsville, South Carolina. One of his articles, headlined "Ironic Sidelights," remarked on Williams's arrest, his "ingenuity" as a photojournalist, the "stupidity" of firefighters unrolling hoses in the rain, and a "high police official" saying "I has no comment." Williams, standing beside Collins, heard a fuller statement from Chief Strom, "About that I has no comment."[57]

Another Williams expedition followed his arrest. Under the pretext of a prisoner visit, Williams entered the county jail, nicknamed "the Pink Palace," to document mistreatment of youth for the *Torch* and the *Afro-American*. "I sneaked in a big ol' 4×5 camera under my coat," and no one noticed. "People at the jail were overburdened; they were used to one or two persons getting arrested. We're talking about a situation where ten, twenty, thirty, forty, fifty, sixty, a hundred people are coming in." He photographed in silhouette two young women pressed against jail bars and left. "It was filthy, mashed-up cigarettes on the floor, the walls dirty, smelled, the paint eroded years ago, rust on the bars," said Williams.

"We submit that there is no justice for us in Orangeburg," said the *Torch*, reporting that a police officer had struck and dragged one young woman to his car and that jailers packed seven juveniles into a six foot by six foot cell from 9 a.m. to 10 p.m. without food or a bunk. The lists of those arrested on October 4 and 7 filled three pages. The fourth page reported that police had arrested Rackley and several young women who used the "White" restroom at the county courthouse. The youngest participants became indispensable. "They would ride their bicycles to Trinity," said

Williams. Children as young as eight were eager to participate. Initially, police took them to jail and required them to "sign a sheet," said Rackley, and "They would go back to church and regroup and march again. So Lurma and her bunch could be arrested three times a day."[58]

The *Afro-American's* Collins used Williams's studio as his home base and Williams's typewriter as his own. Accompanied by Williams and his cameras, Collins reported in depth on Orangeburg, proclaiming, "It is a hotbed of segregationists that will stop at nothing 'to keep the black man in his place.'" It was common for Black journalists to offer each other refuge. "We all were aware that much of the push behind change was stories that would uncover what was going on, to show the unfairness and slap in the face to the Constitution," said Williams, who appreciated Collins's down-to-earth nature and thorough reporting.[59]

On Friday night, the children marched. Collins reported on the October 4 arrests of 318 protesters for breach of peace, many of them elementary and high school students. Nearly 200 law officers blocked their way. Mayor Fair, who refused to participate in a negotiation, vowed, "All demonstrators, whether they are peaceful or not, will be arrested." Of fifty-four children jailed, the majority had been arrested often, some as many as six times, and were held indefinitely. Constitutional rights require release on bail or a trial and conviction, so Perry filed habeas corpus petitions. On Saturday, adults protesting treatment of the juveniles also found themselves in jail. Those arrested included five SC State professors and pastors Curry, Davis, Nelson, and Harold Roland, of New Mount Zion Baptist Church, and Leon Stephenson, of Macedonia Baptist Church. Newman called on "all local ministers not already in jail" to lead their congregations in protests on Sunday.[60]

Briefly in make-a-deal mode, the city attorney offered to release one thousand demonstrators if protests were halted for ninety days. Almost daily arrests cost merchants lost business and wrecked city, county, and state government budgets on the hook for more law enforcement and incarceration personnel and housing and food for prisoners—although jail fare was merely fatback, baloney, bread, and cold grits. Almost daily arrests cost the NAACP too, so far $100,000 in bail bonds, some Black leaders mortgaging their homes for funds. MacArthur Goodwin, an SC State student and NAACP youth coordinator, announced students' willingness to stay in jail "until something gives." Williams once again photographed students penned in the outdoor stockade. The *Afro-American* caption said an officer told one group of students, "Please go home. We don't have any more room for you."[61]

1,600 ARRESTS AND COUNTING

The Orangeburg city council passed an ordinance requiring pickets to fill out a ten-item registration form and to carry a notarized identification card, renewed monthly. On the ordinance's first use, police registered thirty-five picketers and turned away ten, deciding time's up. Police began arresting demonstrators before they could enter the business district. Juveniles had been released to the custody of their parents; their release now required a $100 bail. Adults had been charged with breach of peace and released on $100 bail; charges now included contributing to the delinquency of minors, interfering with police, and traffic violations with bail as high as $6,000. Arrests totaled 1,600, "but we can't stop now," said Newman.[62]

A WCC member approached Williams, who regularly photographed mass meetings at Trinity, still headquarters for the Orangeburg Freedom Movement. "A member of the Citizens' Council offered me five dollars if I would sell him a picture that I took in Trinity of a meeting going on. When I said no, he said, 'Well, I'll give you ten.'" Williams told NAACP leadership. "They were trying to bribe me to get pictures to see who was in the membership meetings. Then they would see who worked some place and try to get to them that way."

On October 7, school superintendent H. A. Marshall notified Rackley by letter that she was relieved of her duties and recommended for dismissal. He cited two sit-in arrests, an arrest for distributing handbills, and a breach of peace arrest as leader and spokesperson for 200 demonstrators. Marshall wrote, "It would appear you have become so rabid in your desire for social reform that you are advocating breaking the laws as a means of calling attention to what you consider your grievances." Rackley felt amused and angered that Marshall described her as "rabid." SLED's Strom described Orangeburg demonstrators as "vicious, vile" and Rackley as "the most wild and dangerous of all."[63]

That night eighty-six students managed a two-block walk before arrests began. They carried schoolbooks and overnight bags, the young men prepared for Wateree Correctional Farm, the young women for confinement with eighty others at the National Guard Armory. The students protested the threat that SC State would close if they continued. On Tuesday, October 8, word circulated of Rackley's impending firing. Outraged coworkers and students skipped school. Seven schools sat empty, students picketing outside. "Save Mrs. Rackley," said their signs. Juveniles were arrested, thirty-seven kept overnight, including Rackley's daughters. On Wednesday, the day of the Negro County Fair, schools remained empty. On Thursday, schools reopened, attendance at no more than twenty-five percent into the next week. And Rackley was back in jail.[64]

The city's segregationists did not budge. The only inch given was an unwillingness at Kress to swear out warrants against sit-in participants. "City Merchants Nix Demands of Negroes" announced the *Times and Democrat* on October 10. An article, an editorial, and a full-page ad—the ad signed by the mayor, city council members, the legislative delegation, sheriff, and police chief—said the shopping district had been "invaded," merchants had been hard hit, and "highly respected Negroes, domestics and others" not participating had been threatened. Acceding to the Movement's demands "if put into effect, would do away with all forms of segregation in the city." The ad ended, "This is our town. Let's work to make it a better one in spite of those who would destroy it."[65]

A first round of trials began on October 14 before an all-White, all-male jury, who found everyone guilty. The judge set a penalty of $100 or thirty days in jail. Police frequently changed the times and days for picket registration in the continuing tug of war. On October 23 sixty high-school students walked downtown to register. They chose Wednesday afternoon, traditionally a half-day for Southern stores. Police arrested the youths, who ranged in age from eleven to seventeen years old, holding those with previous arrests in cell blocks with adult criminals, some for two days and two nights without bail, some denied food and water, according to the *Torch* and a complaint presented to an unreceptive mayor and to Governor Donald S. Russell.[66]

While local and state law enforcement were arresting peaceful protesters, jailing children, and shipping youths to work camps and the state penitentiary, the US Supreme Court reversed the breach of peace convictions from Orangeburg's mass march of March 15, 1960. In a three-line order, the US Supreme Court cited its February 1963 ruling in *Edwards v. South Carolina:* "The Fourteenth Amendment does not permit a State to make criminal the peaceful expression of unpopular views." The *Edwards* ruling concerned breach of peace arrests of 187 high school and college students walking and singing on the South Carolina State House grounds in 1961.[67]

District trustees fired Rackley on October 15. In such situations Williams found himself in the "re-creation business," particularly for *Jet*. "They would take the news that I sent them and then they would give me an assignment to further explore that picture possibility." Williams photographed Rackley at home, reading superintendent Marshall's dismissal letter, and walking the grounds at Whittaker Elementary on a Saturday with daughter Lurma. Williams always tried to sell his photos to more than one buyer, and the *Afro-American* published the photo of Rackley at home, wearing a shift dress, hair in a French twist, eyes downcast to read the letter. "Center of Storm" announced the photo caption, noting Rackley had been accused of "advocating lawlessness." Since 1961, news stories featuring Rackley had appeared statewide and nationally, reporting on her hospital arrest, trespassing charge, civil rights complaint, hospital lawsuit, and, now, her firing and the resulting picketing and the city's overnight jailing of children and youths by the hundreds. Articles often identified her as the movement's leader.[68]

Rackley sued the school district. She became, officially, the coordinator of the Orangeburg Freedom Movement, and Newman hired her to work as state NAACP membership chair, a job she had held in Dillon County after her car accident. Her daughters worried because she drove the countryside in a Corvair that would unexpectedly run out of gas. White officials had decided she had to go. Rackley and Lurma were ordered to juvenile court as a consequence of Lurma's innumerable arrests. Rackley, Lurma, and five other children, unchastened by their court appearances, used the "White" restroom and were arrested and jailed until called back to court. The livid judge threatened reform school until Lurma reached twenty-one if she ever again appeared in his court. Attorney Perry warned Rackley to take the threat very seriously. When Rackley told her daughter this was the time to stop protesting, Lurma replied that everyone had a reason not to protest and that she would continue. In 1964 Rackley accepted a job at Norfolk State University in Virginia but not before she and others sued the Edisto and Carolina theaters for refusing them admission to the ground floor seating of White customers. Within a month of the lawsuit filing, the owner ended his segregation policy.[69]

On November 4, 1963, parents filed applications for their Black children to attend the city's all-White schools. Parents of fourteen Black children and teens requested their transfer to Thackston Junior High and Orangeburg High schools. The school board chair said that no action could be taken within fewer than 120 days. As two more downtown businesses closed, the *Torch* observed, "The power-structure of Orangeburg is willing to see the downtown shopping dry up rather than submit to demands for equality," and warned, "We will work downtown, eat downtown, sleep downtown, or they won't."[70]

Trinity Methodist Church packed in 800 people to hear Roy Wilkins, NAACP executive secretary, speak on November 13. Security was high, with a highway patrol escort and a state plane overhead as Wilkins traveled from Columbia to Orangeburg. He came to celebrate the March on Washington and the US Supreme Court's reversal of the 1960 Orangeburg arrests, to praise the Orangeburg Freedom Movement, and to urge that demonstrations continue. Williams, as usual, documented the visit for the NAACP and news media.[71]

The new year did not deliver "Freedom Now!" The *Torch* said, "Certainly, we understand very well that there is an ordinance against everything a Negro can possibly do in Orangeburg." On Saturday, February 1, 1964, twenty-six young picketers sat on a street's curb. Police arrested them. That led to another school boycott. On Tuesday, police arrested sixteen picketers for supporting the boycott and thus interfering with school attendance. Of 1,200 Black students, 950 did not attend school that day. A glance downtown could assess the economic penalty. The *Torch's* warning had come true; fifteen stores stood empty.[72]

For months the school district did nothing regarding school desegregation. Suddenly, Superintendent Marshall invited select parents to meet with him. The

Torch warned against his handpicking a few children and calling that desegregation. On March 20 parents and their children sued Orangeburg School District 5,
saying that the segregated school system deprived the children of the Fourteenth
Amendment's equal protection of the laws. They found themselves emulating the
petitioners of *Briggs v. Elliott*, a decade after the *Brown* decisions had declared
"separate but equal" unconstitutional.[73]

Just twenty-six years old, Williams found himself photographing generations,
from *Briggs* petitioners to Freedom Fighters. He marked time in other ways, too. Hats
had gone out of style. Men's knee-length, all-weather coats had come into style. Wom-
en's skirts no longer hid their knees. "Automobiles were a dead giveaway," said Williams, fond of his photos of pampered 1940s sedans during Thurgood Marshall's visit
and Fred Henderson Moore's expulsion. Rounded hoods and trunks had given way to
longer, lower, sharper profiles. What remained over time: poster-board-and-marker
picket signs announcing "Segregation Is Obsolete." What was new: Fire hoses. Tear
gas. Overnight stays in Columbia's penitentiary. What was exceptional: at Trinity Methodist Church, Williams photographed the youngest stepping into danger,
children expecting to desegregate Orangeburg's all-White schools, thirteen for high
school, six for elementary and junior high schools. They stood slender and serious
before the church's pews; they had won their lawsuit on August 12, 1964.[74]

June Manning arrived in a police car for her first day at Orangeburg High School.
When her mother drove her, people threw eggs at the car and yelled. Her parents
decided to hire young men at Claflin to drive her to and see her into school. She lived
just a mile away on Claflin's campus—her father was the college president—but the
walk through a White neighborhood was not safe. Nor was school. In class White students pelted her with spitballs, made faces, called her names, used racial epithets—
without penalty. The choir director refused to allow Manning and friend Evelyn
Dash to join until the principal insisted. Among the many teachers over three years,
Manning found a rare exception in the kindness of the Latin teacher, Rosa D. Higgin-
botham. All that seemed normal—eye contact, smiles, idle comments, passed notes,
friendship, mentoring—was converted into "antipathy and hatred toward intrusive
Black people," said Manning. In the halls, "People would jump back as if they didn't
want to be contaminated." A male student cursed Manning and slammed her into

a locker, injuring her leg, which bled, and tearing her stockings. In the cafeteria White students bolted from a table if a Black student sat down. For a few days, until the principal stopped them, the Black students responded with a sit-in, one Black student per table so White students had nowhere to sit.[75]

"I became withdrawn and anxious," said Manning. "I did a pretty good job of erasing memories." She did not push back; she silently bore what she called "an honorable weight." And, in a form of guerilla warfare, she excelled academically. "My coping mechanism was to study. The only way to make them mad at themselves was to score higher" than any other White classmate. "Maybe the teacher would say, 'June Manning made 96!' 'Naw, you mean the nigger?' That gave me a perverse satisfaction." She did not quit. "We saw ourselves as warriors. We were proud to be given that responsibility."[76]

THE VERY LAST

Three decades had passed since the NAACP began winning higher-education lawsuits. No questions of federal law remained unresolved. At the start of 1963 South Carolina stood alone, the only Southern state that had not admitted Black students voluntarily or by court order to any of its public schools—until, on January 16, 1963, the US Court of Appeals for the Fourth Circuit ordered Harvey Bernard Gantt admitted to Clemson Agricultural College. Williams documented the moment for *Jet*, national interest fervid after James Meredith's enrollment at the University of Mississippi involved the death of two men, injuries to 300, and 30,000 US troops and marshals and National Guard troops quelling White rioters.[77]

The oldest of five children, his father an employee of Charleston's Naval Shipyard, his mother a homemaker, Gantt aced kindergarten and skipped second grade, sold the *Baltimore Afro-American*, delivered prescriptions, and worked for a supermarket. He decided in ninth grade to be an architect, played football, graduated second in his class at Burke High School, and earned a National Achievement Scholarship. He reasoned "architecture is practiced mainly by whites" and spent two years at Iowa State University with the assistance of grants that sent Black students out of South Carolina to block in-state desegregation.[78]

Gantt decided that Iowa was too cold and lonely; he said the only Black students were the football players. He wanted to come home. He wrote Clemson of his interest in July 1959; requested a catalog, application, and fee schedule in November 1960; and sent an application in fall 1961. In January 1961, Burke classmate Cornelius Fludd had applied. Fludd had graduated eighth from the top at Burke, was in his first year at Morehouse College in Atlanta, and wanted to study electrical engineering at Clemson. The young men shared an April 1, 1960, sit-in arrest at downtown Charleston's Kress. Perry defended the two dozen participants, and Gantt took the opportunity to ask what it might take to get into Clemson. Gantt applied and applied again, leaving Iowa State in the first quarter of his junior year.[79]

Clemson's foot-dragging and contortions prevented admittance between July 1959 and July 1962. Clemson ignored an inquiry letter, rejected Gantt because of state grants for Iowa, placed a reapplication in a pending file, said his College Board scores arrived late, developed a new admissions policy, discontinued acceptance of transfer students, "held" Gantt's and Fludd's applications in a "strategy of silence," and claimed Gantt's lack of a portfolio and interview (neither an admission requirement) justified refusing admission. Gantt and Perry built a case file. Gantt sued on July 7, 1962. Fludd did not sue.[80]

"He was a best bet, and the NAACP knew it," said Williams. "Any potential suit, I was on the inside track of the NAACP, so I knew what was going on. I started with Gantt at his house, years before he goes to Clemson, before he's discovered by the national press." Williams felt some regret; he had wanted to study architecture at Clemson. "It was a dream I wish I had accomplished myself. Gantt and I talked about it oftentimes." Williams also spoke of that wish to Perry, who said, "Let's see how Gantt does," leaving Williams to wonder if he really wanted another degree, a different career.

An NAACP legal team with Perry and Constance Baker Motley, of the LDF, seemed to guarantee a win. Perry was the son of a Columbia tailor who died when Perry was twelve. He was raised by his grandfather, a brakeman for Southern Railway. He worked his way through SC State and served in Europe during World War II. While a soldier he waited to pick up food at the back window of a depot's café in Montgomery, Alabama. Inside sat Italian prisoners of war, served and eating. He

On January 15, 1963, South
Carolina holds an inaugural
parade for Governor Donald S.
Russell followed by the state's
first integrated inaugural luncheon at the Governor's Mansion. Attending the luncheon
are Matthew J. Perry, left, legal
counsel for the state NAACP;
Rev. Harold Roland, center, pastor of New Mount Zion Baptist
Church in Orangeburg, NAACP
member, and local historian;
and Cecil Williams. Bennie
Brown, a Columbia photographer and friend of Williams,
photographs the three.

never stopped telling that story, which, he said, "reverberated" throughout his days.
A graduate of the second class at SC State's law school, he and one other aspiring
Black lawyer passed in 1951 the new state bar exam, created to block Black law
graduates. He argued five cases and won four before the US Supreme Court. And, a
handy attribute for a lawyer, he possessed an opera-worthy voice. He gave countless
hours to the NAACP free of charge, said Williams, who viewed himself as unofficial-
ly Perry's official photographer.[81]

Motley grew up in New Haven, Connecticut. Her parents were immigrants from
Nevis, a Caribbean island. She graduated from New York University and Columbia
Law School, and, in 1946, was the first female attorney hired by the LDF. During

Harvey B. Gantt's lawsuit seeking admission to Clemson College reaches district court in November 1962 in Anderson County. Cecil Williams and other journalists wait on courthouse steps for photographs and comments. On December 21 district judge Charles Cecil Wyche says that Gantt was not denied admission because of race.

From left: Lincoln C. Jenkins, law partner of Matthew J. Perry, state NAACP legal counsel; J. Arthur Brown, president of the state NAACP; unidentified woman; and Constance Baker Motley, attorney with the NAACP's Legal Defense Fund.

her LDF work she became the first Black woman to appear before the US Supreme Court. She had worked on litigation desegregating six universities when she took on South Carolina. When she left the LDF in 1965 she had argued ten cases before the US Supreme Court and had won nine.[82]

Williams followed Gantt to trial in Anderson County. Some days he accompanied NAACP leadership and stayed at the home of William F. Gibson, a wealthy dentist and NAACP stalwart. Williams ate meals with Gantt and attorneys "who were never tensed up, always jovial." Other nights he stayed at the Black-owned Ghana Motel on state highway 291 in Greenville. Overnight stays were complicated in a segregated state. Williams documented Gantt and his attorneys at Gibson's home, Gantt and his family on the courthouse steps, Gantt and his attorneys on the courthouse steps. Since photographers could not enter courtrooms when court was in session, Williams's job was to hang around. Charleston's *Post and Courier,* Columbia's *State,* and AP journalists hung out too, and Williams enjoyed schmoozing with White journalists. "There was always something to discuss. At that level, people in the press were nice to everyone."[83]

On January 16, 1963, the Fourth Circuit Court of Appeals ordered Gantt admitted. The appeals court described district judge Charles Cecil Wyche's finding that South Carolina "does not prohibit, but discourages, integration of the races in its state-supported colleges" as a novel observation and ruled the refusal to admit Gantt an unacceptable violation of Constitutional rights. Funding out-of-state education instead of admission violated the constitutional right to equal treatment without regard to race, the court said, and was not even in compliance with the "separate but equal" rule preceding the *Brown* decision.[84]

On January 22 Wyche signed the order admitting Gantt. The week before Governor Russell had invited, as the *Greenville News* explained in a headline, "S.C. People—Both White and Negro," to the first integrated event at the Governor's Mansion, a post-inauguration luncheon of barbecue, hamburgers, hot dogs, slaw, pickles, ice cream, and a 600-pound cake. Russell shook hands with Newman as Williams documented greetings. At least one hundred Black South Carolinians attended. That seemed an empty gesture when Russell supported the state asking the Fourth Circuit Court of Appeals to stay its order. The court refused. The state took its appeal to US Supreme Court Chief Justice Earl Warren, who oversaw the Fourth Circuit. He refused to delay Gantt's admission. South Carolina law required closing any public school accepting a Black student and a retaliatory closing of SC State. Clemson attorneys had acknowledged in court that this was unconstitutional. Nevertheless, the state senate debated closing Clemson.[85]

Jet found Gantt irresistible, publishing short articles on his quest thirteen times over seventeen months. Williams received press credentials to attend Gantt's registration—with a catch. *Jet* quoted Clemson's publicity director, who said, "There is no way to give you accommodations on campus." White journalists would stay on campus at the Clemson House, an eight-story hotel set up for the press with coffee, sandwiches, eight teleprinters, and fourteen telephones. To compensate Williams arrived a day early.[86]

Gantt's travels from Charleston to Clemson on January 28 involved a helicopter and patrol cars ahead and behind Gantt's car, a stop in Columbia for Perry and Newman, a stop in Greenville so Gantt's father and minister could disembark, and an arrival, with Perry driving, just four minutes past the 1:30 p.m. Clemson timetable. A multitude awaited Gantt on campus: 160 journalists, about 150 law enforcement officers, a pilot and aircraft for emergencies, and about 100 students, some hecklers, present despite the winter break and orders to stay off campus. Not in attendance: any Black employees. Williams said they had been forbidden to come on campus. "There were only three Black people on the campus of Clemson that day," said Williams. "Gantt, me, and a journalist from the *Amsterdam News*."[87]

The day was cold, in the twenties. "It seemed like five degrees," said Williams. "It took forever to get feeling in my fingers to click pictures." Gantt faced dozens of microphones and so very many White faces. Asked if his admission had been worth the trouble, Gantt replied, "Yes, I think so." This was the photo that Williams wanted. "It was more important to me to get the journalists capturing him. And I liked to get up high, hold my camera up high. I always liked wide angle lenses as well to get an overview. You're the eyes and ears as a journalist; you're trying to take a picture that will describe what's going on." Gantt registered and visited his dormitory room and the School of Architecture, a SLED agent poking him in the back for left and right turns, select journalists trailing him. Clemson's president Robert C. Edwards ended Gantt's first day with "Harvey Gantt is here; he is registered; he is a student."[88]

Ample but less feverish attention was paid to Henrie Dobbins Monteith, an applicant to the University of South Carolina. When Monteith applied on May 13, 1962, the registrar responded that he could not act on the application. She entered the College of Notre Dame of Maryland, after graduating with honors at sixteen years old from St. Frances DeSalles High School in Powhatan, Virginia. She sued the University of South Carolina on October 31, 1962, Perry and Motley among her

Harvey B. Gantt registers at Clemson University on January 28, 1963. Approximately 160 journalists attend as do the 150 law enforcement officers responsible for Gantt's security. South Carolina is the last Southern state to admit a Black student to any public school. Jet *notes that Clemson provides on-campus accommodations, food, teleprinters, and telephones to White journalists but refuses campus accommodations to the two Black journalists attending. Williams positions himself on the steps of Tillman Hall because he wants to document not only Gantt but the drove of White journalists.*

attorneys. At the time, Gantt was awaiting his days in court, and the AP described the two college students' efforts as "an integration assault."[89]

The Monteiths were not as skittish as Gantt with the press. The *Pittsburgh Courier* ran five stories, *Jet* ran eight, one illustrated by Williams. Newspapers from coast to coast kept track with hundreds of bulletins on her lawsuit's progress. Williams and local reporters photographed and interviewed Henrie Monteith at the family compound, owned by grandparents Rachel Hull and Henry C. Monteith. She posed in a white blouse and pleated skirt, standing by some steps or crouched to pet a small and adoring dog, her favorite, according to Williams. "I want very much to correct this social wrong: prejudice," Henrie Monteith told the AP. Her aunt, well-known activist Modjeska Monteith Simkins, said, "Her application will stand."

Henrie Monteith of Columbia applies to attend the University of South Carolina in May 1962. The registrar responds that he cannot act on the application. Five months later, when Monteith sues, USC and Alabama are the the last two segregated public universities. In a class-action ruling, she wins admission, and on September 11, 1963, Monteith, Robert G. Anderson Jr., and graduate student James L. Solomon enroll at USC, "lily-white since 1877," says Jet.

Mother R. Rebecca Monteith said, "We were hoping the authorities would do the honorable thing and act without pressure." Henrie Monteith came from a family of achievers. Her grandmother founded Monteith School. Her mother taught at the Monteith and Perrin Thomas schools; in 1944 she sued for, but did not win, pay equal to that of White teachers. Uncle Henry Dobbins Monteith, a physician, was president of Victory Savings Bank, the state's only Black-owned bank. Aunt Simkins dominated civil rights activism for decades; she and husband Andrew Simkins invested in real estate.[90]

The University of South Carolina responded to the lawsuit by saying Henrie Monteith failed to qualify for admission. However, in court in June 1963, attorneys acknowledged she was rejected because of race. On July 10, 1963, district judge J. Robert Martin ordered Monteith admitted, citing *Gantt* and noting that "failure to admit her . . . deprived her of her constitutional right to equal treatment without regard to race." Martin wrote that "other qualified Negroes . . . are entitled to freedom from racially discriminatory policy," making his decision a class action ruling. Weeks later a dynamite blast outside the home of Dr. Monteith dug a crater five feet long and one foot deep. The Monteiths lived in neighboring houses, and for several nights the physician sat guard on his porch, armed with a rifle—but not this Monday night. Glass shattered at two of the homes. Rebecca Monteith said the "cowardly act" would not stop her daughter's plan to enter the university.[91]

On September 11, 1963, Henrie Dobbins Monteith and Robert G. Anderson Jr., a Greenville native who had completed two years at Clark College in Atlanta, registered for undergraduate studies at the University of South Carolina. James L. Solomon Jr., a veteran and math professor at Morris College in Sumter, registered for doctoral studies. Perry drove the three to the university campus, where they completed their paperwork without observers. The University of South Carolina was the last of the nation's public flagship universities to desegregate.[92]

THE CAUSE

At the beginning of 1964, Newman had reported what he called "breakthroughs," desegregation of a few hotels, motels, theaters, lunch counters and restaurants, as well as "token employment" of Black workers in cities throughout the state. But not Orangeburg, "the most embattled place of all."[93]

In 1965 Thomas Wirth, a White chemistry professor with a doctorate from the California Institute of Technology, came to SC State, its first White professor. In 1966, he was joined by two others, and, by February 1967, the college had said goodbye to all three. When Wirth told the students his contract would not be renewed, four walked out of class, intent on action. A gathering in a dormitory lounge led to all-night vigils in front of Turner's campus home. On Friday morning, February 24, the college's disciplinary committee summoned three students—John Wesley Stroman, Benjamin Bryant, and Joseph Hammond, the state NAACP youth president—and suspended all until August 1970, in effect ending their studies at SC State. The trio had until noon to get off campus. About 200 students held a sit-in at the student center that lasted until 5 a.m., followed by campus police arresting Bryant for being on campus and refusing to leave.[94]

Turner met with class presidents and student body officers, then with the student body, and then granted a rehearing that allowed the three to apply for readmission in August. Still displeased, student leaders called for a class boycott. They wanted their professors back, yes, but far more. They wanted competent instructors from a broader geographic base; an end to compulsory attendance at vespers, assemblies, and classes; and less administrative control over student government and student-teacher relationships. These were young men and women with ambition. They visited relatives in Chicago, Detroit, New York, and Philadelphia and saw a better present than theirs. They had marched for civil rights. They were disturbed that their public college did not measure up in funding, faculty, salaries, and facilities. And they did not like or trust the dictatorial Turner, ferried about in a chauffeured limousine. On Friday, March 3, more than one thousand students skipped class. Trustees decided the school would close if demonstrations and the boycott continued, which they did.[95]

Jerry C. Fryer of Spartanburg worked with Williams at the time. He came to SC State in August 1966 from Carver High School. Mother Florence V. Fryer worked as a housekeeper, father Jeremiah R. Fryer as a laborer with the railroad. During a layoff Fryer's father started a lawn care business. Jeremiah Fryer paid his son when they worked together but, upon his return to railroad work, allowed his son to keep every penny when he worked on his own. Jerry Fryer also drove a school bus. He joined pickets protesting Silver's and Woolworth's segregated lunch counters. And he took photographs, first with Brownies then a Yashica, feeling like a "semi-professional" as he bought film with a professional discount from the Camera House, photographed for Carver High School's newspaper, and developed film in the family pantry. He came to Orangeburg to major in psychology and began shooting 8 × 10 student portraits for $7.50 apiece, "an avenue to put money in my car, a 1953 Plymouth, grey with a mohair interior."[96]

Williams charged $16.50 for a portrait, so "Cecil and I had a little discussion," said Fryer, who knew Williams through older brother Richard E. Fryer, married and a student at Claflin. The consummate businessman made a bargain. "He said, 'Fryer, look here, you will make more money if we charge the same thing. You have access to the studio, use the facility, but let's charge the same thing.' And I did." Williams and Fryer became a team. "Cecil came to take pictures at the school, different functions. I'm right there all the time. It was not 'Fryer, you cover this.' He knew I would be there."[97]

Fryer found Wirth's firing unsettling. Ignoring brotherly advice—"Mom and Dad didn't send you to school to be boycotting class"—he joined the boycott. Williams took a few photos of student gatherings. Fryer photographed speeches in front of the student center. He photographed students collecting money for buses to a Columbia protest. Boycott participation grew to 1,400 of 1,695 students. The four class presidents accepted leadership, and Isaac "Ike" Williams became spokesman for what became known as "the Cause." Senior class president, six foot two inches tall, an earnest charmer, and an ROTC officer, Williams led as many as three rallies a day, attended by hundreds of students. On Monday, March 6, backup arrived. Herbert Wright, the national NAACP youth director, attended a local church rally and announced the NAACP's support. The national NAACP promised legal assistance. The Alumni Association of Orangeburg supported all but return of the expelled students. Turner and the White trustees likely remembered with dread Fred Henderson Moore. Governor Robert E. McNair sent SLED agents and state troopers to Orangeburg, two FBI agents came to town, and Chief Strom ordered twenty officers onto campus.[98]

On Tuesday, March 7, television crews recorded Ike Williams announcing that 720 students had signed up to march the forty-two miles from Orangeburg to Columbia. McNair issued a statement. "I have no intention to meet with any group of students who refuse to attend classes," who did not settle grievances with "authorities." Ike Williams vowed, "The governor is going to have to talk to us one way or another." On Wednesday in Columbia, NAACP leaders met to criticize Turner; they were tired of Turner and of McNair's support of him.[99]

Ike Williams grew up in the Union Heights neighborhood of "The Neck" in Charleston. At 12 years old he became a full participant in Charleston's civil rights movement. He knew firsthand, "We had to fight for every inch we got." In elementary school he had starred as Prince Charming in a school play, and afterward a Navy wife drove the young actors to a drive-in, where the excited children ran to the window to order ice cream. She did not know that segregated Charleston required that they place orders at the back. White youths chased the children back to the car and kicked dents in one of the doors. A few years later, Williams experienced another heartbreak. He discovered that the Boy Scouts segregated camps and transportation to Jamborees. This did not make sense to the Star Scout and holder of the Order of the Arrow. Scouts were supposed to be a "friend to all" and a brother to other scouts. So Ike Williams took action. Under the tutelage of NAACP leader and beautician Mary Lee Davis, he participated in voter education and registration, a boycott of Coburg Dairy, became president of the NAACP youth council, and accumulated eleven protest arrests, one involving nine days at the Charleston County Prison Farm with Newman.[100]

Ike Williams wanted "an end to white dominance in black education," had the full-throttle support of Newman, and had learned brinksmanship young. On Tuesday, Turner met with all the class presidents. At a rally on Wednesday, March 8, Ike Williams conducted enthusiastic choruses of "Which Side Are You On," a union song adapted for civil rights, and called Turner "Tom" Turner, an Uncle Tom who served White politicians and trustees instead of SC State's Black students, faculty, and staff. Ike Williams said, "Our president doesn't know how to be a Negro. He doesn't know what our parents have sacrificed, and for what? A second-rate education." McNair met with Turner, the trustees' chair, the state attorney general, and Strom. At another rally Ike Williams announced chartered buses to Columbia, where SC State students would be joined by protesters from other Black colleges and the NAACP. A *Times and Democrat* editorial advocated closing the school if the capital protest occurred. Turner set a March 10 deadline for the boycott's end. McNair sent an official car to Orangeburg to bring the class presidents to Columbia for a secret meeting.[101]

More meetings followed, yielding an assembly where students accepted a win and cancelled Saturday's protest. They mostly got what they wanted minus the return of the White professors or any immediate plan for improving the quality and geographic reach of faculty. Turner dropped the attendance penalties and cancelled midterms. District court dealt with the expulsions. With McNair's private promise of no state appeal, Perry filed a complaint that the three suspended students had been denied freedom of speech and assembly. A March 14 ruling reinstated them immediately. The boycott was over, and so was Turner's tenure.[102]

TRANSITIONS

In April the state legislature expanded the number of SC State trustees to eight, thus diluting the impact of appointing the public college's first two Black trustees. On May 10, the 61-year-old Turner announced his retirement, which was actually a resignation forced by McNair. The Cause's fatal blow had been preceded by years of dislike for a man that Ike Williams called "a white Negro" and by disgust with South Carolina's neglect of its only public college for Black students. As Ike Williams said, "We're 1,600 black souls crying out for freedom," young men and women who he said were "corralled" for segregation. Parsimonious funding, closure of the law school, a pending closure of the agriculture department, and a mechanical engineering department without engineering graduates had led many to suspect "a conspiracy against Negro education." So did seventy years of White trustees in control.[103]

Cecil Williams disengaged somewhat from the local fray. He liked to say he burned a candle at all ends. He ran a studio, photographed for yearbooks with assistants such as Fryer, and, in the spring, accepted a post at the South Carolina Education Association (SCEA) as photographer and coordinator of professional and public relations. As usual, he stepped into history in the making. The Palmetto Education Association (PEA) and its 9,000 Black teachers merged with the SCEA and its 20,000 White teachers on April 1, 1967. As usual, the state was running late. Only South Carolina and four other Southern states retained segregated teacher organizations. A 1964 resolution by the White teachers' National Education Association (NEA) required that all segregated affiliates merge. The resolution was followed by a 1966 agreement by the NEA and the Black teachers' American Teachers Association. This round it was Black teachers who hesitated, with good reason. Later studies showed that desegregation cost the Black community "the near total disintegration of Black authority" in public education. Integration became "outegration," said Black educators. The SCEA illustrated this by retaining its executive secretary while PEA executive secretary Walker E. Solomon stepped into an associate role. Williams was hired as one of three Black members on a staff of twenty-six. "It was an opportunity, and it was a token job," he said.[104]

While Black educators wrestled over the association merger, Black activists wrestled over the choice of SC State's next president. Alumni wanted M. Maceo Nance Jr. appointed. A veteran, an alumnus with a master's from New York University, and the college's vice president for business and finance, Nance was a popular competitor at the student center's billiard tables. The NAACP wanted Dr. Charles H. Thomas Jr., an SC State education professor with a doctorate from the University of Oklahoma. A former president of Orangeburg's NAACP, Thomas became director of the South Carolina Voter Education Project in 1962 and was among the leaders of the 1963 Orangeburg Freedom Movement. In a private meeting in the governor's office on June 29, 1968, McNair chose Nance as interim president, and the board of trustees concurred.[105]

Nance immediately addressed inadequate funding, requesting close to $1 million to add academic positions and improve salaries and $5.5 million for a building program. In December 1965 he had warned a state legislative committee that the school's accreditation with the Southern Association of Colleges and Schools was at risk and campus limitations prevented admitting more students. Eight hundred applicants had been turned away in 1965. The 1967–68 state appropriations allocated $32.6 million to the state's five majority-White public colleges and universities. SC State received just $2.5 million while Clemson University, the state's other land-grant institution, still 99 percent White, received $7.3 million.[106]

HOTBEDS AND STOMPING GROUNDS

Modjeska Monteith Simkins had seen it all. Born in 1899 and active in civil rights since 1931, Simkins was a founder of the state NAACP conference in 1939, director of Negro Work for the South Carolina Tuberculosis Association from 1931 to 1942, a confidante of Thurgood Marshall, and a state NAACP and Richland County Citizens' Committee (RCCC) officer. She knew what she saw, and she called it by name.

She called Orangeburg and its surroundings "the hotbeds and stomping grounds of the most reactionary element in the state."[107]

The Civil Rights Act of 1964 had led to the desegregation of about half of Orangeburg's restaurants and, after a lawsuit, its Edisto and Carolina theaters but not much more. Orangeburg's drive-ins; doctor's offices; Orangeburg Regional Hospital, its court-ordered desegregation deadline long past; and its one bowling alley remained segregated. Harry Kenneth Floyd Sr., manager of the All Star Bowling Lanes, took ownership of the business in June 1967 along with wife Carolyn R. Floyd. Brother Ernest Custeen "E. C." Floyd and sister-in-law Hanna Floyd operated the air-conditioned snack bar, which seated twenty-one customers at nine counter stools and three tables. The couples displayed a "For White Only" sign and strictly enforced segregation.[108]

They meant it. From August 28 to September 4, 1966, Orangeburg served as host to the American Legion World Series for teens. Ted Williams, the "Splendid Splinter" of the Boston Red Sox and a member of the Baseball Hall of Fame, spoke at the opening banquet. Oakland won. Along with the championship the integrated California team took home the memory of being turned away from the one and only bowling alley in a small town. Floyd told the players that "the white boys could go in, but the Negro boys could not."[109]

In 1968 the city remained home to segregationist mainstays: the South Carolina Independent School Association, which supported private segregated schools; the Orangeburg-Calhoun Counties Citizens' Council; a Truth About Civil Turmoil Committee, a front for the John Birch Society; and WDIX, a radio station that aired WCC editorials. Workers in White-owned businesses felt free to display disdain and resentment of Black customers. "I would test this," said Williams. "I would go into White restaurants, and waitresses would hatefully wait on us. They would throw your change on the counter or take a long time to wait on you. They would treat you very bad to let you know you weren't welcome there. And I would have to say that bowling alley, being one of a kind, it stood out as being segregated. It was offensive, when you walked downtown, that you would see a place with a 'White Only' sign."

Oscar Perry Butler Jr., dean of men at SC State, belonged to an all-Black bowling league. A former SC State basketball star who stood a head taller than anyone around him, he was tired of White business owners and officials who would not employ Black adults as more than a "bag boy, sweeper, or [laundry] presser" and White adults who would not offer Black youths part-time work and prohibited their participation in city recreation. Black people relied on Butler to get things done, said Williams, who thought of the Navy veteran "as more powerful than the presidents." Students trusted Butler, known as a "straight-shooter," said Williams. Butler's actions made an impression on them.[110]

Butler wrote the director of Community Relations Service (CRS) in Washington, DC, in 1965 to complain that his team had to travel to Columbia to bowl and had to seek the required permission from the American Bowling Congress to do so. Why? Because the league's sole local choice was segregated. The Civil Rights Act of 1964 had established the CRS to mediate but not investigate or prosecute discrimination disputes. The CRS replied that bowling alleys might not be covered by the law, which prohibited discrimination in places accommodating the public—hotels, motels, restaurants, and theaters—through Commerce Clause powers to regulate interstate commerce. However, if the bowling alley also served food transported through interstate commerce or eaten by interstate travelers, perhaps the law could be enforced.[111]

This ambiguity lingered as Floyd changed the wording of his bowling alley sign to say "Privately Owned," as a White-owned business withdrew sponsorship of a team, as Butler and businessman Earl M. Middleton asked the mayor and Chamber of Commerce members to intervene, and as Middleton proposed that the bowling alley set aside a night or two for Black bowlers. Butler's complaint moved to the US Department of Justice, the local NAACP consulted with Perry, and James P. Davis, an Air Force veteran and SC State foreign languages major, collected 300 signatures on a petition to picket the bowling alley. The problem remained as SC State asked if a school team could bowl, and as Fabric Services Inc., a contractor that abided by federal regulations, offered sponsorship of a biracial team. Floyd continued to turn away Black students.[112]

On Monday night, February 5, John Stroman and several other SC State students entered the bowling alley through the back door. Stroman—a childhood "pin boy" in the days before automatic pin setters, a league bowler in Savannah, and a

catalyst for the Cause in 1967—sent ahead a White classmate, equipped with Stroman's ball, bag, and shoes. The White student would test what Floyd's use of the
word "private" meant. Recently released from the draft because of a shoulder separation injury, Stroman felt appalled that he could be sent to fight in Vietnam when
he lacked full citizenship at home. Stroman wrote American Machine and Found-
ry, which supplied automated bowling equipment, to complain about Floyd—to
no avail. Stroman also interviewed the White owner of Savannah's Highway 80
Bowling. He told Stroman that he had desegregated to keep his lunch counter in
operation, explaining, "That's interstate commerce."[113]

Harry Floyd locked the door after the students entered. Carolyn Floyd refused
them service at the snack bar. "Everything we touched, if we touched his napkin
holder, his wife would throw it in the trash," said Stroman. Told the bowling alley
was private, the students called over their White classmate, who had been bowling.
An angry Floyd told the bowler that he could not finish his game; he demanded that
the Black students leave. Stroman replied, "We are going to stay here until everyone
else goes," meaning the White customers. Floyd called the police and left for the
city recorder's home to swear out a warrant. Police chief Roger Poston arrived. City
manager Robert R. Stevenson arrived. Poston ordered the All Star closed; the Black
students and White customers left. Afterward Poston, who had thirty officers under
his command, called SLED Chief Pete Strom and Captain Carl Fairey, the highway
patrol's district commander, to ask for additional forces.[114]

On Tuesday night Williams parked his blue Corvette on East Russell Street,
across from the bowling alley. He fumbled as he loaded film in his Hasselblad, noise
in the A&P Shopping Center broadcasting urgency. Stroman had returned with
another group of students. He again led the students into the business, its doors
unlocked after a conversation with Poston and Strom, who said the students would
be arrested. Stroman replied, "Well, we came to go to jail." Floyd asked the students
to leave as police listened. The police then arrested those who stayed for trespassing
on business property after a request that they leave.[115]

Williams had arrived at the tipping point. Word of the arrests had reached the
colleges. SC State students watching a movie at White Hall auditorium rushed to
the shopping center, joined by Claflin students as news spread. The youths jammed

Oscar Perry Butler Jr. raises his hand for calm as he negotiates among students upset with segregation at the All Star Bowling Lanes and with law enforcement officers arrayed against them. Rev. J. Herbert Nelson, smoking, former NAACP state president, listens from the far left. That night, February 6, 1968, students enter the bowling alley and accept arrest. When word hits the campuses, classmates arrive to protest. They are beaten by law enforcement officers, and some react with vandalism.

the parking lot, singing, chanting, and demanding the release of those arrested. Butler persuaded Poston and Strom to put the jailed students into his custody. He hoped that walking them back to the shopping center would convince everyone to return to the campuses. But Strom called in more police and SLED officers. Some carried blackjacks. Highway troopers wore riot helmets and carried riot batons, 28- to 36-inch hardwood sticks. Poston called in the city fire truck. Students taunted the firefighters by lighting matches and challenging them to put out the tiny flames. They recognized that the fire hose's high-pressure water would be another weapon used against them. They were right; that was Strom's plan.[116]

Williams edged into the crowd. "I was right there in the middle of it, getting long shots, close-up shots, different angles, holding my camera up high." He photographed a group that included law enforcement, Butler, and J. Herbert Nelson, pastor of St. Luke Presbyterian Church. Thin, with a diamond-shaped face, glasses, a moustache framing a gap-toothed smile, most often holding a cigarette in hand, Nelson served as president of the NAACP state conference from June 1965 through

December 1967. In June 1967, he told the AP that unrest at SC State had not ended but credited a statewide quiet to the NAACP, saying, "We demonstrate only when we can't negotiate." As Butler held up a hand, hoping to instill calm or at least be able to hear, Williams raised his Hasselblad and photographed the moment.[117]

Glass broke. The sound—like a shot—set off panic among the students and violence among the hundred or so law enforcement officers. Williams believed that a student leaned against or was pressed by the crowd against the glass panes of All Star's double doors. Chief Strom thought a student had kicked in the glass. Strom ordered an arrest, increasing the chaos. "Because everybody jumped and started running, I started running too," said Williams. He saw officers reaching for their batons, others reaching for holstered pistols. Richard Reid, an SC State sophomore, joined the stampede. He jumped on a car hood to avoid being beaten. Reid saw classmate William Stackhouse fall, tried to help him up, then continued running. When Williams reached the Russell Street sidewalk, "I looked back, and two city policemen had started whipping a girl with their billy clubs, a young lady who had fallen to the sidewalk, and they were hitting her."[118]

Fryer, a resident of Bethea Hall, heard that students had been arrested, thought, "I need to be taking pictures," grabbed his Yashica, and arrived after the fire truck. Injustice drew him. "Why are you arrested when it says 'White Only' bowling alley? A lot of the students there have been to Vietnam. It was crazy to me, insane to me that you go fight for this country, risk your life, and you can't go bowl." He photographed a firefighter on his truck, his hand on an uncoiling hose, his gaze directed at the students. He photographed a group of young men, one pointing at the combative police. He photographed an armed officer within the bowling alley. The AP sent out nationwide all three photos on its news wire.[119]

Fryer and Williams weren't the only adult witnesses. Faculty on the edge of the tumult also saw female students clubbed. The county's only Black deputy sheriff stopped a police officer who had pulled his gun after being hit in the head. As the youths retreated, they grabbed a demolition site's bricks and rocks, leaving in their wake broken windows at a furniture shop, a tax office, and two filling stations, and scraped paint and broken windshields at two car dealerships. A Claflin student told Mike Davis, an *Afro-American* reporter, "The violence didn't start, no windows were broken until those damn honkie cops started swinging those billy clubs." Williams agreed. "The only advantage we had, students outnumbered law enforcement. The students aren't hitting police officers; they're not fighting; they don't have any guns." Throughout, the White customers of All Star continued bowling.[120]

And Fryer continued photographing. "This local policeman walked from behind and used the riot stick, three-foot-long wood, and knocked my camera out of my hand, broke my camera. I bent over to pick it up, and in my peripheral vision I could see he was going to hit me, and said, 'Hey, no, no, no, you can have the camera.'" The officer allowed Fryer to pick up the camera and did not demand the film.[121]

Williams stopped at a pay phone to call the AP. That plan ended when a White man, clad in hat and trench coat, interrupted with "I'm US Army Intelligence. I need this phone now!" He showed identification, threatened arrest, and took the receiver. Williams returned to his untouched Corvette; everyone knew the yearbook photographer's car. Later he located six injured students at SC State's infirmary, including Emma McCain, bruised and bleeding about her face and body, and Stackhouse, his head wound so severe that he required a hospital transfer to Columbia. At least thirty-three students suffered injuries severe enough to need medical care, including a coed with a broken arm; nine of them required hospitalization. The city police officer hit by a pipe and a Columbia patrol officer whose eyes had been squirted with an unidentified substance were treated at the hospital and released. Strom, who called the chaos "head-knocking," did not order tear gas because he was concerned about All Star's White patrons.[122]

Back on campus by 9 p.m., students collected back at White Hall. A few threw rocks at passing cars, and a city officer responded by firing a shotgun—onto campus, said the students; into the air, said the officer. Some students gathered at the home of Roland Haynes, an SC State psychology professor and advisor to the campus NAACP. This group decided to approach city officials, ask for a parade permit, and present a list of grievances. Simkins, worried by a call she received around 10:30 p.m., gathered a few members of the RCCC, drove to Orangeburg to investigate, and returned before dawn convinced that worse trouble loomed. But the governor did not seek the advice of Black elders. Newman took pride in his relationships with the powerful, particularly McNair and Strom, but they did not consult him or Nance; Nelson; Thomas, president of the local NAACP; or Rev. Alonzo W. Holman, president of the NAACP state conference. Like McNair, the Black leaders wished for intervention by the Justice Department or the filing of a local lawsuit. It was too late.[123]

The students returned to campus; they did not continue downtown. The damages from vandalism that night amounted to approximately $5,000. They did not loot the businesses. McNair issued statements at 10:30 p.m. and again after midnight, saying that all was under control. In what was surely an overreaction at this point, he mobilized the National Guard around 9:30 p.m. By 10:30 p.m. 250 soldiers (just one a Black soldier) of the National Guard, dressed for combat and armed with M1 rifles with fixed bayonets, were reporting for active duty, as were fifty more highway patrol officers for a total of 100 White highway troopers. After the "long, hot summer" of 1967, McNair's summoning of troops communicated to White residents the state government's protection of their property and to Black residents something completely different, police brutality and death.[124]

AN ARSENAL VERSUS SOUL POWER

The next morning's White-owned newspapers headlined the police officer struck in the head, property damage, and arrests of a dozen or more Black people in a crowd variously estimated at 125 to 700. At a press conference McNair said that he was investigating "outsiders, including Black Power advocates," had no intention of "letting things get out of hand," and had sent the state attorney general to Orangeburg. The AP wrote of "infuriated" students, of a "rampage" and "rioting." Columbia's *State* newspaper tagged the students a "mob," its participants "singing, chanting, and rock throwing" in a three-block area. The AP's Al Lanier made the astonishing claim, despite the state ranking seventh nationally in lynchings, that "South Carolina boasts of being the only Deep South state which has never had a death or serious injury attributed to racial violence."[125]

The heated news coverage omitted beatings of Black students by White law officers. Almost entirely missing were Black sources. The AP interviewed Nance, who said, "I can't condone police brutality," and the AP interviewed Williams, who described a student injured by a tear gas cannister fired at close range into his head.

UPI quoted SC State petitioner James P. Davis, who described the night as "a rebellion against a hardcore Reconstruction-days segregationist."[126]

Nance cancelled classes for Wednesday, February 7. At 9 a.m. he told the 600 students gathered at White Hall, "We need to seal off downtown" to limit conflict and to boycott. Students cheered when Nance said that he and faculty supported them but not the use of violence. Robert Scott, president of SC State's student body; George Campbell, president of the college's NAACP chapter; and Claflin representatives met with Mayor E. O. Pendarvis, Stevenson, and Poston. Denied a permit to march, Scott said, "We've got to try to apply all the pressures we can without being messed up or wiped out." The students debated Nance's and the NAACP's proposal of a boycott but did not call one. They did accept an unheard-of campus visit by Pendarvis, Stevenson, and a representative each from the Chamber of Commerce and the Merchants Association.[127]

That afternoon in White Hall, Pendarvis and Stevenson displayed their discomfort and unfamiliarity with the Black community. The local paper had described the white-haired Pendarvis as a "smooth Southern gentleman" when he was elected mayor in 1965. On stage the owner of E. O. Pendarvis Candy and Tobacco Company used the term "nigra." A student stood and challenged him to say "Negro," with a long e and o. Pendarvis defended his pronunciation. The student instructed him anyway. "Say 'nee,'" which Pendarvis did. "Say 'gro,'" said the student, who then asked the mayor to put the two syllables together, which he did, accompanied by laughter. Stevenson, glasses in hand, paused after disbelieving hoots followed his patently insincere "delighted to be here." He began again this way: "I'll pause when I say this, in order for you to hiss, some of you: But I can truthfully and consciously say it is the philosophy of the city administration that we do treat all our citizens right in this town." Shocked and amused "oohs" followed; the students' personal experiences proved that a lie.[128]

Williams photographed the event and felt offended by Pendarvis and Stevenson insisting that White officials treated Black citizens fairly "when it was anything but. [Pendarvis] had a hard time speaking because about anything out of his mouth was not really true." Nance told Pendarvis, when the mayor deflected mention of police brutality, "I do not condone destruction of property, but for the record, it happened after the young ladies were hit."[129]

At 4:30 p.m. the students presented city officials a list of twelve grievances. They made three immediate requests: end All Star's segregation policy or close it, suspend and investigate the officer who fired his gun on or near campus, and address the issue of police brutality. The students also wanted the city to finally deal with civil rights law and associated societal changes: desegregate Orangeburg's drive-ins, end discrimination in public services, particularly at the health department; accept Medicare at the segregated hospital, which did not participate in Medicare and could not be certified for federal funding while discrimination remained; and establish a biracial human relations committee and a fair employment commission. The AP coverage disparaged the list of grievances as "the price for halting riots."[130]

That evening Holman told the media that the NAACP had asked, as it had in 1967, for the US attorney general to immediately investigate discriminatory treatment at the bowling alley and to enforce the 1964 Civil Rights Act. He said that the local NAACP was not involved in any demonstrations. Newman had traveled to town and failed to persuade the local NAACP to file a lawsuit. "He and McNair and Strom had an understanding to keep things under control," which was common knowledge, said Williams. Simkins saw a serious problem: Black leaders co-opted by seeking close relationships with White politicians. Students in the colleges' NAACP chapters continued their own negotiations. As Williams noted, "Who is the NAACP? The NAACP is us," and the students wanted the bowling alley desegregated immediately.[131]

A siege mentality burgeoned among White locals. White merchants armed themselves and called Poston to demand police protection. Other White residents armed themselves and drove about town, pistols and shotguns jutting from car windows and truck beds. A White man, who lived just off the SC State campus on Lovell Street, shot three Claflin students, saying they had trespassed in his yard. They said they were walking back to Claflin after an SC State meeting. The young men were treated at the hospital for birdshot wounds and left with a Claflin security officer. On the SC State campus near Washington Dining Hall, students from both colleges gathered outside after a meeting. A Dodge Dart zoomed toward them, its White driver firing a pistol. As the car circled back, the students grabbed whatever was at hand and stoned the vehicle. The Dodge raced off campus, followed by B.

E. Evans Sr., a Korean War veteran in charge of campus security. Evans chased the car along US Route 601, ending pursuit by shooting out one of the car's tires and arranging the highway patrol's arrest of the two White brothers in the car, William Robert Carson and Carroll Carson.[132]

McNair further armed the town by sending in two more National Guard units after hearing that the White business district had become what he called an "arsenal." The initial Guard unit, carrying rifles with fixed bayonets and equipped with tear gas and masks, occupied the A&P parking lot. FBI agents arrived. So did more SLED agents, deputy sheriffs, highway troopers, and police officers, all of them White. They guarded downtown streets and surrounded the campuses. The National Guard had received riot training, but the National Advisory Commission on Civil Disorders had warned in 1967 of the 99-percent White force's poor performance due to discrimination, poor leadership, and poor discipline.[133]

Where did this put the students? The beatings haunted and angered them. All Star Bowling Lanes did not open that night, but no remedies had been offered. The mayor refused to appoint a human relations committee, as had been true for years. Officials' unwillingness to acknowledge the validity of grievances underscored their hold on power, and, conversely, the students' lack of power. Hemmed-in by highway patrol troopers armed with loaded riot guns, carbines, and pistols, some students held meetings while others roamed the campuses, remaining within campus boundaries but throwing rocks and bricks at passing cars with White drivers. Claflin students governed access to campus with the password "soul," as in "soul power." A female student, injured the night before, told *Afro-American* reporter Mike Davis that the mayor's comments stunned her. "He said he did not have the power to make businesses integrate, that he just had influence. Well, I've never heard of a mayor that had no power," she said. Troopers stopped the volleys of rocks by blocking streets that surrounded the campuses to eliminate traffic and further confine students.[134]

The morning of Thursday, February 8, brought an appeal from Nance, read in classrooms. Students should stay on campus and refrain from throwing bricks and bottles from the campuses' edges. "Your personal safety is in jeopardy," he warned, as the shooting of Claflin students proved. All Star reopened. A student meeting ended in disagreement. City council followed a closed afternoon meeting with a statement that dismissed, item by item, the students' concerns. The city officials claimed no authority to close a "lawfully operated business," no knowledge of police brutality, and no issue with an officer firing a "warning shot." The council members said that they had no authority over the segregated drive-ins, health department, and hospital, all in the county. They said that private business owners determined their own hiring practices; besides, a fair employment commission would be removed from "the grass roots of this community." And, claiming that the city had complied with local, state, and federal laws, the city council declared that no issues existed in Orangeburg regarding the Civil Rights Act of 1964.[135]

Williams returned to Columbia for work and photo supplies. He and others remained unnerved by the unrest throughout Monday, Tuesday, and Wednesday and deeply worried by the governor's armed response. Thursday evening the signs became ominous. No one had ever experienced roadblocks at the entrances of Claflin and SC State. No one had ever experienced armed troops surrounding campuses. No one had ever experienced armored troop carriers in town. No one had ever experienced the military guarding the water supply, a gasoline supply depot, downtown, and the hospital. Rumors—the shopping center would burn; the city would burn; public utilities would be attacked—fed on images of recent urban rebellions. These included unrest in Newark in 1967, with 26 dead, 700 injured, and $10 million in property damage, and in Detroit in 1967, with 43 dead, 342 injured, and $50 million in property damage. A US Department of Defense report on federal intervention in Detroit listed the use of loaded firearms as a last resort. But Strom authorized troopers to use them.[136]

In Columbia, Simkins and Billie Fleming, president of Manning's NAACP and a member of the state conference's board of directors, met with students fearing violence. Simkins, Fleming, and SC State's two Black trustees met with Henry Cauthen, head of the state Commission on Higher Education. Simkins and Fleming linked anger over the still-segregated bowling alley to long-festering anger over the state's paltry investment in SC State. Simkins asked Nathaniel Abraham Sr. to go to Orangeburg and report back. An Orangeburg native, Korean War veteran, RCCC spokesperson, and Columbia editor of the Black-owned *Palmetto Leader*, Abraham knew Strom.[137]

Williams returned from work late in the afternoon. Troops were arriving and beginning to stop traffic and block roads. Williams reached campus via Goff Avenue and Buckley Street. When he neared Claflin's campus he heard a thunk as a stone hit his car, and then an "Oh, stop! That's Cecil's car." College police allowed him on campus, where he parked and took everyday kinds of photographs. "I found students enjoying themselves, just having fun. Even young ladies were going back and forth. They thought they were invulnerable if they stayed on campus." As light fell, the National Guard could be seen just off campus. Williams left to eat a hamburger, expecting to return. He could not. He found access impossible, every road and entrance blocked. He could not believe it—two campuses surrounded by armed guards as if the colleges were enemy camps or prisons.

DEATH

That night was cold, the forty degrees of the day falling into the thirties. Confined to campus, students tried to build a bonfire at around 7:30 p.m. on Watson Street, near the intersection of Watson, College Avenue, and Russell Street. There, a slanted embankment with steep concrete steps separated SC State's Lowman Field from the sidewalk and street and sixty-six highway patrol officers, forty-five soldiers, and twenty-five SLED agents. Numerous police had set up a command post at the intersection of Russell Street and US 601. Off Watson Street, beyond a brambly hedge that defined campus limits, sat an empty house. Lowman Field separated the embankment from Lowman Hall, a men's dormitory. As time passed troopers reported hearing the sound of small arms (or fireworks). Attempts to spark fires with gasoline-filled bottles failed at a nearby warehouse and at a freight depot. Troopers did not locate any culprits.[138]

Around 9:30 p.m. students vandalized the house, ripping away floorboards and shutters to fuel another bonfire lit by matches and a bottle of gasoline. They sang and shouted and cursed Floyd, the bowling lane owner. They mocked police and firefighters, saying, "Hey, honky, here we are!" They tossed torches made of sticks and sheets. Abraham talked to the students on campus. He talked to Strom, Poston, and Fairey off campus. He begged for a bullhorn to address the students, "to keep my people from being hurt." He was refused, even though Strom's command car contained a public address system and tear gas. Convinced this was an ambush, Abraham called Simkins to say, "It's happening here." Simkins called Cauthen, and Cauthen called the governor. It was too late.[139]

Strom summoned fire trucks, which arrived around 10:30 p.m. The bonfire had died down, but firefighters doused it anyway under the protection of highway patrol officers who jogged to the embankment and onto the campus property. Some stood, some lay on the embankment in shooting position, joined by reporters, photographers, and television crews. Other members of the highway patrol crept onto Lowman Field from the side. A thrown banister hit patrol officer David J. Shealy, who had climbed the embankment to the front of the vacant house. He fell, unconscious and bleeding from the nose and mouth; he seemed a man who had been shot. When firefighter Edward Hoffman arrived minutes later in a rescue truck, Shealy had already been taken by squad car to the hospital. He was treated for a severe nose injury. During the lull the students who had retreated to Lowman Hall headed back toward the embankment. Thomas Kennerly later testified that he and his classmates believed, "Why should we run; we are on our campus."[140]

The troopers shot the students. An eight-to-ten second barrage of bullets struck students as they fled and fell, wounding them in their backs, legs, and the bottom of their feet. All but one of thirty students later identified as shot had been hit in their sides or backs by the gunfire. Lieutenant Jesse A. Spell, in a February 14 statement to the FBI, said students had charged forward, shouting threats, throwing rocks, bricks, and sticks, and he gave the order to shoot. But film showed the young men had strolled back. Thirteen state troopers admitted firing weapons. Two of the thirteen said they heard an order. Four of the thirteen said they shot into the air. Several students said they heard a whistle to start and end the gunfire. No one found weapons among the injured students, nor did anyone find student-owned guns or cartridges on the campuses, nor did anyone report ever seeing any student with a gun.[141]

Fryer liked to be around but not in the middle of an event. He had walked to Lowman Hall to watch from a window as the bonfire burned. He answered the hall phone, and Rev. James Monroe Bradley Jr. demanded, from his view at Trinity Methodist

Governor Robert E. McNair sends 250 members of the National Guard to Orangeburg. Law enforcement officers guard points in the city and surround Claflin University and SC State to confine students. On February 8, 1968, three students die after highway troopers open fire on those returning to an on-campus bonfire. No fewer than twenty-eight students are wounded. All but one of the dead and wounded have been shot in their backs and sides.

From left: Samuel Hammond Jr., 18, SC State; Henry Ezekial Smith, 19, SC State; Delano Herman Middleton, 17, Wilkinson High School

Church, that Fryer "'tell the kids to withdraw from the front of the campus.' He could see law enforcement officers on the sidewalk with their weapons drawn," said Fryer. The young photographer witnessed what came next. "At that point is when the whole sky went blue. They are actually shooting at people." He saw students run toward Lowman Hall or hide behind trashcans. Fryer crouched under a desk's attached counter and stayed there. "It never entered my mind anyone would be shot."[142]

"There was no warning, no command, no nothing. They just started shooting," said Charles Hildebrand, a sophomore shot in the back of the leg, hip, and armpit as he ran. He and others submitted statements to the FBI or testified in court. Warren Koon, an ex-Marine and reporter for the *Charleston Evening Post*, testified, "The first shots I heard were fired by the troopers." Dozier Mobley, an Army veteran and AP photographer, said that he heard no gunfire before the troopers attacked, that the troopers "panicked." Four television photographers also agreed that the troopers had panicked and "swarmed over the embankment," according to a *Los Angeles Times* report. Robert Eaddy, an SC State freshman, dropped to the ground but was hit in the back of his right shoulder. He testified, "We were just walking up there, just watching the fire truck put out the fire we had built in the street. Nobody suspected they could be hurt or anything—and then they [troopers] started shooting." Richard McPherson, a freshman, testified that after being shot in the back of the head, he fell to the ground unconscious, came to, attempted to help another wounded student, and was shot in the back. Two troopers who did not fire at the students testified that they did not hear any shots fired at themselves or other troopers in the time between Shealy's injury and troopers' shotgun blasts of lethal double-aught buckshot or their firing of revolvers and carbines.[143]

Three teens died. Samuel "Sam" Hammond Jr., 18, was helped to Lowman Hall, where he collapsed. Campus police drove the SC State freshman to the infirmary; he was then put in a station wagon and transported to the hospital. He died at 11:20 p.m. A shot in the back, two inches to the left of his spine, killed him. The fatal shots to Henry Ezekial "Smitty" Smith pierced him as he stood near the embankment. Several students saw troopers then strike Smith with a gun butt and beat him with billy clubs. The fatal shots to Delano Herman Middleton had reached him on the steps of Lowman Hall. Troopers dragged Middleton and Smith by their hands and feet to the sidewalk, where photographers recorded them lying in pools of their blood, their shoes beside their feet. Firefighter Hoffman drove the young men to the hospital in his rescue truck. Middleton, seventeen years old and a Wilkinson High School senior, died at 1:10 a.m. Shot six times in the back and side, he died from a bullet that passed just above his heart. Smith, nineteen years old and an SC State sophomore, died at 1:45 a.m. Shot at close range five times, he was wounded in the left side of his neck, the back of the right shoulder, twice in the buttocks, and once through the rib cage, liver, and vena cava. Surgeons Roy C. Campbell and A. B. Wolfe testified to multiple wounds to the youths' backs and sides.[144]

Students with cars started an evacuation. Strom said later, "We didn't have any intention of letting students get off the campus and get in town because in our opinion, Orangeburg would have burned." Students drove the injured to the hospital or just away, to private help or to home, said Williams, sure that rescuers spirited away many more of the wounded, everyone fearful of arrest. Police patrolled the colleges' greens, looking for more bodies.[145]

At home Williams listened to radio and television reports into the morning hours. "The rumor mill started about people killed on campus. Students had been shot. And then the telephone system failed." He thought, "If I had not gone away to get a hamburger, I might have been there when the shooting started." People stayed in their homes, said Williams. "We didn't know if police were running rampant in the streets." Even the most pessimistic felt stunned to hear of death. "I don't think anyone thought law enforcement would open fire on students," said Williams. "The students were on their campus. For the highway patrol to come on their ground was unthinkable; it was unimaginable that the highway patrol would come on their ground and shoot them."

Friday morning began damp and grey. At 7 a.m. an unshaven Williams drove to SC State and walked from Bradham Hall to Lowman Hall. His unease led him to keep his car's engine running and driver's door open, but no guards or barriers existed to stop him. "They [law enforcement] didn't think enough or respect people of color enough to even put up crime scene tape." The sidewalk remained stained with blood; charred wood from the bonfire remained. Shreds of paper and splinters of wood from the bonfire and fabric from clothes littered Lowman Field. "It looked like a battleground." Butler appeared. The two did not speak but began picking up double-aught shell casings. Maintenance workers with an open-bed truck showed up, and the workers began removing evidence of the night. Williams collected pieces of paper and wood. He put twelve shell casings into his pockets, then photographed a few against a nearby building and again back at his studio. He knew the dead and many of the wounded.

That afternoon Williams entered the infirmary. He was not allowed to photograph the disarray, students in shock and emotional distress, volunteers bringing food, parents arriving to take injured students home. "The word was that more would die," said Williams. "People in town felt vulnerable; they were fearful of law enforcement. People were fearful that a stigma was attached to the students that they were the cause of it, that they would be charged with inciting to riot."

President Nance called a 9 a.m. assembly and announced that he had suspended classes. The governor finally took a call from Holman. "You would have thought you were in Vietnam," said Holman of that Friday in Orangeburg. Holman

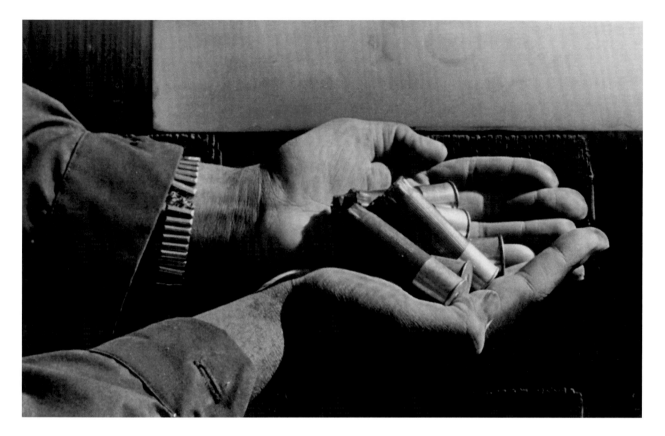

begged McNair to close SC State. He said the governor answered, "'If I close that school, they'll burn it down,'" referring to armed and angry White residents. Holman replied, "You want to take our boys and girls and use them to protect bricks and mortar?" James Forman and H. Rap Brown, of the Student Nonviolent Coordinating Committee (SNCC), made headlines when they named the shootings "the Orangeburg massacre." Brown, who was chair of SNCC, said, "The lesson for us is very clear and evident. If we seek redress of our grievances through peaceful and so-called legal means we will be shot down and murdered." He called for revenge. Both colleges closed indefinitely, and Holman arranged for the NAACP to provide travel funds and bus transportation to Greenville, Spartanburg, and Charleston. Five armored personnel carriers and 600 soldiers in the National Guard took over the town.[146]

Some students remained hospitalized for several days. Robert Lee Davis Jr., a freshman and star football player scouted by professional teams, had walked toward

The morning after what will be called the Orangeburg Massacre, Cecil Williams goes to the bonfire site and recovers the casings from double-aught buckshot. Blood stains the sidewalk; charred wood and shreds of paper and clothing litter the grass field. No one has put up crime-scene tape.

the bonfire to watch firefighters extinguish it. When gunfire began, he dropped and crawled unharmed toward Lowman Hall then stood. A rifle bullet pierced his back, lodging next to his spine. Campus police drove him to the hospital, where he languished on the floor; the segregated ward lacked available beds. Transferred to Columbia, Davis awaited surgery for weeks. Albert Dawson, eighteen years old and a freshman, ran to Lowman Hall when he saw troopers approaching the abandoned house. Upon hearing a shout regarding Smith, he turned toward the embankment. The bullet that hit him in the chest lodged two inches from his heart. He received treatment in Charleston. Ernest Carson, seventeen years old and a freshman, needed recuperation at home after days in the Orangeburg hospital. Shot as he ran and fell, ran and fell again, Carson suffered a total of eights wounds to his legs, heels, and soles. His brothers, Willie and John Carson, found him in the emergency room and challenged police, who arrested them. A patrolman struck John Carson with a rifle butt; it took twenty-two stitches to close his wound.[147]

THE WAY IT WAS TOLD

An official narrative took shape. The AP reported "a brief but bloody exchange of gunfire," an error they did not retract. In his Friday morning statement McNair began, "This is one of the saddest days in the history of South Carolina." In his second sentence, he pivoted to "those who would place selfish motives and interests above the welfare and security of the majority," namely Black Power advocates. The state could come up only with South Carolina native Cleveland Sellers, who had worked with SNCC from 1964 to 1967. Even so the governor continued to sound the Black Power alarm in the weeks that followed. McNair made other factual errors, saying that a "confrontation" took place off campus, not on, and that the highway patrol shot students after "extended sniper fire," and after "an officer had been felled in his efforts to protect life and property," implying an officer had been shot rather than knocked out. He declared a state of emergency and set a 5 p.m. to 6 a.m. curfew.[148]

During a noon press conference McNair argued with NBC correspondent Sidney Lazard, a former foreign correspondent who had been present Thursday night. Lazard challenged McNair's erroneous statements. The *State's* coverage also spun a false narrative. One article described a Thursday night with "a black militancy movement" obtaining weapons while White housewives locked doors and husbands loaded guns. The article ended, "At 1:35 p.m. the battle was over. The war had begun." A hand-drawn map depicted a trooper and a soldier behind North Boulevard and railroad tracks opposed by figures labeled "a student mob" and armed with rifles and a Molotov cocktail. In the days that followed, only out-of-state reporters interviewed the relatives of the dead students or sought out wounded students or hospital workers or morticians. The *Pittsburgh Courier* disclosed eyewitness reports of "brutal and senseless" killings of students who obeyed their college presidents' requests that they stay on campus. Only *Jet* published portraits of the dead and photographs of recuperating students. Williams had provided *Jet* photos of an empty town under curfew and yearbook portraits that he had taken of Hammond, Smith, and Middleton, their deaths a personal loss as they were for so many others. "I knew them. I would see them daily in the student center playing pool, eating a baloney sandwich."[149]

McNair determinedly turned the focus from Strom and himself to Cleveland Sellers, who served as SNCC's program secretary from 1965 to 1967. A native of Denmark, a town twenty-one miles from Orangeburg, Sellers had returned to his home state in October 1967, joined by two other SNCC members hoping to organize students. Sellers was not interested in the segregated bowling alley. He invested in sparking requests for Black history courses and encouraging a thirteen-member Black Awareness Coordinating Committee, organized in fall 1967 at SC State. On Tuesday night, fetched by two women with the committee, he witnessed but did not step in as police beat fleeing students. He attended that night's long discussions about what to do next. Students rejected his suggestion that they block College Avenue with their bodies. On Wednesday night, when he saw four highway patrol cars in front of his home, he slept in a dormitory. On Thursday he told reporters, "Everybody is looking for a scapegoat." Thursday night on campus he saw Smith approach the bonfire then fall as "Bullets seemed to be coming from all directions." Sellers, hit in the side, crawled away from the gunfire. At the infirmary, "Blood was everywhere, on the floor, the walls, the chairs," the injured treated by one nurse, the athletic director, and coaches until classmates could drive them to the hospital.

A deputy arrested Sellers at the hospital. He was arraigned that night for arson, inciting to riot, assault and battery with intent to kill, destruction of personal property, damaging real property, housebreaking, and grand larceny, with bond set at $50,000, and transported to Columbia's state penitentiary.[150]

Eminent educator Benjamin E. Mays wrote in his weekly column for the *Pittsburgh Courier,* "Very little will be done because the victims are not white." Newman wrote in December in his annual NAACP report that the "Orangeburg Crisis Remains Unresolved." These observations held true.[151]

On February 11, 800 Black Orangeburg residents met with local and state NAACP officers, who called for immediate desegregation of the bowling alley, a "no buying quarantine," withdrawal of the National Guard, and suspension of troopers "responsible for police brutality." An NAACP call for long-range actions incorporated student grievances and added such demands as restitution to families of the dead and injured; desegregation of appointed offices, the penal system, and the draft board; and financial and educational investment in SC State. Ramsey Clark, the US attorney general, ordered an FBI probe of the fatal shootings. The US Justice Department filed to intervene in the desegregation of Orangeburg Regional Hospital. The Floyds closed their snack bar but did not escape a Justice Department lawsuit and its result, a temporary restraining order that prevented continued segregation.[152]

The governor met with Nance and the trustees of SC State and pushed White city leaders to form a biracial committee on human relations. That immediately stalled because White officials took charge of Black representation. Strom announced cancellation of an Orangeburg KKK rally. Six hundred soldiers in the National Guard, equipped with live ammunition and accompanied by five armored personnel carriers, occupied the city. An FBI agent visited Williams five times, took six of the shell casings Williams had collected, and failed in his effort to recruit Williams as an undercover informant. One by one the students were buried: Middleton in Orangeburg, Smith in Marion, South Carolina, and Hammond in Fort Lauderdale, Florida. The Fort Lauderdale branch of the NAACP sent a formal protest to Orangeburg's mayor, city council, and police chief. The statement called Hammond "an expected leader" sent to SC State to advance himself. "Brutal tactics of your National Guardsmen, however, have sent him back to us in a coffin." [153]

During protests in South Carolina, North Carolina, and Virginia, Black students carried coffins to represent the dead and wounded. Claflin reopened, and Wilkins came to speak on February 25, the day before SC State reopened. He told an audience of 1,500 that three students "have been murdered here" and called on McNair "to rise up above the usual political posture of South Carolina... and acknowledge that it was a tragic error." Stroman and Davis bowled at All Star Bowling, watched over by federal agents. Token hiring of Black workers downtown occurred. Long-awaited funds came the college's way, including a $6.5 million bond for capital improvements despite opposition from Orangeburg's White legislators. In early March students protested outside the state capitol, held a sit-in before the doors of McNair's office, and attempted to read their grievances from the gallery of the South Carolina Senate. Six participants were arrested.[154]

No autopsies were performed. The Orangeburg County coroner held no inquest, with McNair's permission, although state law required inquests for deaths by unknown or violent causes. A majority-White federal grand jury had refused, on November 7, to indict nine state troopers who had told the FBI that they had fired their weapons at students. The judge sealed these records. The US Justice Department investigated, and, on December 20, filed a criminal information, a formal charging document. Such a presentation of charges avoided a grand jury. This was the same tactic employed in 1946 to prosecute a Batesburg, South Carolina, police chief for beating and blinding Isaac Woodard, a newly discharged World War II veteran. Using an 1870 statute that had protected the civil rights of former slaves, the federal government charged that nine troopers willfully shot into a group of people, wounding or killing them, intending to impose summary punishment, and ultimately depriving them of life and liberty without due process of law. The penalty was one year in prison or a fine of $1,000 or both. Williams was subpoenaed and sat on a courthouse bench waiting, two days in a row, without being called to testify. On May 27, 1969, ten White and two Black jurors acquitted the troopers, five of whom had received promotions before the trial.[155]

In August 1969, given the troopers' acquittal, sixteen plaintiffs dropped a lawsuit against Pendarvis, Poston, and the city police for engaging in violence and intimidation against Black people because of race. In November 1969 a district judge ruled that the parents of the three dead students, who had sued for $400,000, could not hold accountable Silas Pearman, state highway commissioner, but could sue the troopers. In November 1970 an all-White jury cleared the nine troopers in a $300,000 civil suit by the slain students' parents.[156]

Sellers was not tried until September 24, 1970. The years-long delay occurred, in part, due to charges (later dismissed) from Sellers's refusal to be drafted, and in part due to the Orangeburg solicitor's reluctance to bring charges. But McNair insisted. Charges against Sellers, reduced to three counts—incitement to riot, conspiracy to riot, and rioting on February 8—did not hold. Police Chief Poston testified that he did not see Sellers commit any illegal acts. None of the ten prosecution witnesses, all law officers, could connect Sellers to the events that unfolded on February 8, except to say that he was shot. SLED Chief Strom was asked, during his testimony, to cite specific violations of the law by Sellers. He could only say of Sellers that on February 6, during the unrest at All Star Bowling Lanes, "He refused to disperse immediately when ordered by Chief Poston; that's a violation." The judge allowed the rioting charge to be applied to February 6 instead, and Sellers was found guilty for refusing to disperse immediately. Sentenced to one year in prison and a $250 fine, Sellers served seven months.[157]

For Williams, those days and nights in February 1968 negated law and order. The bowling alley's segregation violated civil rights law; it should have been desegregated or closed. "The students knew they had a right to go into that bowling alley." Of enforcers of law, he said, "They grew tired of people exercising their First Amendment rights to demonstrate and finding freedom to do so in their faces. They shot them, and they went home. Sounds like hate."

STRIKE!

Williams's last big assignment of the Sixties sent him to Charleston and teamed him with Chester Higgins, a *Jet* senior editor. Williams again photographed hundreds of chanting picketers and marchers. He again photographed personnel carriers transporting armed National Guard troops that McNair mobilized. But this time the chants combined a celebration of "Soul Power!" with "Union Power!" each anathema to McNair and the all-White state legislature.

Just seven percent of South Carolinians belonged to unions, the lowest percentage in the nation. In the 1920s and the 1930s governors used violence to prevent unions, even ordering the National Guard to shoot to kill picketers during a national strike. The textile industry provided more than half of the state's manufacturing jobs. Until the late 1960s and the beginning of required federal monitoring, White workers held these jobs.[158]

Charleston's history did include a union—the 1944 establishment of a Congress of Industrial Organizations (CIO) affiliate at the Cigar Factory on East Bay Street— and a successful strike. On October 22, 1945, more than one thousand workers, mostly Black women, walked off the job. Their demands included back pay from wages withheld during World War II, a raise of twenty-five cents per hour, a minimum wage of sixty-five cents per hour, and an end to racial discrimination. The National Labor Relations Board ordered the American Tobacco Company to pay its employees $120,000 in back wages. The end of March brought the strike's end. It took workers five months, a week, and a day to win a raise of eight cents per hour.[159]

Williams came to Charleston in April 1969 because Coretta Scott King came to Charleston. She traveled to Charleston for the same reason husband Martin Luther King Jr. traveled to Memphis, where he was assassinated on April 4, 1968. She wanted to support Black workers. He supported striking sanitation workers, all men; she supported striking Black hospital workers, mostly women. The Memphis call, "I Am a Man!" became Charleston's call, "I Am Somebody!"

Charleston's Medical College Hospital (MCH) still practiced segregation, with segregated restrooms, visiting hours, and room assignments; lounges for White nurses and White nurse's aides but not for Black employees; a cafeteria for White doctors and a cafeteria for White employees but not for Black employees; an evident refusal to provide Black people psychiatric services; no Black physicians; and White staff physicians practicing segregation. Unequal pay and no training programs for Black employees confined Black workers to low-skill, low-pay posts. This was illegal. The Civil Rights Act of 1964 had outlawed discrimination on the basis of race, color,

religion, sex, or national origin and prohibited discrimination in public places and
in any program receiving federal funds. In 1965, Executive Order 11246 had reen-
forced the federal requirement of fair employment practices by federal contractors.
MCH received $12 million in federal funds.[160]

In December 1967, five Black women, nurse's aides, and practical nurses at MCH
refused to take patients' vital signs because the new charge nurse ordered them to do
so without providing them the required patient reports. They feared exceeding their
authority; they also feared inadvertently harming patients. A standoff ended when
the women left. They were fired. In 1965 a segregation complaint had placed MCH
under the scrutiny of a compliance committee of the US Department of Health,
Education, and Welfare (HEW). Through the help of Reginald Barrett, a Black
realtor on the compliance committee, the five women got their jobs back.

The firings served as a catalyst for secret meetings. Mary Moultrie, a nurse's
aide at MCH, started conversations with Black leaders, including Isaiah Bennett, a
World War II veteran, Cigar Factory employee, and shop steward of Local 15A, and
Lillie Mae Doster, a Cigar Factory employee who had served as a picket captain,
a union shop steward, and union secretary. Bennett coached union organization.
Doster helped Moultrie catch the interest of New York City's Local 1199, the Drug
and Hospital Employees' Union, which had organized 40,000 hospital workers
there and was considering organizing in the South. Rev. King had called Local 1199
his favorite union, and after her husband's death, Coretta Scott King had accepted
the position of honorary chair of its National Organizing Committee. In October
1968 the MCH hospital workers organized as a union, Local 1199B, with Moultrie
as president and Rosetta Simmons as vice president.[161]

Moultrie possessed a strong, musical voice, which she put to good use as the
strike's spokeswoman. She also possessed a hard-working sense of justice, necessary to sustain her throughout what she called the "bring someone you can trust"
meetings in 1968 and the 113-day strike in 1969. In her teenage years Moultrie had
worked for Esau Jenkins, a Johns Island community leader, in his J&P Restaurant
on Charleston's Spring Street. She accompanied him to NAACP meetings, assisted
him on registration drives, and, with his tutoring, composed speeches about right-
eous demands for change. "I knew I would have to go. I couldn't afford college and

couldn't find a decent job at home," she said. After graduation from Burke High School, she joined a cousin in New York City, earned certification as a licensed practical nurse, made four dollars an hour with benefits at Goldwater Memorial Hospital, and sent money home. In late 1966, she returned to Charleston to care for her ill mother. MCH did not recognize her certification. As an MCH nurse's aide she made $1.33 an hour. She also felt again "the sting of prejudice" at work. She was expected to do hard labor while White nurses socialized. She witnessed coworkers fired at will, even by White nursing students.[162]

Moultrie found a strong strike partner in Rosetta Simmons, the voice of Charleston County Hospital's (CCH) striking workers, the other publicly funded hospital whose workers joined Local 1199B. After Simmons's father died, her mother and aunt raised their children together. With the encouragement of a nun at St. Francis Xavier Hospital, Simmons earned a license as a practical nurse at the Roper School of Practical Nursing. She had decided, "Housekeeping was not my calling. I liked taking care of people." She quit MCH after being labeled "an agitator." She was told, "'You do what I tell you to do or else.' I did the 'or else' and went home." At CCH, she found "the same things: unfairness in pay, job classifications, and raises, not having a voice." Friends with Bennett, she was transfixed by his philosophy: to get fairness people had to come together as one body. She joined the meetings of MCH workers. Simmons began organizing at CCH, convinced, as she said, "Just coming together is a union in itself."[163]

MCH provided the jump-start for a strike. On March 17, 1969, a meeting of fifteen Black employees with hospital president William Mellon McCord and other administrators fell apart. Given an ultimatum—no talk of unions—disappointed workers marched to McCord's office. Soon the hall and offices filled with janitors, housekeepers, cafeteria workers, some occupying the office, answering the phones, even dancing on a tabletop. All left peacefully when ordered to do so by the city police chief. Within a few hours the personnel office called in eleven women, including Moultrie, and one man and fired all of them. McCord, a missionary's son who grew up in the apartheid of South Africa, had a gift for making the situation worse. He sent the employees cartoons of money-clutching, champagne-swilling union bosses. He provided workers a new holiday, Confederate General Robert E.

Lee's birthday. He recruited doctors' wives as volunteers to fill staffing gaps. He thwarted negotiations.[164]

At 5 a.m. on March 20, more than 400 workers did not report to work, and 100 more walked off the job. A judge granted the hospital an injunction prohibiting picketing. Elliott Godoff, director of the National Organizing Committee, announced the support of Coretta Scott King and Ralph Abernathy, King's successor at the SCLC. The backup of both Local 1199 and the SCLC made for a new and heady combination of civil rights and labor. By March 31, 125 workers at Charleston County Hospital had left their jobs to strike. Picketers walked at both hospitals. Abernathy arrived and vowed, at the Fourth Baptist Church, "I've come here to join you in socking it to 'em." The new union quickly added approximately 450 MCH and 100 CCH members and hundreds of local supporters.[165]

On April 2 Simmons delivered a premature girl who died two days later. The union sent a bodyguard to her hospital room after Simmons, known as a striker, was threatened by an MCH nursing supervisor. Simmons returned to the picket line in May. She said, "I couldn't just sit, and I could be much more help." Besides, women were going to jail. Police had arrested Moultrie and thirty other strikers on the MCH picket line on April 11. "As soon as I got there, they shoved me in a paddy wagon," said Moultrie. The women served eleven days. In less than three weeks police arrested more than 500 strikers.[166]

The strike found star power in Coretta Scott King, who had made very few public appearances since her husband's assassination. She spoke at the first union meeting. She suggested Charleston be named Local 1199B. On April 20 she issued a support statement signed by Abernathy, Wilkins, and twelve other prominent civil rights leaders. On April 21 she sent a telegram to be read at a rally: "You in Charleston are demonstrating that my husband's dream still lives." And she showed up. On April 25 Abernathy led 3,000 strikers and their supporters through Charleston, the march ending in his arrest and that of Local 1199 President Leon J. Davis, Local 1199B Vice President Jack Bradford, two Catholic priests, and 180 marchers and picketers. On April 29 Coretta Scott King came to town.[167]

Williams rode with SLED agents to the Charleston Airport to pick her up but only after a thorough search of his camera bag. "They know I'm covering this for

Coretta Scott King, widow of Rev. Dr. Martin Luther King Jr., comes to Charleston on April 29, 1969, to support more than 400 Black women striking for desegregation, better wages, and basic employment opportunities at the Medical College and Charleston County hospitals. The following day she marches with strikers and supporters. Holding the "Human Dignity" sign is Rosetta Simmons, Charleston County Hospital strike leader. To Simmons's right is King; to King's right is Mary Moultrie, Medical College Hospital strike leader. To Simmons's left, in overalls, is Rev. James E. Orange, project coordinator with the Southern Christian Leadership Conference.

Jet, so I travel in their car," as a representative of the national press. *"Jet's* angle was—they would always give me a slant or direction—this was the first major event that Mrs. King participated in after the death of her husband. This meant to them that she would follow in her husband's footsteps."

Moultrie led a motorcade heralding King's arrival. At the airport Martha Simmons "M. S." Alston, treasurer of 1199B, and her son presented King with roses. On the ride into town Williams sat against one back seat window, King against the other. They discussed a mutual friend, Mary Ellen Strong, founder of the *Milwaukee Defender,* Wisconsin's only newspaper for Black readers. King's first step was visiting Abernathy at the county jail, which held more than 200 protesters. That evening she spoke at Emanuel AME Church to as many as 7,000 people listening inside and outside. Using a microphone and a loudspeaker, she said, "My friends, if my husband were alive today, he would be standing with you." When she told her audience, "I want to have the privilege of marching with you," her listeners cheered and pounded each other on the back in congratulations. In a statement released afterward, King said that Charleston, like Selma and Memphis, had become "a national test of purpose."[168]

*Day in and day out, picketers
walk in front of the Medical
College Hospital. The Charleston hospital strike is supported
by Local 1199, the drug and
hospital union based in New
York City, and the Southern
Christian Leadership Conference, led by Ralph Abernathy
after the assassination of Rev.
Dr. Martin Luther King Jr.*

*From left: Julia Davis, retired social worker and wife of Local 1199 president Leon J. Davis; Mary
Moultrie, president of Local 1199B; Coretta Scott King, widow of Rev. King; and Rosetta Simmons. vice
president of Local 1199B.*

Williams photographed King at Emanuel AME's lectern. On Wednesday he photographed her, surrounded by SLED agents in their small-brim Stetsons, as she left
Morris Brown AME to lead 2,000 protesters. King linked arms on her right with
Moultrie, recently out of jail, and on her left with Simmons, recently out of the hospital, as they walked Charleston's narrow streets to the Medical College Hospital. Once
there, all knelt to pray. Williams jogged ahead, as usual wearing two cameras, this
time a Rollei and a 35 mm Nikkormat. "Blacks lined the street, joined the march and
(literally) tried to touch the hem of her garment," wrote *Jet's* Higgins. He remarked
on Charleston's palm trees, Spanish moss, and hot, hard pavement. The march was
peaceful, but Williams documented the forces on call: uniformed SLED agents,
motorcycle cops at corners, and rows of National Guard troops, gas masks obscur-
ing their faces, hips supporting their rifles, the barrels elongated by fixed bayonets.
False fire alarms, small fires, and rock throwing led Abernathy to leave jail on May 2

25c

JET

MAY 22, 1969

THE UNTOLD
STORY OF JULIA'S
TELEVISION SON

DRUG and HOSPITAL UNION

MRS. CORETTA
SCOTT KING:
Wife of slain SCLC
leader takes on his
role as she joins in
Charleston's protests

MRS. KING FIGHTS
FOR BLACK WORKERS
IN CHARLESTON

"The man from Jet," as Cecil Williams sometimes tags himself, comes to Charleston to photograph widow Coretta Scott King. Jet *editors and many of its readers wonder if she will take a leadership role rather than accept the limits of serving as a fundraiser and spokeswoman. Williams's photograph of her speech at Emanuel AME Church—she says, "$1.30 is not a wage; it is an insult"—makes the May 22, 1969, cover.* Jet *asserts the "wife of slain SCLC leader takes on his role as she joins in Charleston's protests."*

On May 11, 1969, Cecil Wil-
liams returns to Charleston
for the Mother's Day March,
a Southern Christian Leader-
ship Conference (SCLC) and
union extravaganza that draws
members of Congress and
union leaders. At a four-hour
rally preceding the march, Rosa
Parks, right, of Montgomery
bus boycott fame, presents a
Mother's Day bouquet to Alberta
Williams, left, a Local 1199B
striker and mother of nine.

and to place an ad in the local paper saying, "This is purely a nonviolent movement."
He warned, "Unless this strike is settled, you will have much more violence." McNair
declared a state of emergency and enacted a 9 p.m. to 5 a.m. curfew.[169]

The *Jet* team made the May 22 cover with Williams's black-and-white head shot
of King wearing a "Drug and Hospital Union 1199" paper cap, her gaze heavenward.
In white letters against a bright orange background, *Jet* announced, "Mrs. King
Fights for Black Workers in Charleston: Wife of slain SCLC leader takes on his role
as she joins in Charleston's protests." Higgins described Charleston as "uptight."
He noted, "One thousand rifle-toting National Guardsmen patrol the tense city,
augmenting 400 helmeted state troopers." Williams, familiar with the destructive
consequences to occupying a city, believed, "As usual, the state government, the
governor's position, they sent tanks down there; the National Guard moved in. They
didn't learn anything from 1968."[170]

Rev. Ralph Abernathy, left, and Andrew Young, right, consult on stage during the Mother's Day rally on May 11, 1969. The Southern Christian Leadership Conference (SCLC) sees the Charleston Hospital Strike as an opportune partnership between a civil rights organization and a union, each opposing economic inequality. SCLC president Abernathy flies in and out of Charleston, to participate in rallies, marches, and arrests. Young oversees the Charleston effort.

Williams returned for a Mother's Day March on May 11, an extravaganza to be led by King and Abernathy. A four-hour rally at the King Street auditorium known as "the Palace" attracted 4,000 people. VIPs packed the stage: five members of Congress; various East Coast union representatives; Rosa Parks, best known for the Montgomery bus boycott; William L. Kircher, director of organization for the AFL-CIO; Walter Reuther, president of the United Automobile Workers; and Gloster B. Current, director of branches for the national NAACP. Williams maneuvered among rows of chairs to photograph Rosa Parks handing an enormous Mother's Day bouquet to Alberta Williams, a striker who had supported nine children on her pay of $1.30 an hour and, like other strikers, now subsisted on union and family support. To photograph the SCLC's Andrew Young, Williams edged around dozens of union officers and members to catch a crouching Young in conversation with Abernathy. "I'm trying to get long shots and closeups. There

*A massive Mother's Day
March—estimates range from
10,000 to 15,000 participants—
includes from left, Rosetta
Simmons, Local 1199B vice
president; Walter Reuther, president of the United Automobile
Workers; Mary Moultrie, Local
1199B president; Rev. Ralph
Abernathy, president of the
SCLC, and wife Juanita Abernathy; Rev. Joseph Lowery,
an SCLC founder, and wife
Evelyn Lowery.*

are so many things happening, I'm continuously shooting." But Coretta Scott King
was not there. She had cancelled to be with her own family.

Williams was ready for the massive march; after all, "This is what I did." He
raced ahead of the leaders: Simmons, Reuther, Moultrie, Rev. Ralph and Juanita
Abernathy, Rev. Joseph and Evelyn Lowery. He photographed them repeatedly.
"You've got to get the key players for whatever the story is about." He dashed here
and there as participants ebbed and surged around civil rights leaders, strikers, SLED agents, and Chicago's Operation Breadbasket Band and its Rangers, a
security force wearing red Stetsons, white safari jackets, and white boots. "Like a
Mardi Gras," said Williams. City and state government officials did not see it that

way. Waiting for potential disaster were 600 soldiers in the National Guard, 100 highway troopers, 140 city police, and uncounted SLED agents. To photograph the packed streets, Williams repeatedly climbed on top of cars, a tried-and-true trick of his. "I would get on the fender, from there get on the hood, from the hood get on the roof. It was not the easiest thing. There were a number of automobiles rolling around Charleston with a dimple on the roof." He got the long view. Calhoun Street overflowed with an estimated 10,000 to 15,000 participants.[171]

Pressure to resolve the strike arrived from many sources. At half-capacity, the hospitals barely functioned. The US Justice Department sent observers. HEW's investigators set a date to cut off federal funds if MCH did not rehire the twelve fired workers and begin an affirmative action plan. The International Longshoremen's Association threatened to close Charleston's port. Arrests totaled nearly 2,000. Abernathy, in jail since June 21 on a charge of inciting to riot, refused to pay bond until the strike was settled at both hospitals. Lost business and tourism in Charleston cost $15 million. Keeping the National Guard, highway patrol, and SLED in Charleston cost $1 million.[172]

The strike ended at MCH on June 26 with strikers promised rehiring, workers a minimum-wage raise from $1.30 to $1.60 per hour, grievance procedures, and a credit union. The strike ended at CCH on July 18 with a minimum wage raise from $1.50 to $1.60 per hour. Forty-two workers were promised immediate rehiring. Also promised was the rehiring at a later date of twenty-one more workers who wanted their jobs back. With union attorneys prohibited during negotiations, the strike ended without strikers' signatures, a memorandum of agreement, or recognition of Local 1199B. Fred Henderson Moore, attorney for 1199B, told strikers and the SCLC, "You've been bamboozled."[173]

This was neither the end of an era nor of a movement. After all, *Brown v. Board* had not ended segregation in public schools and public spaces. The 1964 Civil Rights Act had not ended discrimination in the workplace, although the "first Black" hired or appointed to this or that had entered the lexicon, observed Williams. Clarendon and Orangeburg counties remained, for him, the birthplace and center of the civil rights movement and struggle. He and his Black neighbors "lived in a war zone," he said. They lived as "second-class citizens," he said, under the rule of all-White state, county, and city governments. "If we African-Americans had not asserted ourselves, our history, heritage, and legacy would have been wiped off the face of the Earth—if we had not asserted ourselves and fought for freedom, justice, and equality."[174]

Into a new year and a new decade, Williams added a new apprentice. His instructions to H. Larry Mitchell were basic. "Take this camera, and if you don't know what you're doing, you act like you know what you're doing." Mitchell described his job as taking "the whole gamut" of yearbook photos for SC State, Claflin, and Voorhees. Williams taught Mitchell darkroom work, which Mitchell found dazzling. "You went out; you shot with film. You couldn't see in advance what you'd got. You developed it, and all of a sudden these images popped up. That was amazing to me. Cecil had that process down."[175]

In Williams's Boulevard studio stood tall, grey metal file cabinets. Each cabinet stored hundreds of small manila envelopes, which held negatives: 4×5s from the Crown and Speed Graphic cameras and 6×6s from the Rollei and Hasselblad cameras. Wooden bookcases also stood against the walls. Three-ring binders filled their shelves, each binder holding fifty plastic sheets, each plastic sheet holding in each of its seven rows the strips of 35 mm film from Williams's Nikkormat photography. This room held tens of thousands of images caught by Williams over the years. His documentation of daily life: yearbook portraits, prom portraits, wedding portraits, fires, car wrecks, parties, reunions, celebrations, and celebrities, the ordinary and the joy preserved. And his documentation of a civil rights movement: sit-ins and marches and confrontations, speeches and meetings, heroes and villains, faces and moments and places preserved. Proof of what happened.

Mitchell had a theory about Williams being there. "When you look at it from a spiritual aspect, it had to be divine intervention or some angel watching over him, guiding him."

Williams's mother had her own theory. "Cecil," she used to say, "you try to do the impossible."

Williams, who reveled in being "the man from *Jet*," had faith. "We knew we had important matters to work on." And "I was the person to go to. I was the one in Orangeburg with a camera."

Cecil Williams takes a seat at S. H. Kress & Co. in downtown Orangeburg. Tired of constant claims by White politicians and media that "outside agitators" spark and lead South Carolina protests, Black business owners join the White businessmen's ritual of 10 a.m. coffee. Not one Black person is served. Williams asks a friend to photograph him.

A Ku Klux Klan march or rally in Orangeburg or Elloree is not an unusual event. Ads by the Association of South Carolina Klans run in the local Times and Democrat. Robert Hodges, spokesperson for the association, tells the Times and Democrat, "Klavern 829 in Orangeburg is one of the largest klaverns in the state and very active."

Plans are made, picket signs are written, and freedom songs are sung in the basement of Trinity Methodist Church, 185 Boulevard Street. The 1963 Orangeburg Freedom Movement includes children and teens with their parents' approval. Many youths are not only arrested but jailed with adults. Brenda Williams, an eighth grader and Cecil Williams's sister, sits on the second row, second seat from the left.

The steering committee of the 1963 Orangeburg Freedom Movement includes, from left, Rev. Matthew D. McCollom, superintendent of the Methodist Church's Walterboro district; James E. Sulton Sr., treasurer of the local NAACP; Dr. Harlow E. Caldwell, dentist and chair of the Orangeburg Freedom Movement; Constance Baker Motley, NAACP Legal Defense Fund attorney; John E. Brunson, barber at The People's Barber Shop; Lincoln Jenkins, attorney; Gloria Blackwell Rackley, Orangeburg Freedom Movement leader; J. Arthur Brown, NAACP state conference president; and Dr. Charles H. Thomas Jr., director of the South Carolina Voter Education Project.

Opposite Page: On September 28 Orangeburg city and county jails are out of space. With 175 more arrests made, officials call for buses to take protesters to the state penitentiary in Columbia. Students and adults are transported to the prison and to work camps aboard prison and Army buses, even cattle vans. Returns are celebratory for the Freedom Fighters.

Most marches pass in front of Cecil Williams's studio, Colorama, on Boulevard Street. Children as young as eight years old march and picket downtown during the Orangeburg Freedom Movement. On October 4, fifty-four children are jailed, some ordered held indefinitely. On October 8, thirty-seven juveniles are held in jail overnight. On October 23, sixty-one are arrested on their way to register to picket. Most are younger than 17 years old but are locked up with adult prisoners, some for two days and two nights. Parents protest to the mayor and governor.

NAACP attorneys bail out protesters, defend them in court, and appeal their convictions as violations of the First and Fourteenth amendments. Matthew J. Perry, left; Zack Townsend, seated; and Earl Coblyn defend nearly 2,000 youths and adults arrested during the 1963 protests. Perry serves as the state NAACP's legal counsel. Townsend is a new graduate of the law school at SC State. Coblyn is a professor there. Townsend has just been admitted to the bar when Perry calls to tell him he has 500 clients waiting for him in the Orangeburg jails.

After filling jail cells, officials pen protesters in a stockade at the county jail. Orangeburg police's and firefighters' use of tear gas and fire hoses, mass arrests, and confinement outside in March 1960 had led to national opprobrium, even chastising by President Dwight Eisenhower. That does not stop Orangeburg officials in 1963 from again rolling out the fire hoses and holding protesters outdoors.

Among those shaping the Orangeburg Freedom Movement are Rev. Isaiah DeQuincey Newman, left, field secretary of the state NAACP; Gloria Blackwell Rackley, middle, known as "Miss Movement"; and MacArthur Goodwin, right, a Claflin University student leader. By October arrests of protesters have hit 1,600.

The Torch, *an underground newsletter secretly produced by SC State professor Charles Cottingham, keeps count of arrests and law officers' abuse and provides what it calls "Honor Lists" that name adults, youths, and children "who went to jail for freedom."*

THE TORCH

Volume 1, No. 11   Orangeburg, South Carolina   November 8, 1963

THE TORCH is circulated to inform Orangeburg Citizens of the NAACP activities of the Orangeburg Movement for Freedom.

-o-

NAACP MEMBERSHIP DRIVE IS NOW IN PROGRESS!!! JOIN THE NAACP TODAY!!! JOIN THE FIGHT FOR FREEDOM!!!!

Membership in the NAACP helps:

1. Protect your civil rights.
2. Insure the future of your children
3. Enlarge your economic and cultural opportunities
4. Knock down segregation barriers in all aspects of public life
5. Strengthen democracy in the United States of America
6. Refute anti-American propaganda abroad by correcting racial injustice at home
7. Secure the rights of your fellow Americans
8. Make America truly, "The Land of The Free."
9. Vindicate the American dream of human equality
10. Win the right for freedom now

JOIN NOW

WILKINS TO SPEAK!!

Roy Wilkins, the Executive Secretary of the N. A. A. C. P. will speak at Trinity Methodist Church on November 13, 1963 at 7:30. His speech will highlight the N. A. A. C. P. membership drive now under way in South Carolina. All lovers of freedom are invited to come out to hear Mr. Wilkins.

-o-

HISTORICAL REVIEW OF THE ORANGEBURG MOVEMENT FOR FREEDOM

The Orangeburg Movement under the auspices of the State Conference of the N. A. A. C. P. began its "Strive for Freedom" August 1, 1963. It is a story of determination and solidarity in a deep rooted town of hatred, dictatorship and inhumanity, labeled "segregation."

Negroes, closely knit and determined, have characterized the Orangeburg Movement, with picketing, mass demonstrations, meetings and arrests.

Starting with only 35 pickets, the Orangeburg Movement has grown into the

(Page 2, Col. 1)

-- Cut along this line --

Type of Membership:	
Minimum.............. 2.00( )	
With CRISIS MAGAZINE 3.50( )	
Blue Certificate 5.00( )	
Gold Certificate 10.00( )	
Contributing 25.00( )	
Life Membership 500.00( )	
Youth (under 17) .50( )	
Youth (17 to 21) 1.00( )	
Total..............$........	

"JOIN THE FIGHT FOR FREEDOM"
N.A.A.C.P. Membership Campaign
...................1963
Please Print
Mr.
Mrs.............................
Miss
Address.............................
.....................Telephone........
(include Zone Number)
Signed.............................
Solicitor
(Memberships of $3.50 and Up include Crisis)

-- Cut along this line --

-o-
IT'S A FACT

During the twelve month period beginning August 8, 1962 and ending August 8, 1963 a total of only 242 Negroes registered to vote at the Orangeburg County Courthouse.

During the three month period beginning September 3, 1963 and ending November 4, 1963, 494 Negroes registered to vote. Many times this number were turned away due to the one day registration period per month. Beginning in January the rolls will be open for three days per week. All freedom loving Negroes should take advantage of this additional time and REGISTER TO VOTE.

The ORANGEBURG MOVEMENT is proud to have played a major role in this increased voter registration.

Front row, left to right: Gloria Blackwell Rackley, elementary school teacher and Orangeburg Movement leader, and Arthur Rose, Claflin University art professor.

Second row, left to right: Grace Brooks Palmer, SC State speech professor; Vance Summers Jr., Claflin University student; and John E. Brunson, barber.

Back row, left to right, Willie Ben Ludden Jr., youth field secretary for the national NAACP; Isaac "Ike" Williams, SC State student and state NAACP youth president; and James E. Sulton Sr., local NAACP treasurer.

The Orangeburg Freedom Movement meets regularly to discuss strategy. Sometimes members take a break for Scrabble.

Rev. Isaiah DeQuincey Newman, left, back to camera, and Dr. Charles H. Thomas Jr., right, back to camera, greet students released from Orangeburg's city jail. Newman is field secretary for the state NAACP from 1960 to 1969. Thomas, an SC State education professor, frequently helps fund the bail bond that is paid by the NAACP. Son Reginald "Reggie" Thomas, far left, is among the beneficiaries, as is Isaac "Ike" Williams, fourth from left with pipe. Ike Williams leads "the Cause" in March 1967 when SC State students go on strike for a second time. Among the issues are underfunding of the public college, leading to what Ike Williams calls a "second-rate education."

AND SO MUCH MORE

In the 1950s and '60s, Cecil Williams drove from Orangeburg to Columbia, South Carolina, forty-two miles one way, to deliver his photographs to the Associated Press in the hopes that the AP would put them "on the wire." A nonprofit cooperative owned and governed by its member newspapers, the AP counted on its members to provide their daily newspaper articles and photos, employed a small staff in each state, and used freelance photographers. White-owned newspapers in South Carolina did not employ Black reporters or photographers and seldom covered the events of Black people's lives. Sometimes, thanks to AP distribution, Williams's work countered this omission. Black-owned newspapers such as the *Afro-American* and *Pittsburgh Courier* also turned to Williams when they wanted photographs from South Carolina.

So saying that Williams played a vital role in documenting, outside the photographic studio, the mid-twentieth century life of Black people is to understate the situation. As a Black photojournalist in South Carolina, he was not just rare but singular. On the other hand, to limit a description of him to "photojournalist" is also to understate. He ran businesses. He built houses. He designed his own books. He published others' books. And, as time moved on, he became an indispensable storyteller and interpreter of the civil rights movement in South Carolina.[1]

During the 1970s Williams experimented with what he imagined "life will be like in the 21st century." Inspired by the film *2001: A Space Odyssey*, released in 1968, and by the successful completion of six crewed missions to the moon between 1969 and 1972, he adopted a personal signature, a close-up of the moon, which "seemed to be a symbol of the future." He had always thought of himself as "a futurist." As a child he had dreamed of designing ultramodern cars. As a teen he had dreamed of studying modern architecture at then-segregated Clemson Agricultural College. Self-taught, he began designing Modern houses, large, simple in form and structure, and lacking ornamentation. He built his first Modern home in 1973. *Ebony* magazine devoted a three-page spread in 1977 to his "Space Age" house in Orangeburg, with its black-and-white living room with "specially designed telephones and electronic gadgets of all kinds built into the walls," its bedroom with a "floating bed" and a wall-to-wall photomontage of the moon, its kitchen with a "programmable oven" and a refrigerator whose door "dispenses not only ice cubes but cold water and various beverages," and throughout "windows of black-painted, heat-absorbing mirror glass." A Modern house he designed in 1982 became his photo studio. In 2019 he transformed the studio into the Cecil Williams Civil Rights Museum. A Modern house he designed in 2003 became his home.[2]

Williams studied alternative energy, investing in "what lies ahead." He added photovoltaic panels, a precursor to solar panels, to the first house he built. In 1977 he joined The People Are Coming, a statewide consumers' coalition focused on energy reform. That year Governor James B. Edwards established the South Carolina Energy Research Institute and in 1978 named Williams to the advisory panel. He was the advisory panel's only Black member.[3]

Williams and friends ran a business of the future from 1975 to 1979. Williams, Larry Mitchell, and Alfred Bradley owned 2000 Incorporated, an Orangeburg boutique on John C. Calhoun Drive. At the grand opening Mayor E. O. Pendarvis cut the ribbon, and a guest won a digital watch. A close-up of the moon dominated store ads. The inventory, described as "contemporary ideas for modern living and giving," included arc floor lamps and JVC Videospheres, televisions shaped like space helmets.[4]

Williams published books, a newspaper, and a magazine. In 1976 he began Cecil Williams Photography/Publishing company. By 2018 he had published three of his own photography books, 127 books by other authors, and seventy-nine yearbooks for SC State College, Claflin University, and several high schools. Between 1978 and 1984 he tried magazine and newspaper publishing, producing for Black audiences *Vue South*, a magazine, and *View South News*, a weekly newspaper. "I was the writer, the photographer, the editor, the graphic arts designer," said Williams, but he could not capture the ad base necessary for survival.[5]

He ran for office. In 1984 Williams decided to challenge his childhood foe, US Senator J. Strom Thurmond, "a case of David vs. Goliath," said the Orangeburg *Times and Democrat*. Williams lost in the Democratic primary to Melvin Horace Purvis III, a White nondenominational minister in Florence, by a mere 385 votes. The loss by less than one percent of the total vote resulted in two recounts and Williams's formal protest. He learned that Senate ballots were not distributed to some precincts' voters in eight counties, a report confirmed by Fairfield County's Democratic Party chairwoman. Before the protest hearing a janitor destroyed the Lee County ballots. At the hearing the South Carolina Democratic executive committee acknowledged irregularities but did not find fraud and denied the protest. Williams ran and lost as a write-in candidate in the general election. The 82-year-old Thurmond was reelected for another six-year term.[6]

In the 1990s Williams recalibrated. He had decided to run for office when he began organizing his photographs for his first book. "I began thinking over what things influenced my life—my participation in movements to change things that were going on which were discriminatory," he said. After thirty years as a bachelor, in 1993 he married Barbara Johnson, a teacher at Orangeburg-Wilkinson High School. In 1994 the Orangeburg NAACP branch presented Williams its Freedom Fighter Award. In 1995 Henry N. Tisdale, president of Claflin, presented Williams with the university's Presidential Citation for his contributions to the college and community. And that same year Mercer University Press published *Freedom & Justice,* Williams's first collection of his civil rights photographs. The book also contained his reminiscences and copies of letters, news articles, and documents dealing with local civil rights activities. Williams dedicated *Freedom & Justice* to his wife, several family members, mentor Edward C. "E. C." Jones Jr., tennis star Arthur Ashe—and Senator Strom Thurmond. He directed a wish at Thurmond, that "the images in this book help in understanding our struggle."[7]

Williams ran again for the US Senate in 1996. He was approaching 60 years old. Thurmond was nearly 94 years old, already the US Senate's oldest member. If Thurmond won again, he would become, in May 1997, its longest-serving member.

Williams ran in the Democratic primary against Elliott Springs Close. Although president and chief executive officer of Island Harbor Development in Fort Mill, South Carolina, and part-owner of the Carolina Panthers, a professional football team, Close was most frequently identified by media as the heir of the Springs Industries textiles fortune. Williams lost with 62,424 votes, 38 percent of the total. That impressed Thurmond's team, as did the 148,628 votes Williams had previously received against Purvis. Williams spent little more than the filing fees in both races. The senator met with Williams and invited Williams into the campaign. He wanted Williams's votes. Close dropped by to talk but did not follow through with any invitations or offers.[8]

Williams agreed to join the Democrats for Strom Thurmond Committee and accompany Thurmond on his campaign bus, named the Thurmonator, a play on the word *terminator* and *The Terminator* movies. Williams agreed—as long as he could photograph the man he thought of as "one of the most influential politicians in the state's history, and yes, a segregationist." In kind, Williams accepted Thurmond's presentation of him as a model Black voter. Thurmond's mental and physical infirmities, a scarcely mentioned but ever-lurking issue, were cloaked by his long-tested and frequently uttered campaign clichés and his refusal to debate. South Carolina almost always returned incumbents, and the senator's constituent service meant an impressive number of voters felt they owed him a return to office. Thurmond had his good and bad days, said Williams, who reasoned that Thurmond had changed with the times. Besides, Thurmond had granted him exclusive Thurmonator access. At a Summerville campaign stop when Thurmond became emotional, his voice high and shaky, and pleaded, "Y'all, please send me back one more time," Williams took on a more intimate rescue. He grabbed Thurmond's arm and raised it high in a victory salute—to cheers. Thurmond won his final campaign. He died in 2003, a year after his retirement from the Senate.[9]

Williams's bookmaking projects in the 2000s forced him to face again the transient nature of film as a record. His negatives from decades of work had accumulated, composing a rare civil rights archive. But the fragile film was deteriorating and in need of a safe and permanent home. Unfortunately, libraries and museums were slow to recognize the value of Black civil rights photographers and their photos of the movement. To preserve his images, approximately 400,000, Williams turned to invention. He wanted a speedy way to scan his negatives and thus duplicate his images in a digital format. He built a balsa wood prototype that would hold a digital camera and his film to photograph. He followed that with a metal working model that was too heavy. In 2014 he successfully created a functioning aluminum Film-Toaster, a device that speedily digitized film images, named for its resemblance to kitchen toasters. A bid for permanence seemed possible with the FilmToaster, the establishment of the Cecil Williams Photographic Archive at Claflin University, and President Tisdale's appointment of Williams as director of historic preservation at Claflin. A $50,000 grant from the Gaylord & Dorothy Donnelley Foundation in 2017 made it possible to speed up digitization of Williams's film. Using the FilmToaster, student interns converted 30,000 film negatives to digital format in four months.[10]

Recognition arrived and continued. Williams was given the Preserving Our Places in History Award in 2007 and the Herbert A. DeCosta Jr. Trailblazer Award in 2016, both from the South Carolina African American Heritage Commission. He participated in oral history interviews for the Richland Library in Columbia in 2007, the Library of Congress in 2011, and the Oral History Collection at the University of South Carolina in 2013. He received the Order of the Palmetto, South Carolina's highest civilian honor, in 2017. The Orangeburg *Times and Democrat* named him its Person of the Year in 2018, and he received a Lifetime Achievement Award from the Governor's Awards in the Humanities in 2019. Then Getty Images, a privately owned photo archive that had already licensed commercial use of seventy of Williams's photographs, stepped up. The Getty Images Photo Archive and the philanthropic community Stand Together committed $500,000 to Claflin University and three other HBCUs in 2022, the funds dedicated to research, restoration, and digitization of images and the creation of an HBCU collection at Getty Images.[11]

Williams's livelihood came not from photojournalism but from his studio, yearbook work, and other businesses. His identity, though, was defined by his work as a civil rights photographer. He frequently described his photojournalism as "covering a revolution," his depictions of Black life as documents on "living in a war zone" or "living as second-class citizens." However, the strengths of Williams's photographic trove exist in multiple spheres. He photographed the NAACP's everyday activism—everyone who was anyone speaking from a stage, shaking hands, posing for a group shot. He photographed high school and college life—classes, club meetings, dances, sports events, awards ceremonies, graduation ceremonies, and just being on campus with friends. He photographed beauty queens. He photographed friends. He photographed himself and his cars.

When Williams documented Black life in the mid-twentieth century, he documented activism. The ordinary became extraordinary—schoolchildren, teachers, barbers, laborers, launderers, cooks, and professors in marches downtown, prayers at the city square, picketing on hot city sidewalks, and incarceration in a stockade. Williams's ability to overcome the bias of film and photographic chemicals—their calibration to White skin—enabled him to capture the intent and intensity of Black faces and the light and bright and dark of Black skin.

The most familiar images of the civil rights movement came from White photographers documenting the 1960s violence in Alabama and Mississippi for White-owned media. Matt Herron, of *Life*, *Look*, and *Newsweek* magazines, photographed Freedom Summer. James Karales, of *Look* magazine, photographed the Selma to Montgomery march. Bill Hudson, of the AP, and Charles Lee Moore, of *Life* magazine, photographed violence in Birmingham.

This was dangerous work for anyone. But for Black photographers, assaults by White protesters were guaranteed, and police protection was nonexistent. The destruction of an expensive camera could be career-ending. Some Black photographers worked on contract, as Williams did for *Jet*. Many took freelance assignments with no guarantee of publication and pay, documenting local events for faraway Black-owned media while not infrequently holding more than one job. Doris Adelaide Derby, a field secretary for the Student Nonviolent Coordinating Committee and photographer for Southern Media Inc. in Jackson, Mississippi, photographed the funeral of the four girls killed in the bombing of the Sixteenth Street Baptist Church in Birmingham. James Gibson Peeler, owner of Peeler's Portrait Studio in Charlotte, North Carolina, and freelancer for the *Afro-American*, photographed

Charlotte marches and sit-ins. Ernest C. Withers Sr., owner of Ernest C. Withers Sr. Photographers in Memphis, Tennessee, and freelancer for *Ebony* and *Jet*, photographed the Emmett Till murder trial in Sumner, Mississippi.[12]

A lucky few held staff posts that contributed to their recognition. Alexander M. Rivera Jr., reporter and photographer for the *Pittsburgh Courier* and the National Negro Press Association, investigated South Carolina and Georgia lynchings and, in federal court in Charleston, South Carolina, photographed attorneys, petitioners, and supporters at a *Briggs v. Elliott* hearing. The much-celebrated Gordon Parks, the first Black staff photographer for *Life* and the first Black director of a Hollywood studio film, photographed the *Briggs* doll test, during which Black children compared dark-skinned and light-skinned baby dolls and chose the doll they preferred. He also photographed life under Jim Crow in Mobile, Alabama. Moneta John Sleet Jr., staff photographer for *Ebony* magazine, frequently photographed the Rev. Dr. Martin Luther King Jr. Sleet won a Pulitzer Prize in 1969, the first Black man and first Black photojournalist to do so, for his portrait at King's funeral of widow Coretta Scott King and daughter Bernice King.

Black-owned publications reached fewer people, thus so did the photographs. Black-owned newspapers bestowed photo credits erratically, so many published photos are unattributed. Black photographers' studios burned. Their photo archives were discarded by themselves or their descendants. We do not know who and what we are missing. This may seem the way of the world, but an incomplete and thereby biased record of the past creates a skewed present and future.

In his ninth decade Williams sustains a workday that flows from 10 a.m. to 10 p.m. seven days a week. He does not joke when he says, "I'm a workaholic." Having secured preservation of his film negatives, he intends to fully identify people, places, and events, a large and daunting task. He initiated a capital campaign for his nonprofit Cecil Williams Civil Rights Museum, its funding sources as varied as the Southern Poverty Law Center, BMW, and the South Carolina Arts Commission. He expects to ensure a larger, lasting venue.

There is more. At least twice a month Williams shows his photographs and tells the stories behind them anywhere and everywhere. He travels to schools, churches, civic meetings, libraries, and museums throughout the state. "I believe more is to be done to tell the true story of a civil rights movement that included far more than a few larger-than-life heroes," said Williams. Always mission-driven, Williams wants to amplify and augment the historical record with what he considers a fuller and truer story of the civil rights movement. He wants to further interpret those decades by correcting errors, filling in the gaps, and bringing forth the forgotten. He is an authority. He does not hesitate to say, "I was there; I took the pictures."

NOTES

In the endnotes below, several South Carolina newspapers are frequently cited. After the initial reference, citations for these newspapers do not include the state or the city, unless the city is part of the newspaper's full name. South Carolina newspapers with these shortened citations include the *Florence Morning News*, in Florence; the *Greenville News*, in Greenville; the *Herald* and *Evening Herald* in Rock Hill; the *Index-Journal* in Greenwood; the *State* and the *Columbia Record* in Columbia; and the *Times and Democrat* in Orangeburg. The *Afro-American*, founded and published in Baltimore, Maryland, also included regional editions in Washington, DC; Philadelphia, Pennsylvania; Richmond, Virginia; and Newark, New Jersey.

THE 1940S

1. While Cecil Williams could walk the garden's acreage, he could not use the pond that served as a swimming pool; it was not desegregated until 1969. Henry P. Leifermann, "Not Yet Still Means Never: Orangeburg, South Carolina," *New South*, 24, no. 4 (Fall 1969): 71.

2. Alfred Leroy Williams, born February 20, 1933, studied music at State A&M before leaving for New York City. A well-known bartender at Harlem's Baby Grand Lounge, he often played saxophone with artists from the nearby Apollo Theater. He died March 24, 1999. "Alfred Leroy Williams," *Times and Democrat* (Orangeburg, SC), March 27, 1999, 9; George Rufus Greene Jr., interview by author, January 4, 2022.

3. Frederick Douglass, "Lecture on Pictures," in *Picturing Frederick Douglass: An Illustrated Biography of the Nineteenth Century's Most Photographed American* (New York: W.W. Norton & Company, 2015), 127, 130–31.

4. $7.50 in 1949 is valued at $94.28 in 2023 dollars.

5. For a comprehensive review of Jim Crow laws state-by-state, see Stetson Kennedy's unusual and thorough *Jim Crow Guide to the USA: The Laws, Customs, and Etiquette Governing the*

Conduct of Nonwhites and Other Minorities as Second-Class Citizens (Tuscaloosa: University of Alabama Press, 2011). The Jim Crow Museum, at Ferris State University in Big Rapids, Michigan, attributes the use of "Jim Crow" to a song popularized by Thomas Dartmouth "Daddy" Rice, a White singer and dancer who performed in Blackface makeup. See "Who Was Jim Crow," Jim Crow Museum, Ferris State University, accessed February 17, 2023, https://www.ferris.edu/HTMLS/news/jimcrow/who/index.htm.

6. Kim Parker et al., "Race and Multiracial Americans in the U.S. Census," in *Multiracial in America: Proud, Diverse, and Growing in Number*, Pew Research Center, accessed February 17, 2023, https://www.pewresearch.org/social-trends/2015/06/11/.

7. Ibid.; Jennifer L. Hochschild and Brenna M. Powell, "Racial Organization and the United States Census 1850–1930," *Studies in American Political Development*, 22, no. 1 (2008): 59–96; Daniel J. Sharfstein, "Crossing the Color Line: Racial Migration and the One-Drop Rule, 1600–1860," *Minnesota Law Review* 592 (2007): 651.

8. S.C. Const. of 1895, art. III § 33; S. C. Const. art. XI § 7, December 4, 1895.

9. I. N. Rendall Harper Jr. left Orangeburg at 13 to attend St. Emma Military Academy in Powhatan, Virginia. He graduated from Duquesne University in Pittsburgh, Pennsylvania, was among the first Black employees working in sales for IBM, and, in 1977, founded the American Micrographics Company. I.N. Rendall Harper Jr., obituary, *Pittsburgh (PA) Post-Gazette*, 9 May 2020, accessed February 13, 2022, https://obituaries.post-gazette.com/obituary/.

10. Berry Brewton, "The Mestizos of South Carolina." *American Journal of Sociology* 51, no.1 (1945): 34, 36–37.

11. R. Scott Baker, *Paradoxes of Desegregation: African American Struggles for Educational Equity in Charleston, South Carolina, 1926–1972* (Columbia: University of South Carolina Press, 2006), 31–33, 76–82.

12. Wrighten v. Board of Trustees, 72 F. Supp. 948 (E.D.S.C. 1947); Gil Kuvojich, "Equal Opportunity in Higher Education and the Black Public College: The Era of Separate But Equal," *Minnesota Law Review*, 1387 (1987): 128.

13. Thurgood Marshall to James Myles Hinton and Harold Boulware, September 30, 1947, part 26, series A, reel 18, frame 454, NAACP Papers; Modjeska Monteith Monteith Simkins, newspaper column transcript, *Journal and Guide*, May 24, 1947, Modjeska Simkins Papers, South Caroliniana Library, University of South Carolina, Columbia. Wrighten graduated in 1952 and practiced law in Charleston and Walterboro, South Carolina.

14. Carrie Butler was 15 years old when she became pregnant by the 23-year-old James Strom Thurmond. Their child Essie Mae Washington grew up in the care of an aunt and uncle in Pennsylvania, was introduced to her mother in 1938, and to her father in 1944. Thurmond served in the state senate from 1933–1938, as governor of South Carolina from 1947–1951, ran for president in 1948, and served as a US senator from 1956–2003. Essie Mae

Washington-Williams and William Stadiem, *Dear Senator: A Memoir by the Daughter of Strom Thurmond* (New York: Harper Collins, 2005), 15, 41–42, 67, 101, 115.

15. Plessy v. Ferguson, 163 U.S. 537 (1896); Patricia Sullivan, *Lift Every Voice: The NAACP and the Making of the Civil Rights Movement* (New York: The New Press, 2009) 157, 159.

16. NAACP, *A Study of Educational Inequalities in South Carolina* (NAACP/Harmon Foundation: 1936), 16 mm film, 3 reels, National Archives and Records Administration, College Park, MD.

17. Lloyd L. Gaines Digital Collection, University of Missouri School of Law, accessed October 10, 2021, https://scholarship.law.missouri.edu/gaines/; *State ex. rel. Gaines v. Canada*, 113 S.W. 2d 783 (Mo. 1938); *Missouri ex rel. Gaines v. Canada*, 305 U.S. 337 (1938).

18. *University v. Murray*, 169 Md. 478 (1936). Murray graduated in 1938 and practiced law in Baltimore. *Sweatt v. Painter*, 210 S. W. 2d 442 (Tex. Civ. App. 1948). In 1952 Sweatt left law school without a degree. In 1954 he earned a master's from the University of Atlanta Graduate School of Social Work. Afterward, he worked for the NAACP and the Urban League.

19. McLaurin v. Oklahoma State Regents for Higher Education, 87 F. Supp. 526 (1948), 87 F. Supp. 528 (1949); McLaurin v. Oklahoma State Regents, 339 U.S. 637.

20. Sipuel v. Board of Regents of Univ. of Oklahoma, 190 P. 2d 437 (Okla. 1948), 199 Okla. 586; 1948 Okla. 17; 322 U.S. 631 (1948). Sipuel practiced law in her hometown of Chickasha, Oklahoma.

21. Peter F. Lau, *Democracy Rising: South Carolina and the Fight for Black Equality Since 1865* (Lexington: University Press of Kentucky, 2006), 110, 114; Claudia Smith Brinson, *Stories of Struggle: The Clash Over Civil Rights in South Carolina* (Columbia: University of South Carolina Press, 2020), 1–30.

22. Robert L. Carter, *A Matter of Law: A Memoir of Struggle in the Cause of Equal Rights* (New York: New Press, 2005), 62; Joseph Armstrong "Jay" DeLaine Jr., interview by the author, April 2003; Ferdinand Pearson, interview by the author, April 2003; Phynise "Piney" Pearson Witherspoon, interview by the author, 2004; Jesse Pearson, interview by the author, 2004.

23. Joseph Armstrong DeLaine, fifty-second installment, *AME Christian Recorder*, Joseph A. DeLaine Papers, South Caroliniana Library; Harry Briggs et al, to the Board of Trustees for School District no. 22, Clarendon County, Board of Education, 11 November 1949. A copy of the petition can be found at Petition, 1949, Nov. 11 (Clarendon County, SC), Harry Briggs et al. to the Board of Trustees for School District No. 22 (Clarendon County, SC), DeLaine Papers, accessed February 17, 2003, https://digital.tcl.sc.edu/digital/collection/jad/id/373/.

24. *Plessy v. Ferguson*; Seventy-Second Annual Report of the State Superintendent of Education of the State of South Carolina, 1940, January 20, 1941, 144, 145, 148.

25. Resolution Adopted by S.C. Conference of the NAACP, October 9-11, 1948, part 26, reel 18, frames 801-2, NAACP Papers.

26. A 4 × 5 Speed Graphic in the late 1940s cost from $95.00 to $160, the equivalent of $1,194 to $2,011 in 2023 dollars.

27. Jesse Pearson, interview by the author, 2003.

28. Harry Briggs et al., to the Board of Trustees for School District no. 22, Clarendon County, Board of Education, 11 November 1949. A copy of the petition can be found at Petition, 1949, Nov. 11, (Clarendon County, SC) Harry Briggs et al. to the Board of Trustees for School District No. 22 (Clarendon County, SC), DeLaine Papers, South Caroliniana Library, accessed February 17, 2003, https://digital.tcl.sc.edu/digital/collection/jad/id/373/; Joseph Armstrong DeLaine, fifty-second installment, *AME Christian Recorder*, DeLaine Papers.

THE 1950S

1. The 1947 Journey of Reconciliation, organized by the Fellowship of Reconciliation and the Congress of Racial Equality, was the forerunner to CORE's 1961 Freedom Rides. Smith v. Allwright, 321 U.S. 649, (1944); Elmore v. Rice, 72 F. Supp. 516 (E.D.S.C. 1947); Rice v. Elmore, 165 F. Supp. 2d 387 (4th Cir. 1947); Brown v. Baskin, 80 F. Supp. 1017 (E.D.S.C. 1948); Baskin v. Brown, 174 F. 2d 391 (4th Cir. 1949).

2. Eighty-Third Annual Report of the State Superintendent of the State of South Carolina, 1951 (Columbia: South Carolina Budget and Control Board, 1951), 12, 234–36, 238.

3. Eighty-Third Annual Report, 59, 236, 237; Wrighten v. Board of Trustees, 72 F. Supp. 948 (E.D.S.C. 1947). The eight colleges and universities for Black students in South Carolina included Benedict College and Allen University in Columbia, Friendship Junior College and Clinton Normal and Industrial Institute in Rock Hill, Morris College in Sumter, Voorhees School and Junior College in Denmark, and Claflin University and State A&M, renamed South Carolina State College in 1954, in Orangeburg.

4. William C. Hine, *South Carolina State University: A Black Land-Grant College in Jim Crow America* (Columbia: University of South Carolina Press, 2018), 2–3, 10–11. Until its name change the school was formally called The Colored Normal Industrial Agricultural & Mechanical College of South Carolina. Lauritza Salley Hill, *African Americans of Orangeburg County* (Charleston, SC: Arcadia Publishing, 2012), 24, 30; Claflin University Fact Book, 2014–2016, Office of Institutional Effectiveness, Orangeburg, SC, 3.

5. Hine, *South Carolina State*, 116–18; Rosenwald School Building Program in South Carolina, 1917–1932, National Register of Historic Places, National Park Service, accessed November 22, 2021, http://www.nationalregister.sc.gov/MPS/MPS050.pdf; Daniel Aarons and Bhaskar Mazumdar, "The Impact of Rosenwald Schools on Black Achievement," Federal Reserve Bank of Chicago, October 2009, accessed February 18, 2023, https://files.eric.ed.gov/fulltext/ED509827.pdf; Brinson, "Separate, Never Equal: White Schools, Colored Schools," *Stories of Struggle*, accessed November 22, 2021, https://storiesofstruggle.com/. Julia Washington later married M. Maceo Nance, president of SC State College from 1967 to 1986.

6. "South Carolina's Plot to Starve Negroes," *Jet*, October 20, 1955, 8–13.

7. George Rufus Greene Jr., interview by the author, January 4, 2022.

8. Sweatt v. Painter, 339 U.S. 629 (1950); McLaurin v. Oklahoma State Regents, 339 U.S. 637 (1950); Henderson v. United States, 339 U.S. 816 (1950).

9. Trezzvant W. Anderson, "World News," *Pittsburgh Courier*, June 17, 1950, 2; Sweatt v. Painter; James L. Hicks, "All-Out War Mapped," *Afro-American*, July 8, 1950, 1, 2. "End of Jim Crow Predicted," *Pittsburgh Courier*, June 17, 1950, 1, 4; "233 Students Now in Dixie Colleges," *Afro-American*, November 18, 1950, 20.

10. W. Lewis Burke and William C. Hine, "The South Carolina State College Law School: Its Roots, Creation, and Legacy," in *Matthew J. Perry: The Man, His Times, and His Legacy,* ed. W. Lewis Burke and Belinda Gergel, (Columbia: University of South Carolina Press, 2004), 21.

11. Williams's one-dollar flashbulb would cost $12.57 in 2023 dollars. Adam Burns, "Timetable (1940)" in "The Champion," American-Rails.com, accessed February 18, 2023, https://www.american-rails.com/champion.html#gallery[pageGallery]/1/.

12. Briggs v. Elliott, Complaint Against Segregated Schools, Civ. A. No. 2657, (E.D.S.C. 1950), accessed November 22, 2021, https://www.archives.gov/exhibits/documented-rights/exhibit/section5/detail/briggs-complaint.html.

13. "People Are Talking About," *Jet,* August 11, 1955, 45; "Forecast," *Jet,* February 21, 1952, 19; "S.C. NAACP Makes New Demand," *Jet,* August 13, 1953, 30; "Near-Blind S.C. Wife," *Jet,* August 11, 1955, 17; Simeon Booker with Carol McCabe Booker, *Shocking the Conscience: A Reporter's Account of the Civil Rights Movement* (Jackson: University Press of Mississippi, 2013), 84.

14. Alexander M. Rivera, "Dixie Holds Breath," *Pittsburgh Courier*, June 9, 1951, 1, 2; Rivera, "Courier Catches Highlights," *Pittsburgh Courier*, June 9, 1951, 2; Albert J. Dunmore, "Old Year Had Its Setbacks Too!" *Pittsburgh Courier*, December 29, 1951, 2.

15. Alexander M. Rivera, interview by Kieran Taylor, November 30, 2001, C-0297, transcript, Southern Oral History Program Collection, University of North Carolina at Chapel Hill, Chapel Hill, North Carolina; Simeon Booker, "From the Notebook," *Jet*, December 26, 1957, 13; "Renowned Photojournalist Alex Rivera Dies," North Carolina Central University, October 24, 2008, accessed February 18, 2023, https://nccueaglepride.com/news/2008/10/24/; Sid Bedingfield, *Newspaper Wars: Civil Rights and White Resistance in South Carolina, 1935-1965* (Chicago: University of Illinois Press, 2017), 144–48; "Newspaper Publishers Evaluate Desegregation," *Afro-American*, January 28, 1956, 2.

16. Testimonial Honoring Parent Plaintiffs and Their Children, June 17, 1951, part 26, reel 19, frames 343–49, NAACP Papers.

17. Brinson, Stories of Struggle, 50–53.

18. Edward C. "E. C." Jones Jr., Cecil Williams, photograph, Joseph A. DeLaine Sr. and His Family Looking at Their Burned Home, October 10, 1951, South Caroliniana Library, accessed February 18, 2023, https://digital.tcl.sc.edu/digital/collection/jad/id/870/rec/33; B.B. DeLaine,

interview by the author, 2003, 2004; FBI, File# HQ 44-3077, 24 March 1952, 26-28; Ophelia DeLaine Gona, *Dawn of Desegregation: J. A. De Laine and Briggs v. Elliott* (Columbia, University of South Carolina Press, 2011) 154–55.

19. Joseph Armstrong "Jay" DeLaine Jr., Brumit Belton "B. B." DeLaine, interviews by the author, 2003, 2004; James Morris Seals, interview by the author, April 2003; Juanita Richburg Wells, interview by the author, 2006; Brinson, *Stories of Struggle*, 52–53, 81, 83, 85–88, 90.

20. Rebekah Dobrasko, "South Carolina's Equalization Schools 1951-1960," accessed November 30, 2021, http://www.scequalizationschools.org/history.html.

21. Rhiannon Walker, "Althea Gibson, Arthur Ashe: Complete List of American Tennis Association Winners," August 4, 2017, accessed September 2, 2022, https://andscape.com/features/; "Negro Tennis Talent Praised," *State*, November 14, 1951, 16.

22. "1950 Tennis Champ, ATA," *Indianapolis (IN) Recorder*, September 2, 1950, 11.

23. Brenda Lillian Williams earned a bachelor's from SC State, a master's in hospital administration from Virginia Commonwealth University, in Richmond, Virginia, and served as vice president with the Regional Medical Center of Orangeburg and Calhoun counties. She died February 7, 2021; "Brenda L. Williams, June 22, 1952," Glover's Funeral Home, accessed February 19, 2023, https://www.gloversfuneralhome.com/obituary/Brenda-Williams.

24. Greene, interview by the author

25. John Egerton, *Speak Now Against the Day* (Chapel Hill: University of North Carolina Press, 1995), 549–50; Bedingfield, *Newspaper Wars*, 124–27; Brinson, *Stories of Struggle*, 14–16, 177.

26. United States Commission on Civil Rights, Equal Protection of the Laws in Public Higher Education, 1960 (Washington, DC: US Government Printing Office, 1961), 83

27. Brown v. Board of Education of Topeka (1), 347 U.S. 483, 1954; Brown v. Board of Education of Topeka (2), 349 U.S. 294, 1955.

28. Al Walburn, "Citizen Council Is Formed," *Times and Democrat*, August 11, 1955, 1, 12; Bob Pierce, "Citizens Councils, NAACP Draw Lines," *State*, September 21, 1955, 13, 19; "Citizens Councils Form Statewide Organization," *State*, October 11, 1955, 1; "Probe of NAACP Work On Campus To Be Asked," *State*, September 23, 1955, 35; "Mixing Protests," *State*, August 26, 1955, 1, 9; W. D. Workman, "Citizens Groups Form," *Greenville News*, September 18, 1955, 4; "Lieutenant Governor Addresses Elloree Lions," *Times and Democrat*, October 11, 1955, 1.

29. "NAACP Hopes to Top Racial Barriers," *Times and Democrat*, August 18, 1955, 1; "Negroes Desire Names Off," *Times and Democrat*, August 12, 1955, 1: "Negroes Ask Off NAACP," *Times and Democrat*, August 19, 1955, 1; "Citizens Council Is Formed."

30. "Huge Crowd at Citizens Meeting," *Times and Democrat*, August 30, 1955, 1, 10; "Office Opened," *Times and Democrat*, September 3, 1955, 1; "Plot to Starve Negroes."

31. Rivera, "Courier Exposes Carolina 'Squeeze,'" *Pittsburgh Courier*, September 17, 1955, 1, 4.

32. John H. McCray, "Those Dred Scott Overtones," *Afro-American*, November 24, 1956, 4; McCray, "NAACP Aid Routs Elloree Hate Group," *Afro-American*, April 14, 1956, 3.

33. "NAACP Official Blasted by Klan," *Times and Democrat*, December 4, 1955, 1; "Mayor Knew Nothing," *Times and Democrat*, December 5, 1955, 7; Subcommittee on Constitutional Rights, "Elloree, S.C." in "Intimidation, Reprisal and Violence," *Civil Rights-1959, Hearings Before the Subcommittee on Constitutional Rights*, 86th Cong. 1959, 1580; McCray, "NAACP Leader Dares Klan," *Afro-American*, December 17, 1955, 1, 2; "Overhaul City Hall," *Crisis 72*, no. 10 (November 1965): 293 ; McCray, "Tired of Starving," *Afro-American*, December 24, 1955, 5.

34. "Petition Signatures Dropping," *Times and Democrat*, September 10, 1955, 1. Redemptorists, a Catholic order whose priests came to Orangeburg in 1930, served as missionaries in needy communities. The Redemptorists established Christ the King as an all-Black congregation and school. Cecil J. Williams, *Freedom & Justice: Four Decades of the Civil Rights Struggle As Seen by a Black Photographer of the Deep South* (Macon, Georgia: Mercer University Press, 1995), 78–79, 96.

35. Candace Cunningham, "Ahead of Their Times: Black Teachers and Their Community in the Immediate Post-Brown Years" (master's thesis, University of South Carolina, 2016), 10; "Test Case on NAACP Pressure," *State*, September 8, 1955, 3.

36. Rivera, "Organize S.C. Boycott," *Pittsburgh Courier*, September 24, 1955, 1, 4; Carl Rowan and Richard P. Kleeman, "Boycott Becomes New Segregation Weapon," *Minneapolis (MN) Star Tribune*, January 30, 1956, 11; Earl Brown, "Let's Battle Back," New York *Amsterdam News*, November 5, 1955, 10.

37. McCray, "Tired of Starving"; "Owner Surrenders," *Jet*, October 13, 1955, 12; "A Way of Life," *Times and Democrat*, October 16, 1955, 4.

38. "City Employees Allowed to Join," *Times and Democrat*, September 8, 1955, 1; Nicholas Rademacher, "Pursuing and Impeding: Civil Rights and the Redemptorist Mission in Orangeburg, South Carolina, 1930–1955," *U.S. Catholic Historian* 39, no. 4 (2021): 101–25; Williams, *Freedom and Justice*, 78; "Life Is Threatened," *Times and Democrat*, December 11, 1955, 1; Rivera, "Courier Exposes Carolina 'Squeeze,'" 1; "SC Seeks Probe of NAACP," *Jet*, October 13, 1955, 24; "Probe of NAACP Work On Campus To Be Asked"; "Petition Signers Stand Pat," *Afro-American*, September 17, 1955, 5.

39. Family of Matthew D. McCollom, interview by the author, 2008.

40. *Ibid.*; "This is SCLC," Southern Christian Leadership Conference, n.d., Civil Rights Movement Archive, accessed May 17, 2022, https://www.crmvet.org/docs/61_sclc_this-is.pdf. McCollom, "Reaching Out for Spiritual Reality," n.d., McCollom Papers, H. V. Manning Library, Claflin University.

41. "Mrs. Hazel F. Pierce," *Times and Democrat*, January 14, 1982, 16; "Sunlight Club," *Times and Democrat*, March 7, 1976, 19.

42. "NAACP Secretary Disavows Statement," *Times and Democrat*, August 25, 1955, 1; "Citizens Group to Meet," *Times and Democrat*, August 29, 1955, 1, 8.

43. John E. Brunson purchased the shop in 1975. "Local Barber Hangs Up His Shears," *Times and Democrat*, June 1, 1988, 11; "John E. Brunson," *Times and Democrat*, March 31, 1998, 14.

44. NAACP, "Lynching of School Boy," Manuscript Division, Library of Congress, accessed September 5, 2022, https://www.loc.gov/exhibits/naacp/the-civil-rights-era.html#obj9; "Chicago Boy, 14, Kidnapped," *Jet*, September 8, 1955, 3–4; "Nation Horrified," *Jet*, September 15, 1955, 69; Theodore Coleman, "100,000 View Battered Body," *Pittsburgh Courier*, September 10, 1955, 1; William Huie, "Shocking Story of Approved Killing," *Look*, January 24, 1956, 46–49; Jill Collen Jefferson, "Journalist William Huie Concealed Lynchers," *Mississippi Free Press* (Jackson), September 1, 2021, accessed November 22, 2021, https://www.mississippifreepress.org/15462; Gene Roberts and Hank Klibanoff, *The Race Beat: The Press, the Civil Rights Struggle, and the Awakening of a Nation* (New York: Alfred A. Knopf, 2006), 101–3; "100 Photographs: Emmett Till," *Time*, July 10, 2016, accessed November 22, 2021, https://time.com/4399793/. Mamie Till Bradley married Gene Mobley on June 24, 1957, and changed her last name to Till-Mobley.

45. "Acts to Bypass Integration," *Florence (SC) Morning News*, March 10, 1955, 1; "S.C. Determined to Resist," *Columbia Record*, November 4, 1955, 7; Workman, "Timmerman Hits Both Parties," *Charlotte Observer*, October 18, 1955, 1; "NAACP May Owe State $7,300," *Columbia Record*, November 11, 1955, 8; McCray, "How They Manage to Do It," *Afro-American*, November 19, 1955, 4; "Shotgun Blasts," *Afro-American*, October 8, 1955, 18; "Council Squeezes Nonpetitioner Too," *Afro-American*, October 8, 1955, 18.

46. Rivera, "Organize S.C. Boycott"; Rivera, "Fight Squeeze With Boycott," *Pittsburgh Courier*, October 8, 1955, 1, 7; Rivera, "Courier Exposes Carolina 'Squeeze,'" 1; "White Council Squeeze Eases," *Afro-American*, October 15, 1955, 3; Earl M. Middleton with Joy W. Barnes, *Knowing Who I Am: A Black Entrepreneur's Struggle and Success in the American South* (Columbia: University of South Carolina Press, 2008), 93.

47. "World Today," *Pittsburgh Courier*, October 15, 1955, 4; Lou Falkner Williams, *The Great South Carolina Ku Klux Klan Trials, 1871–1872* (Athens: University of Georgia Press, 1996), 44–45; Equal Justice Institute, table 2, "Lynchings in the South," table 6, "Most Active Lynching Counties," in *Lynching in America: Confronting the Legacy of Racial Terror*, 3d ed. (Montgomery, AL: Equal Justice Initiative, 2017).

48. "Flames Raze Church," *Afro-American*, October 15, 1955, 22; "S.C. Whites Burn Church," *Jet*, October 20, 1955, 3–5; "Plot to Starve Negroes"; "How He Outwitted Lynchers," *Jet*, November 3, 1955, 6–8.

49. Hattie Mobley, "J. J. Sulton and Sons Lumber Company," *WPA Federal Project Materials on African American Life, South Carolina*, South Caroliniana, accessed February 19, 2023, https://digital.tcl.sc.edu/digital/collection/wpafwp/id/2167/; "J.J. Sulton Mill Destroyed," *Times and Democrat*, February 15, 1943, 3; Joyce W. Milkie, "Family Business," *Times and Democrat*, February 18, 1996, 21, 26.

50. "Civil Rights Pioneer," *Times and Democrat*, April 19, 2008, 1, 5; Cecil Williams, O*ut-of-the-Box in Dixie: Cecil Williams' Photography of the South Carolina Events That Changed America* (Orangeburg, SC: Cecil J. Williams, 2007), 100.

51. McCollom, "Reaching Out for Spiritual Reality."

52. James Tracy, *Direct Action: Radical Pacifism from the Union Eight to the Chicago Seven* (Chicago: University of Chicago Press, 1996), 88–90.

53. "Solid South Split," *Times and Democrat*, November 28, 1955, 1, 6.

54. Workman, "Relations Go Bad," *Greenville News*, December 4, 1955, 1, 8.

55. "NAACP To Use Claflin Gym," *Times and Democrat*, November 24, 1955, 1; Rivera, "Fight Squeeze,"; "State College Students Voice Several Protests," *Times and Democrat*, March 29, 1956, 1.

56. Middleton, *Knowing Who I Am*, 76, 90–91. Middleton opened Middleton and Associate Realtors in 1960. In 1974 he won a seat in the state legislature and served for ten years. Williams believes that Laler Cook De Costa, an SC State professor, not Julius I. Washington, went to Montgomery.

57. "Montgomery Bus Boycott, December 5, 1955, to December 20, 1956," Martin Luther King Jr. Research and Education Institute, Stanford University, accessed February 20, 2023, https://kinginstitute.stanford.edu/encyclopedia/.

58. McCray, "They Now See the Light," *Afro-American*, January 28, 1956, 1. Among the Black activists murdered in 1955 in Mississippi was the Rev. George W. Lee, who worked for voting rights in Belzoni, Mississippi, and was shot dead by assailants in a car that pulled up beside his. "Miss. Pastor Slain; Blame KKK Gang," *Pittsburgh (PA) Courier*, May 21, 1955, 1, 4; "Church Blasts Terror Reign in Mississippi," *Kingsport (TN) Times-News*, December 25, 1955, 10.

59. "Put Yourself on Record," *State*, August 21, 1955, 11; Workman, "Councils of Citizens to Form Group," *Greenville News*, October 11, 1955, 1; Workman, "Relations Go Bad."

60. Fred Henderson Moore, interview by the author, 2008; Fred Henderson Moore, interview by Felice Knight, in *Champions of Civil and Human Rights in South Carolina*, (Columbia: University of South Carolina Press, 2016), 2: 25–26. Moore did not know the cause of his disability and would sometimes offer a variety of explanations.

61. Moore, interview by the author.

62. Census Bureau, Historical Statistics on Educational Attainment in the United States, 1940–2000, Table 3, accessed November 22, 2021, https://www.census.gov/data/tables/2000/dec/phc-t-41.html; Moore, interview by the author; Moore, *Champions*, 2:32–33.

63. "Probe of NAACP At SC State Asked," *State*, January 25, 1956, 17; "Complete Text of Resolution," *Times and Democrat*, January 25, 1956, 1.

64. "Peace Feelers Out," *Afro-American*, February 11, 1956, 19.

65. Rademacher, "Pursuing and Impeding," 123; McCray, "Would Speed the End of Jim Crow," *Afro-American*, February 4, 1956, 4; "Bill Passed to Close Colleges," *State*, March 25, 1956, 60; Tom MacRae, "Turner Denies Report," *Times and Democrat*, March 27, 1956, 1.

66. McCray, "Hang S.C. State Prexy in Effigy," *Afro-American*, April 7, 1956, 1; Hine, *South Carolina State*, 233; "Head Denies Legislator 'Hung,'" *State*, March 27, 1956, 18; "This Time It is Hughes," photo, *Afro-American*, April 14, 1956, 3 "This Figure," photo, *Afro-American*, April 14, 1956, 6; "No Comment on State Resolution," *Greenville News*, March 27, 1956, 5.

67. "Set Up Pickets," *Greenville News*, March 31, 1956, 1; "Not for Pursuit of Happiness," *Afro-American*, April 14, 1956, 3; "Probe of NAACP Work On Campus To Be Asked," *State*, September 23, 1955, 35.

68. "SC Educators Challenge State," *Afro-American*, March 31, 1956, 16; "Police at SC State," *Afro-American*, April 14, 1956, 8; "Students Remain Out of Classes," *Times and Democrat*, April 12, 1956, 12.

69. "Police at SC State," *Afro-American*, April 14, 1956, 8; "Students Remain Out," 12.

70. "State College on Strike," *Times and Democrat*, April 10, 1956, 1; "Some Students Return to Class," *Times and Democrat*, April 11, 1956, 10; "Students Remain Out," 12; "Strike Ends at SC State," *Times and Democrat*, April 13, 1956, 10; "Strikers Will Return," *State*, April 13, 1956, 1, 2; "Students Walk Out," *Greenville News*, April 14, 1956, 6; "Ultimatum is Issued," *Times and Democrat*, April 14, 1956, 1, 3.

71. "State Expelled the Cream," *Sumter (SC) Daily Item*, June 26, 1956, 7, 13; "NAACP Wants College Closed," *Columbia Record*, June 26, 1956, 16; McCray, "Jackie Is Right," *Afro-American*, February 11, 1956, 4.

72. Moore, interview by the author.

73. McCray, "Jeer S.C. President," *Afro-American*, May 5, 1956, 1, 2; "Ouster Protested," *Index-Journal* (Greenwood, SC), April 27, 1956, 10; "Strike Situation Seen Ended," *State*, April 28, 1956, 15.

74. Five dollars would be worth $54.99 in 2023: $50 to $75 would be worth $549.74 to $824.92. Francis H. Mitchell to Cecil Williams, May 4, 1956, in *Freedom & Justice*, 12.

75. "S.C. Ousters Confirmed," *Afro-American*, July 7, 1956, 1, 2; "Yesterday in Negro History," *Jet*, August 25, 1966, 11; Hine, *South Carolina State*, 236–42; McCray, "NAACP Probe Flops," *Afro-American*, September 8, 1956, 1, 19; Moore, interview by the author. Moore finished his bachelor's in June 1957 and then completed law school at Howard University in Washington, DC.

76. "Probe of NAACP at SC State Opens Wednesday," *State*, July 17, 1956, 13; "NAACP Activity Probed Further," *Times and Democrat*, August 20, 1956, 1; "Another Probe," *Gaffney (SC) Ledger*, August 30, 1956, 8; Hine, *South Carolina State*, 242; McCray, "NAACP Probe Flops."

77. On June 22, 1954, in Columbia, South Carolina, a White woman invited Sarah Mae Flemming to sit beside her on a city bus. When Flemming sat, she was ordered to the back of the bus by the driver and struck by the driver when she left the bus from the front door. She sued South Carolina Electric and Gas, which operated the bus line. The Fourth Circuit ruled that the

separate but equal doctrine had been repudiated. Flemming v. SCE&G, 239 F. 2d 277 (4th Cir. 1956). This was a precedent for the Alabama decision, Browder v. Gayle, 352 U.S. 903. Moore was testing compliance. "Bus J.C. Laws Dead," *Afro-American*, December 8, 1956, 3; "Students Continue," *Afro-American*, December 15, 1956, 12; McCray, "Stupid, Scared," *Afro-American*, January 26, 1957, 4; McCray, "We Don't Like It," *Afro-American*, February 16, 1957, 16; "Negro Who Lost Orangeburg Job," *Index-Journal*, November 14, 1957, 11; "Negro Integration Leader Buried," *Times and Democrat*, August 29, 1958, 5.

78. Mitchell to Williams, 12.

79. "NAACP Aid Routs Elloree Hate Group"; "Negro Student Strike," *Southern School News 2*, no. 11 (May 1956): 14; Modjeska M. Simkins, biographical sketch, 1964, Isaiah DeQuincey Newman Papers, South Carolina Political Collections, University of South Carolina, accessed February 20, 2023, https://digital.tcl.sc.edu/digital/collection/idn/id/5520; Martha Elizabeth Cunningham Monteith, biographical note, South Carolina Political Collections, accessed February 20, 2023, https://d2sw33rowd4mod.cloudfront.net/findingaids/scpc/Monteith.pdf.

80. "18 Negro Teachers Resign," *Sumter Daily Item*, May 17, 1956, 1; W. E. Solomon, "The Problem of Desegregation in South Carolina," *The Journal of Negro Education* 25, no. 3 (1956): 315–23, accessed November 16, 2021, https://doi.org/10.2307/2293441. Solomon served as executive secretary of the Palmetto Education Association, the Black teachers' organization. Elizabeth Lewis Cleveland, interview by the author, 2006; Juanita Richburg Wells, interview by the author, 2006.

81. "Martyred Teachers," *Jet*, n.d. 1957, 23, 24, in *Out-of-the-Box in Dixie*, 280; Stan Opotowsky, "Big Pocketbook Squeeze," *Afro-American*, March 16, 1957, 3.

82. "Negro Teachers Resign," *Times and Democrat*, May 17, 1956, 14; Wilkins to Hinton, May 21, 1956, part 20, reel 11, 000856, NAACP Papers; Henry Lee Moon, "Teachers Reject Anti-NAACP Oath," May 17, 1956, part 20, reel 11, 0193, NAACP Papers; "Eighteen Teachers Challenge," *State*, September 11, 1956, 1, 8; "24 New Teachers Hired," *Afro-American*, September 8, 1956, 3; Bryan v. Austin, 148 F. Supp. 563 (E.D.S.C. 1957); "Elloree Teachers' Suit," *Columbia Record*, January 24, 1957, 2. Teachers were also fired in other South Carolina counties, including Charleston and Williamsburg.

83. McCray, "Makes a Difference," *Afro-American*, November 3, 1956, 4; Workman, "Law Against NAACP Repealed," *Greenville News*, April 25, 1957, 17; "Law to Bar NAACP Teachers," *Florence Morning News*, May 7, 1957, 1; "Segregation Lines Held," *Columbia Record*, December 31, 1957, 1; "Dismissal of NAACP Case Sought," *State*, May 18, 1957, 13; "Barratry Bill Signed," *State*, February 9, 1957, 20.

84. Dawson v. Mayor City of Baltimore, 220 F. 2d 386 (4th Cir. 1955); "Use of Edisto Beach State Park," *Gaffney (SC) Ledger*, May 26, 1955, 15; Workman, "Uncertain Future," *Herald* (Rock Hill, SC), March 22, 1955, 2; Clark v. Flory, 141 F. Supp. 248 (E.D.S.C. 1956); "The Black Beach," Historic Charleston Foundation, accessed November 15, 2021, https://

www.historicmosquitobeach.com/home/history/. Within segregated parks, Black visitors had access to Campbells Pond at Cheraw State Park, Chesterfield County; Hunting Island, Beaufort County; Lake Greenwood State Park, Greenwood County; and Mill Creek, which neighbored Poinsett State Park, Sumter County.

85. "Autherine Lucy: Failed Integration Bid Left Lasting Legacy," *Judiciary News*, United States Courts, accessed December 7, 2021, https://www.uscourts.gov/news/2021/02/09/; "Before Little Rock: Mob Violence in Clinton, Tennessee, 1965," *Life*, September 17, 1956, accessed December 7, 2021, https://www.life.com/history/school-integration-clinton-history/. For a personal look at Little Rock, see Daisy Bates, *The Long Shadow of Little Rock: A Memoir* (Fayetteville: University of Arkansas Press, 1986).

86. Opotowsky, "Klan Tries to Muscle In," *Afro-American*, March 9, 1957, 3; "SC Klan Head Bagwell," Gaffney (SC), January 4, 1958, 4; Workman, "Klan Disregards State Mask Law," *Greenville News*, July 31, 1956, 1; "15 Leave Academy," *Afro-American*, July 21, 1956, 3; "Probe Kershaw Burnings," *Greenville News*, December 2, 1956, 1; "Camden Musician Flogged," *Florence Morning News*, December 29, 1956, 1; "Sol. Taylor Undecided," *Greenville News*, June 28, 1957, 43.

87. "Six-Foot Cross Burned," *Evening Herald*, January 18, 1957, 1; "Segregation Lines Held," *Columbia Record*, December 31, 1957, 1; "Bomb S.C. Home," *Jet*, December 5, 1957, 5; "Two Bombs Failed," *Columbia Record*, December 7, 1957, 1; "Jury Acquits Painter, McCullough," *Gaffney (SC) Ledger*, July 19, 1958, 1.

88. A later photo of Williams's ran twice in *Jet*. That photo showed a Conoco sign above the door. The Continental Oil Co., known as Conoco, responded by asking the distributor to remove the sign. "Experience Pays Off," *Jet*, November 9, 1961, 29; "Jet Pix Causes Action," *Jet*, January 11, 1962, 28.

89. "Red Shirts Hurl Corruption Charges," *Evening Herald*, April 28, 1958, 1; Workman, "Constitutional Hurdles," *Evening Herald*, May 21, 1958, 17.

90. "Neal Keeps His Gun," *Greenville News*, January 12, 1959, 1; "Race Fear," *Evening Herald*, April 17, 1959, 1, 2; "Elloree Rally," *Times and Democrat*, May 5, 1959, 1, 5.

91. FBI, Citizens Councils, Savannah Division, January 27, 1958, December 17, 1958, Internet Archive, n76, n82, accessed February 20, 2023, https://archive.org/details/CItizensCouncilMovement/CitCouncils-Savannah/page/n53/mode/; "Citizens Council Elects Manning and Smith," *State*, February 20, 1959, 33.

THE 1960S

1. Colorama Photography, ad, *Times and Democrat*, July 4, 1963, 7.

2. "Jet Stringer Takes Bride," *Jet*, May 21, 1959, 41.

3. Kennedy Wins," *State*, November 9, 1960, 1,7; "Kennedy Wins Election," UPI, November 9, 1960, UPI Archives, accessed February 21, 2023, https://www.upi.com/Archives/1960/11/09/.

4. Marvin Sykes, "Woolworth Made Target," *Greensboro (NC) Record*, February 2, 1960, B1.

5.   Miles Wolff, *Lunch at the 5 & 10* (Chicago: Ivan R. Dee, 1990), 11–35.

6.   James T. McCain, interview by the author, February 1994.

7.   August Meier and Elliott Rudwick, *CORE: A Study in the Civil Rights Movement, 1942-1968* (Chicago: University of Illinois Press, 1975) 4–13.

8.   "Negro Demonstrations Spread to Rock Hill," *Times and Democrat*, February 13, 1960, 1; C. A. Ivory, Summary of Sitdown Demonstrations, Rock Hill, SC, part 20, reel 10, frame 680, NAACP Papers.

9.   Thomas Walter Gaither, interviews by the author, February 2003 and September 12, 2011.

10. Ibid.; "Gaither Travels," *Claflin College Panther*, May 1960, Gaither scrapbook; James Farmer, *Lay Bare the Heart: An Autobiography of the Civil Rights Movement* (New York: New American Library, 1985), 188–89.

11. Gaither, interview by the author; "CORE Rules for Action," Congress of Racial Equality, accessed April 16, 2022, https://www.crmvet.org/docs/corerules.pdf; Gaither, "Orangeburg: Behind the Carolina Stockade," in *Sit-Ins: The Students Report*, CORE, May 1960.

12. Gaither, "An Orangeburg Story," n.d, draft for *Sit-Ins: The Students Report*, CORE, May 1960, Gaither personal papers.

13. "Second Demonstration," *State*, February 27, 1960, 13.

14. "Orangeburg Sitdown Staged," *State*, February 26, 1960, 1; "Word of Caution," *Times and Democrat*, February 26, 1960, 4.

15. Gaither, "Orangeburg Story"; Charles Frederick McDew, interview by the author, 1993.

16. Allen University, private and affiliated with the AME Church, and Benedict College, private and affiliated with American Baptist Churches USA, are in Columbia. Morris College, private and operated by the Baptist Educational and Missionary Convention in South Carolina, is in Sumter. Voorhees School and Junior College, private and affiliated with the Episcopal Church, is in Denmark.

17. "Fear of Unknown," *Jet*, April 7, 1960, 12–15.

18. Bob McHugh, "Lunch Counter Issue Spread," *Florence Morning News*, March 1, 1960, 3; "Negro Sitdown," *State*, March 2, 1960, 1, 7; "Segregation Disorder," *State*, February 18, 1960, 1. "Mayor Issues Warning," *Times and Democrat*, March 2, 1960, 1, 5. Gaither interview by author, December 13, 2013; McDew, interview by author, 2017; "At Least 40 Negro Students Arrested," *Evening Herald*, March 15, 1960, 1; "Five Sitdowners Are Jailed," *State*, March 16, 1960, 1, 5; "350 Negro Marchers," *Sumter Daily Item*, March 16, 1960, 1, 15.

19. Gaither interview by author, December 13, 2013; McDew, interview by author, 2017; "At Least 40 Negro Students Arrested," *Evening Herald*, March 15, 1960, 1; "Five Sitdowners Are Jailed," *State*, March 16, 1960, 1, 5; "350 Negro Marchers," *Sumter Daily Item*, March 16, 1960, 1, 15.

20. William V. Shannon, "Sitdowns in the South," *New York Post*, April 1, 1960, 39.

21. Gaither, "Orangeburg Story,"

22. "425 Negro Protesters Jailed," *State*, March 16, 1960, 1; Saunders Redding, "Negro Youth Impatient," *Jet*, April 21, 1960, 12–18.

23. Police Brutality, part 25, reel 30, frame 493, NAACP Papers.

24. Isaiah DeQuincey Newman, Newman Reports, part 20, reel 10, 683, NAACP Papers; "400 Negroes in Outdoor Cage," *San Francisco Chronicle*, March 16, 1960, 1; "Sit-In Student Freedom Fighters," *Jet*, April 21, 1960, 13; "Deplores All Violence," *Rock Island (IA) Argus*, March 16, 1960, 1; Trezzvant W. Anderson, "Sit-In Toll: 1,359 Arrests," *Pittsburgh Courier*, April 16, 1960, 29.

25. Earl M. Middleton became licensed to broker real estate and insurance and formed his own companies, including Middleton and Associates Realtors and The Middleton Insurance Agency. In 1974 he won a seat in the state legislature and served five terms.

26. Williams and Dean Livingston later became friends, Williams loaned his Hasselblad Distagon lens to Livingston for *Times and Democrat* photos. Livingston served as the paper's publisher from 1962 to 1999, and Williams spoke at his 2014 funeral.

27. "Two Negroes Turned Down," *Sumter Daily Item*, April 27, 1961, 15.

28. "Two Negroes Attempt to Register," *Columbia Record*, April 27, 1960, 3; Harry H. Lesesne, *A History of the University of South Carolina, 1940–2000* (Columbia: University of South Carolina Press, 2001), 138.

29. "Role of the NAACP in the Sit-Ins," part 21, reel 22, frame 299, NAACP Papers; "NAACP Units Continue Support of Students," press release, part 21, reel 22, frame 254, NAACP Papers.

30. "Color Bar at Church," *Newsday*, October 9, 1961, 4; "Turned Away," *Ft. Lauderdale (FL) News*, October 9, 1961, 34; "2 Turned Away," *Lancaster (PA) Intelligencer Journal*, October 9, 1961, 2; "Mayor Labels Church Incident as NAACP Stunt," *Times and Democrat*, October 9, 1961, 10.

31. "History of the Selective Service System," History and Records, Selective Service System, accessed September 19, 2022, https://www.sss.gov/history-and-records/. At the height of the Vietnam War, Black people composed 11 percent of the nation's population, Black men 16.3 percent of draftees, 27 percent of combat troops, and 25 percent of combat casualties and deaths. L. Deckle McLean, "The Black Man and the Draft," *Ebony*, August 1968, 61–65; Cleveland Sellers, "Black Men and the Draft," June 8, 1967, Student Nonviolent Coordinating Committee, accessed April 16, 2022, https://www.crmvet.org/docs/670608_sncc_draft.pdf.

32. Ibid.; In later years draft boards' racial discrimination was successfully challenged in court. Cleveland L. Sellers Jr. v. Marvin R. Laird, 395 U.S. 950 (1969); Clay v. United States, 397 F. 2d 901 (5th Cir. 1968), Clay v. United States, 403 U.S. 698 (1971).

33. Gloria Blackwell Rackley, interview by author, September 26, 2004.

34. Ibid.

35. Sadye K.M. Logan, ed., *The Spirit of an Activist: The Life and Work of I. DeQuincey Newman* (Columbia: University of South Carolina Press), 2014, xvii-xxvii.

36. Ibid.; Gloria Blackwell Rackley, interview by the author; Gloria Rackley Blackwell, Lurma Rackley, Jamelle Rackley-Riley, "The Rackleys, Wild Women of Orangeburg," interview by Marvin Lare, January 17, 2005, in *Champions of Civil and Human Rights in South Carolina*, vol. 3, https://digital.library.sc.edu/exhibits/champions/volume-2-contents/volume-1-part-4/. Note: Blackwell is the maiden name. The correct name order is Gloria Blackwell Rackley.

37. Ibid.; Gloria Blackwell Rackley, interview by the author; Gloria Rackley Blackwell, Jamelle Rackley-Riley, Lurma Rackley, "Roots of a Storm," interview by Lare, January 17, 2005, in *Champions*, vol. 2, accessed February 22, 2023, https://digital.library.sc.edu/exhibits/champions/volume-2-contents/volume-1-part-4/.

38. Ibid.; Rackley v. Board of Trustees of Orangeburg Hospital, 310 F. 2d 141 (4th Cir. 1962).

39. "Lawyer Jailed Then Released," *Newport (VA) News Daily Press*, November 2, 1961, 30; "Judge Says He's Sorry," *Alabama Tribune* (Montgomery), November 17, 1961, 2; "Judge Says He's Sorry," press release, November 3, 1961, part 20, reel 10, frame 769, NAACP Papers.

40. "Mother Files Anti-Bias Suit," *Jet*, April 5, 1962, 5; "S.C. College Professor Sues," *Jet*, April 25, 1962, 25; "Immediate Race Mixing Is Sought," *Times and Democrat*, March 27, 1962, 8; "Desegregation Action," *Tampa Bay (FL) Tribune*, April 11, 1962, 45; "Rackley Graduate," *Tallahassee (FL) Democrat*, June 2, 1963, 13; Rackley v. Board of Trustees of Orangeburg Regional Hospital, 238 F. Supp. 512 (1965). Title VI of the 1964 Civil Rights Act and Medicare required equal access at any hospital receiving federal funding. To stay segregated the Orangeburg hospital had not adopted Medicare.

41. Rackley, interview by the author; "The Rackleys," *Champions*, vol. 3; Richard Reid, "Gloria Rackley-Blackwell Story," *Times and Democrat*, February 22, 2011, 6.

42. "Local Negro Complains," *Times and Democrat*, April 27, 1962; Rackley, interview by the author.

43. Taylor Branch, *Pillar of Fire; America in the King Years, 1963–1965* (New York: Simon & Schuster, 1998), 77–78, 84.

44. Abraham Lincoln, "Emancipation Proclamation," National Archives, https://www.archives.gov/milestone-documents/; "NAACP Plans 'Big Attack,'" *Greenville News*, May 22, 1963, 1.

45. "Gressette Gives Reply to NAACP," *State*, June 7, 1963, 1.

46. Claude Sitton, "Token Desegregation," *New York Times*, June 7, 1963, 154; Newman, Monthly Report of Field Secretary, South Carolina Conference of Branches, NAACP, June 10–August 17, 1963, 2–6, Newman Papers, South Carolina Political Collections, University of South Carolina, accessed February 22, 2023, https://digital.tcl.sc.edu/digital/collection/idn/id/1380; Brown v. School District No. 20, Charleston, SC, 226 F. Supp. 819 (E.D.S.C. 1963).

47. "Demonstrators Warned," *Times and Democrat*, June 2, 1963, 1; Newman, Monthly Report, 3–5; "Demonstrations Due to Start," *Times and Democrat*, July 29, 1963, 10; "Negroes Slate Requests," *Times and Democrat*, August 21, 1963, 1, 7. Other Orangeburg Freedom Movement members, active or honorary, included Lincoln Jenkins, a Columbia attorney; J. Arthur

Brown, president of the NAACP state conference; Charles H. Thomas Jr., a South Carolina State education professor; and Constance Baker Motley, the first female attorney with the NAACP's Legal Defense Fund.

48. George Collins, "Orangeburg Protest Backed by Leaders," *Afro-American*, October 12, 1963, 1, 2.

49. "Jelly Belly the Jailer," *Torch*, October 31, 1963, 2; "Hello, we bin waitin' for yo!" and "Information Please?" *Torch*, September 26, 2–3, 1963, private collection of Cecil J. Williams; "Service for Former SCSC Professor," *Times and Democrat*, April 18, 1995, 12.

50. "Record of Arrests," *Torch*, September 19, 1963, 1; "More Demonstrations Likely," *Index-Journal*, October 1, 1963, 7; "Did You Know?" *Torch*, August 28, 1963, 2; "Mystery of the Vanishing Police," *Torch*, September 5, 1963, 1-2; "Do You Know That," *Torch*, September 5, 1963, 2.

51. "No More Mourning," *Torch*, September 26, 1963, 1–2; "Historical Review of the Orangeburg Movement for Freedom," *Torch*, November 8, 1963, 1–2.

52. Bill Black, "175 Arrests," *State*, September 29, 1963, 71; "Demonstrators Arrested," *Times and Democrat*, September 29, 1963, 12; Collins, "City in Ugly Turmoil," *Afro-American*, October 19, 1963, 1, 2.

53. Collins, "City in Ugly Turmoil."

54. "More Demonstrations Likely"; Collins, "Ironic Sidelights of the Orangeburg Story," *Afro-American*, October 19, 1963, 3. Earl W. Coblyn, a graduate of Suffolk University Law School in Boston, served on the faculty of the South Carolina State Law School from 1961 to 1966. He and Zack Townsend opened an Orangeburg law office when the law school closed.

55. Robert McHugh, "Officers Arrest 305," *State*, September 30, 1963, 1, 7.

56. "Russell Says SC Troopers to Keep Orangeburg Safe," *Charlotte (NC) News*, October 2, 1963, 4; "More Arrests," *Delta (MS) Democrat-Times*, October 2, 1963, 15; "Dedicated to those honorable people who have presented their very bodies," *Torch*, October 3, 1963, 1–4.

57. Collins, "Ironic Sidelights."

58. Ibid; "The Army for freedom grows," *Torch*, October 20, 1963, 1–3; "They Went to Jail!" *Torch*, October 20, 1963, 4-5; Rackley, interview by the author.

59. Collins, "City in Ugly Turmoil," Afro-American, October 19, 1963, 1.

60. Collins, "S.C. Arrests Rise to Total of 1,348," *Afro-American*, October 12, 1963, 1–3; "Orangeburg Protests Backed," *Afro-American*, October 12, 1963, 1, 2; Collins, "City in Ugly Turmoil." Collins rose to editor-in-chief of the *Afro-American* then switched to broadcast. In 2003 the Library of America, National Committee for Excellence in Journalism, and Smithsonian Institute jointly cited him as one of the best American journalists of the twentieth century. Frederick N. Rasmussen, "George W. Collins, Pioneering Broadcaster," *Baltimore Sun*, August 4, 2014, accessed February 23, 2023, https://www.baltimoresun.com/obituaries/.

61. "Stockaded Students," *Afro-American*, October 12, 1963, 3. After graduation from Claflin University and the University of South Carolina, MacArthur Goodwin worked for the state Department of Education, participated in the founding of the South Carolina Governor's

School for the Arts and Humanities, and served as president of the National Art Education Association. "MacArthur Goodwin," J.W. Woodward Funeral Home, n.d. 2016, https://www.legacy.com/us/obituaries/thestate/name/.

62. "Pickets Now Required To Register With Law," *Times and Democrat*, October 12, 1963, 1; Collins, "Arrests Total More Than 1,600," *Afro-American*, October 19, 1963, 1, 18.

63. "School Board Delays Action on Dismissal," *Index-Journal*, October 15, 1963, 8; Rackley v. School District No. 5, Orangeburg County, 258 F. Supp. 676 (E.D.S.C. 1966); Rackley, interview by the author; "Picket Law Gets Reading," *Columbia Record*, October 8, 1963, 1, 2.

64. "Negro Schools Picketed," *Birmingham News*, October 8, 1963, 2; "Negro Schools Closed," *Times and Democrat*, October 9, 1863, 1; "Picket Law"; "Teacher Release," *Columbia Record*, October 8, 1963, 1, 2; "S.C. City Reopens Schools," *Charlotte (NC) News*, October 10, 1963, 5.

65. "Demonstrators Warned," 1; "Threats and Intimidations Reported Here," *Times and Democrat*, October 10, 1963, 1; ; "We Stand With Our Merchants," editorial, *Times and Democrat*, October 10, 1963, 1, 10; "A Message to You," ad, *Times and Democrat*, October 10, 1963, 11; "Yes, It's a Fact," *Torch*, October 24, 1963, 1.

66. "School Board Delays Action on Dismissal"; "Negro Leaders Protest Arrest," *Times and Democrat*, October 25, 1963, 7; "Yes, It's a Fact"; Jack Bass, "Russell Hears Protest," Columbia *Record*, October 26, 1963, 7.

67. "SC Ruling Gets Praise of NAACP," *Afro-American*, November 2, 1963, 3; State v. Brown 240 S.C. 357 (1962); Edwards v. South Carolina, 372 U.S. 229 (1963).

68. "Center of Storm," *Afro-American*, October 19, 1963, 3. The *Afro-American* erroneously attributed the photo to reporter Collins, who wrote an accompanying article, "Ironic Sidelights."

69. *Rackley v. School District No. 5.* In 1966 the district court, establishing that Rackley's supervisors had rated her capability and performance "excellent," ordered back pay and re-employment. As to her protest arrests, *Edwards v. South Carolina* had eliminated them as a cause for firing. Lare, "The Rackleys," *Champions 3*; "Orangeburg Grid [*sic*] For Showdown," *Mobile Beacon-Alabama Citizen*, October 26, 1963, 26; Thomas v. Orangeburg Theaters, Inc. 241 Supp. 317 (E.D.S.C. 1965).

70. "Integration Is Coming!!!" *Torch*, November 8, 1963, 2; "Negro Pupils' Transfer Efforts," *Times and Democrat*, November 13, 1963, 5; "It has been rumored," *Torch*, December 19, 1963, 1.

71. "Urged to Keep Up Demonstrations," *Times and Democrat*, November 14. 1963, 8; "Surface Calm Prevails," *State*, February 27, 1968, 13; Collins, "City in Ugly Turmoil."

72. "More Negroes Arrested," *Danville (VA) Bee*, February 5, 1964, 8; "What Is Obstructing Traffic?" *Torch*, February 13, 1964, 1; "Orangeburg, South Carolina—An Untiring Struggle," *Torch*, February 13, 1964, 1.

73. Adams v. School District Number 5, Orangeburg County, SC, 232 F. Supp. 692 (E.D.S.C. 1964).

74. "School Desegregation," *Torch*, February 13, 1964, 1–2; Adams v. School District Number 5, 444 F. 2d 99 (4th Cir. 1971).

75. June Manning Thomas, interview by author, August 3, 2022. June Manning Thomas, *Struggling to Learn: An Intimate History of School Desegregation in South Carolina* (Columbia: University of South Carolina Press: 2021), 153, 158, 162, 163.

76. *Struggling to Learn*, 163. Thomas followed Furman University's first Black student, Joseph Vaughn, as one of the first three Black female undergraduates. After the Orangeburg Massacre she transferred to Michigan State University. She is Mary Frances Berry Distinguished University Professor Emerita of Urban Planning at the University of Michigan.

77. "Court Ruling Upholding Gantt Appeal," *Greenville News*, January 17, 1963, 11. In January 1963 Gantt entered Clemson Agricultural College. In June 1963 federalized National Guard troops made it possible for Vivian Malone and James Hood to enter the University of Alabama. In September 1963 the University of South Carolina became the nation's last state flagship university to desegregate. Public schools in Charleston also desegregated that fall.

78. Harvey B. Gantt, interview by Lynn Haessly, January 8, 1986, interview C-0008, Southern Oral History Program Collection, University of North Carolina at Chapel Hill.

79. Ibid. H. Lewis Suggs, "Harvey Gantt and the Desegregation of Clemson University, 1960–1963," in *Integration with Dignity: A Celebration of Harvey Gantt's Admission to Clemson*, ed. Skip Eisiminger (Clemson, SC: Clemson University Digital Press, 2003), 18-19, 21, accessed February 22, 2023, https://tigerprints.clemson.edu/cgi/.

80. Suggs, "Harvey Gantt," 20, 22–27; Gantt v. Clemson Agricultural College of South Carolina, 208 F. Supp. 416 (D.S.C. 1962), 320 F. 2d 611 (4th Cir. 1963).

81. Robert Moore, "Matthew J. Perry's Preparation," in *Matthew J. Perry: The Man, His Times, and His Legacy*," ed. W. Lewis Burke, Belinda Gergel (Columbia: University of South Carolina Press, 2004), 71; Matthew Perry, interview by the author, June 2001; "Council Honors Judge," *State*, June 14, 2001, 1. In 1976 Perry became the first Black federal judge appointed from the Deep South.

82. "Constance Baker Motley: Judiciary's Unsung Rights Hero," *Judiciary News*, United States Courts, February 20, 2020, accessed February 22, 2023, https://www.uscourts.gov/news/2020/02/20/; "Constance Baker Motley, James Meredith, and the University of Mississippi," *Columbia Law Review* 117, no. 7, accessed February 22, 2023, https://columbialawreview.org/content/. Motley was the first Black woman to win a seat in the New York State senate and the first appointed a federal judge.

83. William F. Gibson served as president of the NAACP state conference from 1977 to 1997 and as chairman of the national NAACP from 1985 to 1995.

84. Gantt v. Clemson, 320 F. 2d 611.

85. W. B. Ragsdale Jr., "Courts Refuse to Delay Gantt's Admission," *Greenville News*, January 22, 1963, 1; "S.C. People—Both White and Negro—Break Bread at Governor's House by Thousands," *Greenville News*, January 16, 1963, 1; Charles H. Wickenberg, "100 Negroes at

Luncheon," *State*, January 16, 1963, 1, 11; Bob Talbert, "Russell-ed Up the Grub," *State*, January 16, 1963, 15; Bert Lunan "11,000 Tons of Food, *State*, January 16, 2003, 15; "Chief Justice Denies Appeal," *Pantagraph* (Bloomington, IL), January 22, 1963, 1; Orville Vernon Burton, "Dining with Harvey Gantt" in *Matthew Perry*, 196; "Gantt Wins Appeal," *Herald*, January 16, 1963, 1; "Closing Move Said Doomed," *Sumter Daily Item*, January 23, 1963, 1; "Legislation to Close Clemson," *Greeneville (TN) Sun*, January 23, 1963, 6.

86. "U.S. Press Starts Gathering," *Greenville News*, January 27, 1963, 10; "Clemson Bars Negro Newsmen from Facilities," *Jet*, February 7, 1963, 6.

87. Herbert Johnson, "Press Is Main Group," *Greenville News*, January 29, 1963, 1, 2; Jerome V. Reel Jr., "Clemson and Harvey Gantt" in *Integration with Dignity*, 48; "Students Receive Gantt With Some Heckling," *Greenville News*, January 29 1963, 2. Student comments included references to zoos, a coon, and a noose. James E. Booker of the New York *Amsterdam News* attended.

88. Bill Collins, "Gantt Will Begin," *Greenville News*, January 29, 1960, 1; "From Automobile into History," *Index-Journal*, January 29, 1963, 1; "Clemson Enrolls Gantt," *Long Beach (CA) Press-Telegram*, January 28, 1963, 1.

89. "Negro Girl Asks to Attend USC," *Greenville News*, July 31, 1962, 12; "USC Nixes Application," *Sumter Daily Item*, July 31, 1962, 1; "Negro Sues for Entry to USC," *Evening Herald*, November 1, 1962, 2.

90. "Always Decisions," *Jet*, July 25, 1963, 17; "Negro Girl Sees Self as Knight," *Sumter Daily Item*, November 2, 1962, 1; "Negro Girl Seeks to Enter South Carolina University," *Gaffney Ledger*, August 2, 1962, 6.

91. "McLeod Leaves for Gantt Case," *State*, January 8, 1963,1; "USC Mixing Issue," *Columbia Record*, June 21, 1963, 1, 2; "Full Text of Judge's Decision," *State*, July 11, 1963, 6; "Federal Officers Enter Blast Case," *Columbia Record*, August 27, 1963, 1, 2.

92. "USC to Admit Negro," *State*, July 11, 1963, 1, 9.; "Univ. of S.C. Accepts First Negro," *Pittsburgh Courier*, August 17, 1963, 5. Robert G. Anderson Jr. became a social worker in New York City. Henrie Monteith Treadwell became Director of Community Voices at the Morehouse School of Medicine in Atlanta, Georgia. James L. Solomon became director of the South Carolina Department of Social Services.

93. Newman, Annual Report, 1964, South Carolina Conference of Branches, NAACP, 10, accessed February 22, 2023, https://digital.tcl.sc.edu/digital/collection/idn/id/1380.

94. Hine, *South Carolina State*, 293–4; Philip Harrison, interview by Sonny DuBose, October 2007, in Sonny DuBose and Cecil Williams, *Orangeburg 1968: A Place and Time Remembered* (Orangeburg, SC: Cecil Williams Photography/Publishing, 2008), 109; John Faust, "College Students May March on Governor," *Times and Democrat*, March 8, 1968, 1, 11; John Wesley Stroman, "The Real Story Hasn't Been Told," interview by Lare, February 10, 2005,

in *Champions*, vol. 4, accessed February 22, 2023, https://digital.library.sc.edu/exhibits/champions/volume-4-2/part-i/.

95. Faust, "College Students May March on Governor"; "College to Shut If Protests Continue," *Baltimore Evening Sun*, March 4, 1967, 2; Del Booth, "Boycotters Plan Hike," *Index-Journal*, March 7, 1967, 1.

96. Jerry C. Fryer, interview by the author, February 17, 2022.

97. Ibid.

98. "Students Vow to Continue," *Greenville News*, March 7, 1967, 14; "Class Boycott Continues," *Times and Democrat*, March 7, 1967, 1, 2; Hine, *South Carolina State*, 295.

99. "Governor's Statement," *Times and Democrat*, March 8, 1967, 1; Sam E. McCuen, "Williams: Ultimatum Given," State, March 9, 1967, 49.

100. Isaac "Ike" Williams, interview by author, 2004; Isaac "Ike" Williams, "Tipping Points," interview by Lare, February 23. 2005, *Champions*, vol. 3, accessed February 23, 2023, https://digital.library.sc.edu/exhibits/champions/volume-3-2/part-5/.

101. Isaac "Ike" Williams, interview by author; "Boycott Group Undeterred," *Columbia Record*, March 9, 1967, 1; "Plan for Student March," WLTX-TV News Story 223, March 1967, Moving Images Research Collections (MIRC), University of South Carolina, accessed February 22, 2023, https://digital.tcl.sc.edu/digital/collection/localtvnews/id/62/; Paul Clancy, "No March, No Boycott," *State*, March 11, 1967, 1, 2; "Enough Is Enough," *Times and Democrat*, March 9, 1967, 1; "Cause Doesn't Count," *Times and Democrat*, March 10, 1967, 1; Philip G. Grose, *South Carolina at the Brink: Robert McNair and the Politics of Civil Rights* (Columbia: University of South Carolina Press, 2006), 191.

102. "No March, No Boycott," 1, 2.

103. "First Negro Trustees," *Jet*, May 12, 1966, 47; "Turner to Quit," *State*, May 11, 1967, 1, 7; "SC State Head Resigns," *Sumter Daily Item*, May 11, 1967, 20; Faust, "Boycotting Students," *Times and Democrat*, March 9, 1967, 1; "Complications at State," *Greenville News*, May 20, 1967, 4; "Chartered," *State*, August 11, 1967, 1.

104. "A Brief History of the NEA," National Education Association, accessed May 18, 2022, https://www.nea.org/about-nea/mission-vision-values/history-nea; Levona Page, "Bi-Racial Education Group," *State*, July 13, 1967, 39. The 1967 interim plan to merge was made official on January 27, 1968. Michael Fultz, "The Displacement of Black Educators Post-Brown," *History of Education Quarterly* 44, no. 1 (Spring 2004): 14.

105. "Full Petition Predicted," *State*, April 17, 1967, 15; Evan Faulkenbury, *Poll Power: The Voter Education Project and the Movement for the Ballot in the American South* (Chapel Hill: University of North Carolina Press, 2019), 1–3.

106. "More Funds Sought," *Times and Democrat*, October 14, 1967, 2; Paul Clancy, "Fulfill Commitment, College Chief Urges," *State*, December 14, 1967, 52; Hon. John Conyers Jr., *The

Ides of February: 1 Minute of Violence in Orangeburg, 90th Cong., 2nd session, Cong. Record, 114, pt. 10, 12704, accessed February 23, 2023, https://www.govinfo.gov/content/pkg/GPO-CRECB-1968-pt10/pdf/GPO-CRECB-1968-pt10-2-3.pdf. Clemson became a university in 1964.

107. "I Woke Up This Morning," Richland County Citizens Committee broadcast, February 12, 1968, Modjeska Monteith Simkins Papers, South Carolina Political Collections, accessed February 22, 2023, https://digital.tcl.sc.edu/digital/collection/simkins/id/33.

108. Thomas v. Orangeburg Theaters, Inc., 241 F. Supp. 317 (E.D.S.C. 1965); United States v. All Star Triangle Bowl, Inc., 283 F. Supp 300, (E.D.S.C. 1968).

109. "Eight Legion Teams Attend Kickoff Banquet," *Times and Democrat,* August 28, 1966, 9; "Oakland Tight on Discipline," *Times and Democrat,* September 3, 1966, 6.

110. Oscar P. Butler, letter to the editor, *Times and Democrat,* February 8, 1968, 4.

111. Jack Bass and Jack Nelson, *The Orangeburg Massacre* (Macon, GA: Mercer University Press, 2002), 17–18; Heart of Atlanta Motel, Inc. v. United States, 379 U.S. 241 (1964); Miller v. Amusement Enterprises, Inc., 391 F. 2d 86 (5th Cir. 1967); Miller v. Amusement Enterprises, Inc., 394 F. 2d 342 (5th Cir. 1968).

112. Bass, *Orangeburg Massacre,* 19–21; "2 State College Students to Study, Travel Abroad," *Times and Democrat,* May 11, 1968, 7.

113. Newman, 1967 Annual Report, November 30, 1967, South Carolina Conference of Branches, NAACP, 4, accessed February 22, 2023, https://digital.tcl.sc.edu/digital/collection/idn/id/1253; Stroman, "The Real Story Hasn't Been Told," *Champions.* Stroman told Lare that the White student bowled on February 5.; Hine and Bass placed the White student in the bowling alley on January 29.

114. Stroman, "The Real Story Hasn't Been Told," *Champions*; Bass, *Orangeburg Massacre,* 16, 22–23; Frank K. Myers, "Operator Hits Police Action," *Times and Democrat,* February 7, 1968, 1, 3; McNair Press Conference, Orangeburg, WIS-TV News Story 68-5007, February 7, 1968, MIRC; accessed February 22, 2023, https://digital.tcl.sc.edu/digital/collection/p17173coll18/id/152/rec/3; Grose, *At the Brink,* 204.

115. Stroman, "The Real Story Hasn't Been Told," *Champions*; John Stroman, interview by Damon Foreman, n.d., Orangeburg Massacre Oral History Project, College of Charleston, in *Orangeburg 1968,* 168.

116. Stroman, "The Real Story Hasn't Been Told," *Champions*; Bass, *Orangeburg Massacre,* 28–29; Stroman, *Orangeburg 1968,* 168; Grose, *On the Brink,* 207.

117. "NAACP Leaders Watchful," *State,* June 22, 1967, 13.

118. "Call Out of Guard," *State,* February 7, 1968, 1; Pat Watters and Weldon Rougeau, "Events at Orangeburg: A Report Based on Studies and Interviews in Orangeburg, South Carolina, in the Aftermath of Tragedy," Southern Regional Council, February 25, 1968, 4, accessed February

23, 2023, https://files.eric.ed.gov/fulltext/ED019380.pdf; Richard Reid, "Reflections 50 Years After," *Times and Democrat*, February 8, 2018, accessed February 23, 2023, https://thetandd.com/news/.

119. Fryer, interview by the author.

120. Harrison, interview by DuBose, *Orangeburg 1968*, 110; "Guardsmen Ready," *Index-Journal*, February 7, 1968, 1; Mike Davis, "'Soul' Password on College Campus," *Afro-American*, February 17, 1968, 12; Bass, *Orangeburg Massacre*, 31–32, 43.

121. Jerry Fryer said the city later paid for repairs to his camera.

122. "Policeman Injured," *Times and Democrat*, February 7, 1968, 1, 9; Davis, "'Soul' Password on College Campus"; *Orangeburg Massacre*, 32; Watters, "Events at Orangeburg," 5; Grose, *At the Brink*, 209.

123. "Racial Violence," *Kannapolis (NC) Daily Independent*, February 7, 1968, 1; "Negroes Protest," *Hackensack (NJ) Record*, February 7, 1956, 32; *Orangeburg Massacre*, 31–32; Modjeska Simkins, interview by Jacquelyn Hall, July 28, 1976, interview G-0056-2, Southern Oral History Program, accessed February 22, 2023, https://docsouth.unc.edu/sohp/G-0056-2/G-0056-2.html.

124. "Call Out of Guard," *State*, February 7, 1968, 1, 2. The first Black trooper, Israel Brooks Jr., joined in 1967. Bass, *Orangeburg Massacre*, 43.

125. Grose, "We Have No Intentions Of Letting Things Get Out of Hand," *State*, February 8, 1968, 15; McNair on Orangeburg Protests, WLTX-TV News Story 369, February 7, 1968, MIRC, accessed February 22, 2023, https://digital.tcl.sc.edu/digital/collection/p17173coll18/id/82/rec/1; "Racial Violence"; Al Lanier, "Rampage in Orangeburg," *Sumter Daily Item,* February 7, 1968, 3; Equal Justice Initiative, "African American Lynching Victims by State, 1877–1950," in *Lynching in America*, accessed January 10, 2022, https://lynchinginamerica.eji.org/report/.

126. Phyllis Austin, "Students Present Demands," *Sumter Daily Item*, February 7, 1968, 1; Jack Bass, "Economic Boycott Threatened," *Charlotte Observer*, February 8, 1968, 7; "S.C. Students on Rampage," *Durham (NC) Sun*, February 7, 1968, 27.

127. Bass, "Economic Boycott Threatened"; "SC Students Set Price," *Charlotte (NC) News*, February 7, 1968, 20.

128. "E.O. Pendarvis," *Times and Democrat*, September 15, 1965, 1; Bestor Cram and Judy Richardson, *Scarred Justice: The Orangeburg Massacre 1968* (Boston: Northern Light Productions, Independent Television Service, National Black Programming Consortium, 2009).

129. "*Scarred Justice.*"

130. Phyllis Austin, "Orangeburg Students Present Grievances," *Columbia Record*, February 7, 1968, 1.

131. "NAACP Said Not Involved," *Florence Morning News*, February 8, 1968, 2; "National Guard Called"; Bass, *Orangeburg Massacre*, 41–42.

132. Davis, "'Soul' Password on College Campus;" Grose, *At the Brink*, 210; Frank K. Myers, "All Hell Breaks Loose," *Times and Democrat*, February 9, 1968, 1, 10; Conyers, "Ides of February," 12701-02; Reid, "Reflections 50 Years After"; John L. McCoy, letter to the editor, "Anti-McNair," *Times and Democrat*, March 18, 1968, 4.

133. Grose, *At the Brink*, 210; "Militia Men Activated," *Times and Democrat*, February 8, 1968, 1; "State on Top of Situation," *Times and Democrat*, February 8, 1968, 1; "White National Guard," *New York Times*, April 14, 1967, 30.

134. Davis, "'Soul' Password on College Campus"; Conyers, "Ides of February," 12702; David W. Bledsoe, "Three Students Hurt," *State*, February 8, 1968, 1. The bricks and stones came from demolition and construction projects on and off campus.

135. "Students Urged to Remain on Campus," *Index-Journal*, February 8, 1968, 1; "Council Statement Replies to Grievances," *Times and Democrat*, February 9, 1968, 1.

136. McNair, "Riot Report," *State*, March 6, 1968, 17; "Incident Sparks Callout of Guard," State, February 7, 1968, 1; Grose, *At the Brink*, 214–15; Cyrus R. Vance, *Final Report Regarding Detroit Riots*, September 12, 1967, Office of Assistant Secretary of Defense, Washington, DC, 48; accessed February 22, 2023, https://www.archives.gov/files/declassification/iscap/2015-071-doc02.pdf.

137. Simkins, interview by Hall.

138. Ibid.; Myers, "All Hell Breaks Loose"; "Pleas for Peace," *State*, February 10, 1968, 7; Bass, *Orangeburg Massacre*, 56–58; James L. Wooten, "3 Dispute Gov. McNair on Killing of Negro Students," *New York Times*, May 27, 1969, 30.

139. Myers, "All Hell Breaks Loose"; "Pleas for Peace"; *Orangeburg Massacre*, 56–58; Wooten, "3 Dispute Gov. McNair on Killing"; Nathaniel Abraham Sr., interview by DuBose, September 13, 2007, *Orangeburg 1968*, 88.

140. "Government Rests Case," *Florence Morning News*, May 23, 1969, 1. The news story refers to Thomas Kimberly; the correct name is Thomas Kennerly.

141. Grose, *At the Brink*, 221; Bass, *Orangeburg Massacre*, 223–24; Nelson, "No Shots Before Police Fired," *Los Angeles Times*, May 21, 1969, 9; "Race Tensions Remain High," *Pittsburgh Courier*, February 24, 1968, 1. Black-owned newspapers reported as many as fifty students shot.

142. Fryer, interview by the author. Fryer became a labor organizer for the American Federation of Government Employees (AFGE). He was elected president of AFGE Local 3892 and then president of AFGE Education Council 252.

143. Tom Wicker, "Jackson State and Orangeburg," *New York Times*, October 4, 1970, 179; James Wooten, "Troopers Blame Students," *New York Times*, May 23, 1969, 19; "Troopers' Shots Depicted," *New York Times*, May 22, 1969, 25; Wooten, "3 Dispute Gov. McNair on Killing"; Bass, *Orangeburg Massacre*, 66–68; Nelson, "Orangeburg Students Unarmed," *Los Angeles Times*, February 18, 1968, 31. Mobley said he was misquoted in an AP story that ran February 9.

144. Bass, *Orangeburg Massacre*, 74–75; Wooten, "3 Dispute Gov. McNair on Killing"; Nelson, "Orangeburg Students Unarmed."

145. Myers, "All Hell Breaks Loose."

146. Alonzo W. Holman, interview by author, 2004; "SNCC Says They'll Appeal," *State*, February 10, 1968, 5; "Calls for Revenge," *Chicago Tribune*, February 10, 1968, 16; "Curfew Set," *Austin (TX) American-Statesman*, February 10, 1968, 1, 6; "Emergency Extended," *State*, February 11, 1968, 1, 2.

147. Bass, Will Police Bullet "End Pro Prospects," *Charlotte Observer*, February 28, 1968, 25; "Six Students Still in Hospital," *State*, February 10, 1968, 5; Bernard Garnett, "Untold Story of Fatal Riot," *Jet*, March 7, 1968, 17; Garnett, "Orangeburg Tension High," *Jet*, February 29, 1968, 6–8; Garnett, "Youths Say Troopers Shot," *Jet*, March 7, 1968, 16–23; James Hoagland, "South Carolina Youth's Wounds Studied," *Washington Post*, February 12, 1968, in Congr. Record 114, pt.10, 12710; Bass, *Orangeburg Massacre*, 70, 75–76.

148. Kent Krell, "Three Negroes Die," *Jefferson City (MO) Post-Tribune*, February 9, 1968, 2; "Saddest Day, Governor Says," *State*, February 10, 1968, 6; "Curfew Order Text;" *State*, February 10, 1968, 6; "Black Power Group Blamed by McNair," *State*, February 10, 1968, 6.

149. Pat Robertson, "Rioting Tolls Death Knell," *State*, February 10, 1968, 7; Eugene Sloan, "Peaceful Adjustment Ends As Guns Crackle," State, February 10, 1968, 6; "Map Outlines Violence Areas," *State*, February 10, 1968, 6; Watters, "Events at Orangeburg," 19–20; "Student Slayings Arouse Nation: Eyewitnesses Rap Troopers," *Pittsburgh Courier*, February 17, 1968, 1, 4; "Untold Story of Fatal Riot," 16–23.

150. Hine, *South Carolina State*, 308; Cleveland Sellers with Robert Terrell, *River of No Return: The Autobiography of a Black Militant and the Life and Death of SNCC* (Jackson: University of Mississippi, 1973), 209–19; Dr. Cleveland Sellers, interview by Jack Bass, February 8, 2001, March 12, 2001, *Orangeburg 1968*, 137. Cleveland Sellers received a pardon in 1993 from the State Probation, Parole, and Pardon Board. He served as president of Voorhees College in Denmark, South Carolina, from 2008–2015.

151. "King Says All Shot in Back," *Abilene (TX) Reporter News*, February 14, 1968, 23; Benjamin E. Mays, "Not on a White Campus," *Pittsburgh Courier*, March 9, 1968, 6; Newman, Annual Report, December 1, 1968, SC Conference of Branches, NAACP, 3–5, accessed February 23, 2023, https://digital.tcl.sc.edu/digital/collection/idn/id/1219/.

152. "Uneasy Quiet Follows," *State*, February 10, 1968, 1, 2; "800 Negroes Ask Removal of Guard," *State*, February 12, 1968, 1, 2; "Bowling Alley Can't Continue Segregated," *Times and Democrat*, February 24, 1968, 1; "Bowling Alley Integration Sought in Suit," *State*, February 11, 1968, 1, 2.

153. William Cotterell, "1 of 3 Negroes Killed in Orangeburg Buried," *Shreveport (LA) Times*, February 13, 1968, 3; Patty Mummert, "Sam Hammond Shot in Back," *Fort Lauderdale (FL) News*, February 14, 1968, 16. A death notice for Henry Ezekial Smith could not be found.

154. "Rocks Thrown," *Times and Democrat,* February 16, 1968, 1, 2; "NAACP Director Urges Restraint," *Greenville News,* February 26, 1968, 2; Roy Wilkins Speaks in Aftermath of Orangeburg Massacre," WIS-TV News Story 68-256, February 25, 1968, MIRC, accessed February 27, 2023, https://digital.tcl.sc.edu/digital/collection/p17173coll18/id/149/rec/1; "Police Were Wrong," *Florence Morning News,* February 26, 1968, 3; "Negro Bowls at Alley," *Pittsburgh Courier,* March 9, 1968, 1, 4; "$6.5 Million State Project Voted," *State,* May 7, 1968, 15; "Disturbance Rocks Quiet SC Senate," March 8, 1968, 21, 30; "Demonstrations to Protest Orangeburg Massacre," WLTX News Story 155, March 7, 1968, MIRC, accessed February 24, 2023, https://digital.tcl.sc.edu/digital/collection/localtvnews/id/421/.

155. Bass, "Shot in Back," *Charlotte Observer,* February 13, 1968, 8, 9; Eugene Sloan, "Jury Refuses Indictment," *State,* November 8, 1968, 1; "Criminal Information Filed," *State,* September 27, 1946, 1; "Nine SC Highway Patrolmen Named in Civil Rights Suit," *Columbia Record,* December 21, 1968, 23; James Wooten, "9 Troopers Freed," *New York Times,* May 28, 1969, 1, 23; Bass, "Five Defendant Patrolmen Promoted," *Charlotte Observer,* May 23, 1969, 9.

156. "Suit Against Local Police Is Abandoned," *Times and Democrat,* August 5, 1969, 1. Fred Henderson Moore represented the plaintiffs, including Cleveland Sellers. "Court Airing of Bloody Incident," *Times and Democrat,* May 18, 1969, 5; "Parents Should File Suit," *Herald,* November 18, 1969, 8; "Carolina Patrolmen Cleared," *New York Times,* November 14, 1970, 16.

157. Sellers, *River of No Return,* 264–65; Bass, *Orangeburg Massacre,* 208-10. The defense attorneys wanted a directed acquittal since Sellers' rioting charge was only for February 8, 1968. But the judge ruled against them after the prosecution cited a state Supreme Court decision that an indictment did not need to be precise as to the time of an alleged crime. Fred Henderson Moore served as one of Sellers's attorneys.

158. Ray Belcher, *Greenville County, South Carolina: From Cotton Fields to Textile Center of the World* (Charleston, SC: History Press, 2006), 109; Archie Vernon Huff Jr., *Greenville: The History of the City and the County in the Piedmont* (Columbia: University of South Carolina Press, 1995), 302–5; "1934: Southern Workers Spark Massive Textile Strike," *American Postal Workers Union,* August 31, 2013, accessed May 21, 2023, https://apwu.org/news/; Gary Fink and Merl E. Reed, eds., *Race, Class, and Community in Southern Labor History* (Tuscaloosa: University of Alabama Press, 1994), 54, 56–57; Textile Workers Union v. Darlington Mfg. Co. 380 U.S. 263 (!965).

159. "Charleston's Cigar Factory Strike, 1945-1946," Lowcountry Digital History Initiative, Lowcountry Digital Library at the College of Charleston, South Carolina, accessed February 23, 2023, https://ldhi.library.cofc.edu/exhibits/show/cigar_factory/introduction.

160. John E. Wise, interview by Leon Fink, February 1980, box 146, Retail, Wholesale and Department Store Union, Local 1199 Drug and Hospital Union, Hospital Division Records, Kheel Center for Labor Management Documentation and Archives, Martin P. Kheel Center, Cornell University; Moultrie, interview by the author, July 2, 2008.

161. Lillie Mae Doster, "Birthing 'We Shall Overcome,'" interview by Felice Knight and Marvin Lare, *Champions*, vol. 1, accessed February 23, 2023, https://digital.library.sc.edu/exhibits/champions/volume-1-2/part-3/.

162. Mary Moultrie, interview by the author, 2008; Brinson, *Stories of Struggle*, 217.

163. Rosetta Simmons, interview by the author, July 2, 2008; Brinson, *Stories of Struggle*, 217–18.

164. Brinson, *Stories of Struggle*, 218, 221–24, 232–34, 238, 264, 267.

165. Al Lanier, "Hospital Strikers Are Backed," *Durham (NC) Sun*, April 1, 1969, 24; Brinson, *Stories of Struggle*, 225–32, 239.

166. Lanier, "Hospital Strikers Are Backed."

167. Brinson, *Stories of Struggle*, 241–44; "Strikers Resume Picketing," *Columbia Record*, April 23, 1969, 13; "Mrs. King Steps into Hospital Strike," *Dayton (OH) Daily News*, April 29, 1969, 5.

168. "Daily Notes," *Canonsburg (PA) Daily Notes*, April 30, 1969, 9; Chester Higgins, "City Blacks, Union Members Idolize King's Widow," *Jet*, May 22, 1969, 14–20; "Charleston Like Selma, Says Mrs. King," *Jet*, May 15, 1969, 5, 6.

169. "Racial Trouble," *Petersburg (VA) Progress-Index*, May 2, 1969, 18; Higgins, "City Blacks," 20.

170. Higgins, "City Blacks," 16–17.

171. "850 Officers to Guard," *State*, May 11, 1969, 15.

172. "Charleston Port May Face Walkout," *Greenville News*, June 13, 1969, 22; "Strike Ended," *El Paso (TX) Herald Post*, June 30, 1969, 7; *Stories of Struggle*, 261–63.

173. *Stories of Struggle*, 269–73.

174. On November 3, 1970, Herbert Ulysses Gaillard Fielding, of Charleston; James Felder, of Sumter; and I. S. Leevy Johnson, of Columbia; won election to the state legislature, the first African-Americans to serve since 1902. H. Larry Mitchell worked on the 1974 election of Earl M. Middleton to the state legislature. In 1981 Mitchell returned to Orangeburg and opened Mitchell's Photography with three brothers. In 1984 Mitchell himself ran and won one term in the legislature.

175. H. Larry Mitchell, interview by the author, April 4, 2021.

AND SO MUCH MORE

1. Studio photographers in mid-twentieth century South Carolina included E. C. Jones in Sumter, Walter N. Boags and Joseph and Rachel Coards in Charleston, and Richard Samuel Roberts and John Williamson Goodwin Jr. in Columbia.

2. "Space Age Home," *Ebony*, June 1977, 86–92; "Place of the Future to House the Past," *Times and Democrat*, August 19, 2019, 1.

3. "PSC Hearing Delayed," *Greenville News*, April 3, 1977, 57; "Edwards Creates Energy Institute," *State*, April 27, 1977, 31.

4. "Grand Opening," *Times and Democrat*, December 7, 1975, 33; "You're Invited," ad, *Times and Democrat*, December 5, 1975, 15.

5. Williams, *Out-of-the-Box in Dixie*; DuBose and Williams, *Orangeburg 1968* Cecil Williams, *Unforgettable: Light Hope Bravery* (Orangeburg, SC: Cecil J. Williams, 2018).

6. In 1983, Harvey Gantt, Williams's former photo subject and first Black graduate of Clemson, became the first Black mayor of Charlotte, North Carolina. Rev. Isaiah DeQuincey Newman, former NAACP field secretary and a frequent photo subject of Williams's, won a special election to become South Carolina's first Black state senator since 1887. "S.C. Man Seeks Senate Seat on Write-In," *Charlotte Observer*, August 29, 1984, 28; "Local Photographer Aspires to Dispel Thurmond Legend," *Times and Democrat*, February 16, 1984, 17; "Recount Today in Senate Race," *Index-Journal*, June 14, 1984, 13; Clark Surratt, "Purvis Is Winner in Recount," *State*, June 21, 1984, 35; "Second Recount Ordered," *Herald*, June 22, 1984, 8; "Williams: Irregularities in Primary," *Times and Democrat*, June 26, 1984, 16; "Ballots for Lee Subpoenaed," *Sumter Daily Item*, July 12, 1984, 2; "Purvis May Face Write-In Candidate," *Columbia Record,* July 18, 1984, 16.

7. "Johnson-Williams," *Times and Democrat*, March 28, 1993, 26; "Local Photographer Aspires"; Williams, *Freedom & Justice*. Barbara Johnson-Williams earned a bachelor's in elementary education, a master's in special education, and an Ed.S. in educational administration, all from SC State. She has served as president of the Orangeburg NAACP branch since 2011 and in 2013 joined the Medical University of South Carolina's board of trustees.

8. "Election At a Glance," *Hilton Head Island (SC) Packet*, June 13, 1996, 3; Surratt, "Purvis Is Winner in Recount."

9. "Cecil Williams Not Afraid of Criticism," *Times and Democrat*, December 21, 1995, 1, 5; "Last Minute Filings," *Greenville News*, May 1, 1996, 7. In 1993 James E. Clyburn Jr., an SC State contemporary of Williams, won election to Congress, the first Black person to serve South Carolina in Congress since 1893.

10. "FilmToaster Photography," Cecil Williams Photography, accessed October 2, 2022, https://www.filmtoaster.photography/our-team; "Claflin Interns Help Preserve History," *Times and Democrat*, July 10, 2017, 1.

11. "Claflin University Selected as Recipient," *Atlanta (GA) World*, January 25, 2022, accessed October 2, 2022, https://theatlantavoice.com/.

12. In 2019 a consortium purchased the archive of Johnson Publishing Company, which owned *Jet* and *Ebony*, and donated the archive to the Getty Research Institute and the Smithsonian National Museum of African American History and Culture for broad public access. The FBI approached Ernest C. Withers, as it had Cecil Williams. Williams refused an informant role. Withers accepted and passed on tips and photographs between 1969 and 1970. "Double Exposure," *Memphis Commercial Appeal*, September 12, 2010, 43–49.

INDEX

Page numbers in *italics* refer to illustrations.